NAVIGATING APPLIED SPORT AND EXERCISE PSYCHOLOGY

In recent years, more students have chosen to study sport and exercise psychology with a view to building careers as applied practitioners. While sport and exercise psychology master's graduates leave university with the necessary theoretical knowledge to inform their practice, they are often left wanting to know more about creating and navigating a career within the field.

Navigating Applied Sport and Exercise Psychology provides readers with an honest and contemporary insight into the work and experiences of trainees and early career practitioners. This book delves further into the more complex and nuanced experiences of being an applied practitioner. Using case studies and reflections, the chapters explore key topics including working within multi-disciplinary teams, maintaining ethics and integral practice during challenging conversations and supporting mental health in high-performance environments.

Written by trainees and early career practitioners, this book is vital reading for students, early career practitioners, and anyone interested in sport psychology.

Erin Prior is a BPS Chartered, HCPC registered Sport and Exercise Psychologist. As an applied practitioner, Erin works with a range of individuals, teams, and organisations across various sports. Alongside her applied practice, Erin is completing her PhD which is focused on athlete mental health, at Loughborough University.

Tim Holder, PhD, is an HCPC Registered Sport and Exercise Psychologist, BPS Chartered and a BASES Fellow. He is an applied sport psychology consultant and supervisor to students working towards practitioner status in the UK. Tim is the Programme Leader for the MSc in Applied Sport Psychology at the University of Winchester, UK.

NAVIGATING APPLIED SPORT AND EXERCISE PSYCHOLOGY

Reflections and Insights from Emerging Practitioners

Edited by Erin Prior and Tim Holder

Routledge
Taylor & Francis Group

NEW YORK AND LONDON

Designed cover image: LoveTheWind

First published 2023
by Routledge
605 Third Avenue, New York, NY 10158

and by Routledge
4 Park Square, Milton Park, Abingdon, Oxon, OX14 4RN

Routledge is an imprint of the Taylor & Francis Group, an informa business

ISBN: 978-1-032-20502-1 (hbk)
ISBN: 978-1-032-20501-4 (pbk)
ISBN: 978-1-003-26389-0 (ebk)

DOI: 10.4324/9781003263890

Typeset in Bembo
by MPS Limited, Dehradun

CONTENTS

ABOUT THE CONTRIBUTORS

Anna Abraham, University of Ottawa, Canada, Anna is a Registered Psychotherapist (CRPO) with a passion for mental health advocacy in sport. She is currently the Varsity Mental Health Coordinator and Counsellor for the University of Ottawa and the Educator of Performance Psychology at the School of Dance. She has the rewarding opportunity of supporting clients through a variety of issues related to mental well-being and performance.

Fionnuala Barnes, Liverpool John Moores University, England, Fionnuala is a Performance Psychologist, completing a Professional Doctorate in Sport and Exercise at Liverpool John Moores University. Alongside her doctorate, Fionnuala works within Professional and Olympic sporting organisations supporting athletes, coaches, and the wider support team to learn, develop, grow, and ultimately be the best version of themselves on any given day. Blending art and science, Fionnuala aims to develop mindset skills and practices while encouraging others to connect with what really matters to them, embrace curiosity in challenge, thrive under pressure, and believe in their potential. Life is special. Enjoy the journey. **Twitter: @fionnualabarnes**

Harley de Vos, University of Sydney, Australia, Harley is an endorsed sport and exercise psychologist in Australia. Since 2020, he has been working in sport and performance psychology with one of Australia's leading sport and performance psychology providers, Condor Performance Psychologists. Harley provides targeted evidence-based sport and performance psychology interventions with athletes from grassroots to elite levels across an array of sports including cricket, football (various codes within Australia and internationally), basketball, golf, and tennis. Harley also works with non-athlete high-performing populations, such as Special Forces candidates, medical professionals, law enforcement personnel, and aeromedical professionals. In addition to his applied work, Harley is currently undertaking his PhD at the University of Sydney and affiliated with the Australian Institute of Sport. His PhD is focused on exploring and understanding the relationship between mental health and sleep in elite Australian athletes. **Twitter:** **@harley_dv**

Alban Dickson, Edinburgh Napier University, Scotland, Alban is a Sport & Exercise Psychologist presently completing a PhD at Edinburgh Napier University, Scotland, within the School of Applied Sciences. His current research explores psychosocial development in youth football. In applied practice he adopts Acceptance & Commitment Therapy and Personal Construct Psychology as part of his approach, working across Scottish Governing Bodies of Sport and individual clients. In addition, Alban has contributed to teaching on accredited MSc Psychology of Sport programmes and delivers Scotland's Mental Health First Aid on behalf of NHS Scotland. **Twitter: @AlbanDickson**

Joseph G. Dixon, Staffordshire University, England, Joseph is a dual-chartered Sport & Exercise and Occupational Psychologist who has worked with elite athletes and teams across a variety of different sports. Since 2013 he has been Lead Psychologist with Stoke City Football Club in the English Premier League and Championship Division whilst completing a PhD focusing on challenge and threat states in athletes. During this time, he has also worked within both Men's English Premiership Rugby and with Elite Para Football teams at the English Football Association. He currently combines his work in applied practice alongside a Lecturing role in Sport & Exercise Psychology at Staffordshire University. **Twitter: @DrJosephDixon**

Karla Drew, Staffordshire University, England, Karla is a BPS Chartered, and HCPC Registered Sport and Exercise Psychologist. As an applied practitioner, Karla provides sport psychology provision to a range of individuals ranging from youth to professional athletes across a number of sports including track-and-field, archery, snooker, netball, and swimming. Alongside her applied practice, Karla is a Lecturer in Sport and Exercise Psychology at Staffordshire University and teaches across a number of applied and professional practice modules at both undergraduate and postgraduate levels. Karla's current research focuses on career transitions in sport and applied sport psychology practice. **Twitter: @KarlaLDrew**

Megan Gossfeld, University of West Alabama, United States of America, Megan is a counsellor at the University of West Alabama where she provides sport psychology services to student-athletes in addition to general mental health counselling. Megan also offers mental training sessions to individual athletes and groups through her private practice Headway Mental Performance Consulting, LLC. **Twitter: @MeganGossfeld**

Charlotte Hinchliffe, England, Charlotte is a BPS Chartered Psychologist and HCPC Registered Practitioner Psychologist in the field of Sport and Exercise

Psychology. Charlotte currently works part-time for the English Institute of Sport, where she is contracted as a Performance Psychologist working with the British Para-Swimming Team. Alongside her employed work, Charlotte also has her own business (Charlotte Hinchliffe Sport Psychology) providing sport and performance psychology support to private clients. Charlotte has also completed a PhD, focusing on the role of sport psychologists in supporting effective talent development. Charlotte's experiences of working across both the applied and research domains within sport psychology have fostered an interest in bridging the research-practice gap, aspiring for sport psychology research to be more relevant and useful for practitioners. **Twitter: @SportPsychHinch**

Jennifer A. Hobson, Staffordshire University, England, Jennifer is a BPS Chartered and HCPC Registered Sport and Exercise Psychologist, working as the Lead Academy Psychologist at Stoke City, FC. She is also a Post Graduate Researcher at Staffordshire University, exploring the Theory of Challenge and Threat States in Athletes (TCTSA) in youth academy football players to establish how TCTSA variables change over time and whether they predict performance and mental health outcomes. **Twitter: @JenHobSporty**

Guy Matzkin, Israeli Archery Association, Israel, Guy is secretary general of the Israeli Archery Association (IAA), and former head coach of its national program. A graduate of the University of Edinburgh's performance psychology program, he is an accredited psychologist with the Israeli registry, and works as a performance psychologist with the Israeli Paralympic Committee alongside a range of athletes and organisations.

Ismael Pedraza-Ramirez, German Sport University Cologne, Germany, Ismael Pedraza-Ramirez is a Specialist in Applied Sport Psychology (SASP-FEPSAC). He is completing his PhD at the German Sport University Cologne at the Psychology Institute. His research focuses on the psychological and cognitive elements of esports performance. Besides his academic involvement, he is a full-time embedded performance coach for a professional esports organisation. His work as a performance coach in esports began in 2016 when he integrated psychology into this new performance domain, bringing his experiences from his work in traditional sports. Additionally, as an Applied Department Coordinator, Ismael is part of the Managing Council of the European Network of Young Specialists in Sport Psychology (ENYSSP). **Twitter: @IsmaPedraza**

Erin Prior, Loughborough University, England, Erin is a BPS Chartered and HCPC Registered Sport and Exercise Psychologist. As an applied practitioner, Erin works with a range of individuals, teams, and organisations across various sports. Alongside her applied practice, Erin is a Doctoral Researcher and University Teacher at Loughborough University. Her current research focuses on athlete mental health within elite sport, with previous research exploring areas such as athletes' experiences of performance blocks, and expertise in sports parenting. Erin uses her applied experience to inform both her research and her teaching. **Twitter: @EPSportsPsych**

Bernadette Ramaker, Germany, Bernadette is accredited as SPORT-PSYCHOLOOG VSPN® and Specialist in Applied Sport Psychology (SASP-FEPSAC). Bernadette is currently working as a full-time embedded performance coach for a professional esports organisation. She works closely with players and coaching staff, facilitating all processes regarding physical and mental well-being and performance enhancement on both individual and team levels. Before Bernadette joined the esports scene at the start of 2020, she had been active as a self-employed applied sport psychologist in the Netherlands since 2016 working with athletes from a variety of traditional sports disciplines, such as speed skating, CrossFit, field hockey, beach volleyball, (wheelchair)tennis, and basketball. Additionally, Bernadette is part of the Managing Council of the European Network of Young Specialists in Sport Psychology (ENYSSP) as an Applied Department Coordinator as well as being actively involved in the Equal Esports Council, which has a monitoring and advisory function within the Equal Esports Initiative. **Twitter: @b_ramaker**

Clara Swedlund, Scotland, Clara is a Trainee Sport and Exercise Psychologist enrolled in the British Psychological Society's independent training pathway. She is also a fitness coach and competitive bodybuilder, which makes her specifically interested in the field of exercise psychology and its application to the fitness industry. Clara currently consults as an applied psychologist with individuals who want to improve their relationship with physical activity, as well as with fitness professionals who want to enhance their coaching services by applying exercise psychology principles to their work. **Twitter: @ceswedlund, Instagram: @the_exerpsych**

Betsy Tuffrey, England, Betsy Tuffrey is a Chartered Sport and Exercise Psychologist, registered with the HCPC. Her applied experiences have fallen largely in football academy settings, international para football, and cricket academies. As the founder of Seed Psychology Ltd., Betsy practices within many sporting contexts, as well as enjoying experiences with the military and in corporate settings. Betsy's practice interests include rational emotive behaviour therapy, brief contact therapy, and single-session therapy. Betsy also has a research interest in the use of mindfulness in performance contexts. **Twitter: @seedpsychology**

Steven Vaughan, Liverpool John Moores University, England, Steven Vaughan is in the process of completing a Doctorate in Sport and Exercise Psychology at Liverpool John Moores University. He is a mature student in the process of transitioning career from senior leadership in healthcare. As a trainee Sport & Exercise Psychologist, he has gained applied practice experience in multiple sports including cycling, cricket, karate, running, and snowboarding. He provides support to athletes ranging from recreational to elite and professional. Steven's research relates to cognitions and mental performance within endurance sport. **Twitter & Instagram: @sjvpsych**

Beth Yeoman, England, Beth is in her final year of the Qualification in Sport and Exercise Psychology with the BPS. During Beth's applied practice she has worked in a variety of sports supporting both individuals and teams. Sports include golf, cricket, tennis, athletics, and rugby. This work has included a wide age span; however, the main focus of Beth's experience has been working with youth athletes. Specifically, working within a county cricket academy and through private consultancy. She enjoys introducing youth athletes to mental skills, celebrating their strengths, and helping them achieve their full performance potential. Alongside applied practice, Beth has published research on the use of smartphone video analysis within golf and the impact this has on a player's focus of attention and performance. The aim of the research Beth publishes is to inform real-world applied practice. **Twitter: @beth_yeoman**

ACKNOWLEDGEMENTS

Tim

To Ann – thanks for your support and patience – you have always been there for me when the going gets tough. Couldn't do any of it without you – if nothing else at least it provides us with a bit of a Brucie Bonus.

To Mum and Dad – still can't believe what you have done for me in my life. Your continued support always helps keep things in perspective.

To all those I have had the privilege to supervise into applied practice (you know who you are) – I have learnt more from you than I have ever given to you – thank you for being open, honest and committed to the journey towards being a practitioner. I am thankful that you all are valued colleagues and friends.

Erin

To Tom – thank you as always for your unwavering love and support, especially as I take on more and more projects...

To Mum and Dad – my twin pillars without whom I could not stand – these words don't seem like enough but thank you for all the love and support you continue to give in every aspect of my life.

To my fellow trainees and early career practitioners – those who contributed to this book and those who didn't – thank you for putting yourselves out there, sharing your stories, and striving together to move our profession forwards.

Finally, to the team within my own book chapter – thank you for welcoming me into the wonderful world of your sport and for allowing me to be part of your journey.

INTRODUCTION

Erin Prior and Tim Holder

Introduction

Tim: Applied sport psychology has a number of case study-type books that are already available. So, what do we think it is about this book that adds to what is already out there for practitioners?

Erin: *Firstly, I think there are several great books that offer inspiration in the form of case studies. You can grab them from your bookshelf and learn about interventions delivered by experienced practitioners that have come before you. But what we've found is that these traditional case study textbooks – while informative – are quite methodical, quite polished. What we are looking to do with this book is be a bit more candid and open about some of the ups and downs, the less polished moments – because there are definitely a range of challenges and barriers that practitioners can face throughout their careers.*

Tim: I think it's really obvious when you read case studies and applied literature, that it tends to be a very sanitised, possibly even unrealistic – but academically written – view of what happens on the ground. One of the great strengths of this book is that it's written by people who are working in applied practice in the early stages of their development, and they're sharing the things they've come across, the challenges they are meeting and overcoming, and how they're going about doing that. I think the candid nature of that is a significant addition to what is already out there in the literature that's guiding applied practice and practitioners.

Erin: *As we've discussed throughout creating this book, there can be real benefit in learning from the more challenging moments in a practitioner's career. So, with this book, we are hoping to create a resource for trainee and early-career practitioners (and maybe even experienced practitioners!), that prompts honest reflection and learning.*

DOI: 10.4324/9781003263890-1

Tim: It's our intention that this book will provide readers with the opportunity to investigate and understand the reality of working on the ground with other human beings in a sporting or exercise context and explore some of the fascinating insights that you can get from people's real-world experience.

Erin: *And something we've really encouraged all the authors to do is to be open, to be honest, to be candid, and to sit with some of those awkward moments where things might not have quite gone to plan, the moments that can be difficult to reflect on. All the authors have really embraced this vulnerable way of writing and have shared with us experiences that have been meaningful to their practice. We also chose trainee and early-career practitioners rather than more experienced practitioners to give a different perspective that we hope will resonate with readers. We hope early-career practitioners can gain a sense of reassurance from the stories within this book, that they may feel understood, and recognise that there is a group of people – across the world – who are going through this profession and facing some of these challenges, and that they're not on their own in that.*

Tim: Looking at the structure of the book, we chose a particular way of dividing up the sections to reflect real-world experience. Maybe you could share a little on that?

Erin: *So, we start with case studies in the first section which looks at a practitioner's intervention and approach to working with an individual or maybe a team and taking us from the conceptualisation of the intervention through to the delivery. Unlike other case studies, we've also encouraged authors to include reflective elements sharing their thoughts on the intervention or piece of work. I think the real benefit of these case studies is that we explore a range of different approaches but from the perspective of someone who is earlier in their career, and who is still trying to figure things out. It might not always go to plan, and that's okay, because we're going to learn from that – and hopefully collectively reading this book, we'll learn and develop.*

Tim: These case studies are the authors talking to an experience that they have found particularly insightful or challenging, or where they have been more creative and inventive in how they've worked with clients. The vibrancy of these case studies is what we hope is going to come across to the readers of this book, so that each of the authors are jumping off the page.

Erin: *The second part of the book is where we take a slightly different approach, which is more novel than previous books. Here, authors have written reflections, giving us an insight into the human experience of applied practice. What is it actually like being a practitioner and navigating through the profession in those early years? The authors are very open and honest in sharing their personal reflections on a range of experiences, ethical issues or challenges they've come across. It's a real opportunity for readers to connect with other practitioners over shared or similar experiences, but with the variety of reflections across the chapters, it's also an opportunity to learn from some different scenarios which readers may have not yet experienced. With these reflections you get a real feel for who the author is as a practitioner. Their stories are jumping from the page because the authors are really sharing some deep reflections about their practice.*

Tim: And one of the unique features of this book is that the authors are coming from different training backgrounds in different parts of the world. So, what might be insight for some readers is how a North American training experience might be significantly different from a training experience in the UK, or someone from Australasia and how they are training. So, these stories are coming from around the world.

Erin: *The writing style also varies across the book both within the book sections and between the sections. We really wanted to give the authors the freedom to let their voice be heard and express their experiences in a way that gets to the heart of the story they want to tell. So, this book may be unlike previous academic texts in the sense that there is a variation of writing style and approach across the book. We felt that it was really important for the way we approach the book to reflect the reality of our profession – that we all have different ways of working, and different ways of expressing our ideas.*

Tim: The restrictions and the structure that often comes with an academically focused, scientific writing style, probably don't maximise the potential in communicating practitioner experiences. Having a variety of writing styles enables the communication of the authors' experiences to be more compelling as well as more varied for the reader. So, what readers will notice in this book is a different way of signposting the evidence base which is underpinning the work that is going on. Whilst there will be traditional academic sources that are referenced throughout both the case studies and reflections, what readers will also find are other resources that are being recommended by the authors. These resources might be a podcast, or a piece in a popular psychology book that's been published which has drawn from academic evidence but isn't the academic evidence itself. We hope that these resources will be accessible and useful for the reader to develop their own practice.

Erin: *I think it was really important for us to think about how we were using those references and signposting readers to a wide range of resources, as that's where our knowledge and learning becomes much richer. So, we were really clear that although this is an academic book, that the focus was really how the book could be used in an applied way. How can this book be useful for practitioners who are in an applied environment, so that they can pick it up and really take something away that informs their practice?*

When thinking about how to use this book, we really want to encourage readers to dip in and out of the sections based on their interests and perhaps guided by current challenges they are facing. But we also encourage readers to be open-minded. There may be some chapters that don't jump out at the reader initially, or some chapters that may not seemingly resonate quite as much as others. By diving into those chapters, readers may be surprised what they can learn from practitioners with different view or experiences – you never know when something is going to strike a chored a make a big difference to your practice.

Tim: We hope that all the chapters will stimulate readers in different ways and for different reasons. What we want readers to do is to engage with chapters in preparation for future applied practice and use the reflective questions at the end of each chapter to think about how some of the experiences shared may inform their work.

CASE STUDIES: AN INTRODUCTION

Tim: We wanted to include case studies in this book to introduce readers to different ways of working and different approaches to the work of an applied practitioner, looking at how practitioners organise their thinking about a client and design appropriate interventions. When reading through these case studies, readers are encouraged to reflect on their own practice and recognise any similarities and differences from the case studies.

Erin: *I think it's really important to be thinking 'what can I learn from this that might confirm some of the ways I'm working and give me more confidence in my approach?' or 'is there something new and a bit different that I can try with one of my clients that may enhance my work?'. Using the case studies for information and inspiration and seeking out some of the signposted resources can be a great guide when conceptualising interventions. A broad range of topics are explored throughout the case study section, so I think there will be something for everyone. Chapter 1 focuses on fostering a sense of belonging as a female practitioner in a male-dominated sporting organisation and then we've got Chapter 2 which talks about something quite significant for readers to consider which is identifying a gap in service provision and considering whether you could be the person to fill that gap by creating a role for yourself either independently or within an organisation. This chapter focuses on creating an athlete mental health support role which was not available to university performance athletes at the time.*

Tim: Chapter 3 explores a practitioner's experience of working closely with and through sports parents and considers how a practitioner can conduct one-to-one sessions with clients online, in a time where we may be moving away from the more traditional approach to working with all clients in-person.

Erin: *Chapter 4 gives readers an insight into using Rational Emotive Behaviour Therapy (REBT). This chapter gives readers a detailed view of what it is like to use REBT with a client – in this case, a young footballer. The author also provides a commentary*

DOI: 10.4324/9781003263890-2

on her experience of implementing REBT which gives readers a rich understanding of what this approach may involve.

Tim: Chapter 5 considers how a Sport & Exercise Psychologist can adapt their skills and knowledge to work in other performance domains such as military and healthcare settings. This chapter gives readers an insight into ways in which they can broaden their career options as applied psychologists.

Erin: *We've then got Chapter 6 where we are introduced to the world of esports. This is a performance domain which is rising in popularity, and where it is becoming more and more common for a sport psychologist to be part of the staff team. This chapter gives us a great look at how sport psychology can be applied to esports and draws some interesting comparisons between this new domain and traditional sport.*

Tim: Finally, in the case study section of the book is a chapter which explores the novel experience of a performance psychologist who is working in a coaching role. In this chapter, the practitioner discusses how they created a psychologically informed environment and helped prepare the Israeli archery team for the Olympic Games in Tokyo. They reflect on both what a performance psychologist can bring to a coaching role, but also how practitioners can work closely with coaches to bring psychology work into training and competition settings.

Erin: *So, when thinking about how we would encourage readers to approach this case study section, it's been a goal of ours that the book can be used as a resource for practitioners to dip in and out of as required. There are some really nuanced messages across the chapters, so we hope readers engage with each chapter and reflect on what they can take away and use to inform their practice moving forward, with the help of the reflective questions posed at the end of each chapter.*

1

FINDING YOUR VOICE: A PRACTICAL SELF-CASE STUDY OF AN EARLY CAREER PRACTITIONER INTEGRATING INTO A PROFESSIONAL FOOTBALL ACADEMY

Fionnuala Barnes

> *True belonging has no bunkers. We have to step out from behind the barricades of self-preservation and brave the wild*
>
> *– Brené Brown.*

Introduction

Self-case studies have been advocated as catalysts for personal and professional development within the field of counselling education (Fraser & Wilson, 2010). Ultimately, in taking the time to consider one's own experiences, perceptions, and actions, a self-case study aims to explore and enhance a therapists' self-awareness to aid interpersonal effectiveness during their consultancy relationships. This account presents a practical self-case study of an early career practitioner finding her way to integrate into a professional football organisation. In doing so, it explores the role of belonging and connection, recognising the twists and turns as one navigates through the multidimensional construct of self, in an ever-changing and interdependent web of social relationships. This case study aspires to stimulate your thoughts and encourage discussions with those that you work with, to bring about takeaways for you to reflect upon and apply in your own career as a practitioner. Presented throughout this self-case study is a combination of evidence-based theory and research, interwoven with expressions of my experiences, involvements, and understandings to bring this area of exploration to life. I hope my experiences and curious questions motivate a new way of looking at the role of connection and belonging as we integrate into new work environments.

DOI: 10.4324/9781003263890-3

The Importance of Relationships

Relationships are at the centre of who we are as human beings. They go far deeper than any words can offer. Relationships extend all the way to our nervous system. In the presence of others, we experience a change in what is going on inside of ourselves. There is a shift in our psychophysiology as we relate with others (Porges, 2001). True to the psychologist, Chris Peterson's clear-cut quote, 'other people matter'. As we interact with others, these micromoments in our social and environmental world influence how our nervous system responds to either encourage connection or encourage protection. The emotions we catch, quite simply, have consequences. Next time you are with friends or family, notice what happens to your autonomic state. In their presence, how does their energy influence your internal sensations? For example, do you feel calmer, relaxed, energised, or perhaps nervous, uneasy, or unsettled? How does your psychophysiological experience differ when in the presence of work colleagues?

It is well regarded within the field of sport psychology and indeed, spanning wider across counselling, psychotherapy, and clinical psychology, that the relationship between the client and the psychologist, regardless of technique used, significantly contributes to therapeutic success (Rogers, 1965). It is no surprise that this relationship between a client and therapist plays such a critical role in the client reaching their goals, when we consider the deeply interconnected nature of human beings, influencing each other in a multitude of ways and providing the opportunity to have new socially learned experiences of connection, acceptance, and compassion. As Daniel Goleman advocates, we are hardwired for connection, with even the most routine encounters acting as regulators in the brain, impacting the way our brain develops and performs (Goleman, 2007). Exploring this in greater depth, Daniel Siegel's book 'Mindsight' offers a thought provoking read on how we can spend time to understand our inner selves, the link between our mind and body, and notably, what we can achieve by being receptive, rather than reactive, in our relationships with others (Siegel, 2001).[1] While this innate need for connection brings with it great strengths, it also highlights the dangerous consequences for disconnection. The experience of disconnection has the potential to thwart the basic human need of relatedness; at best disconnection can elicit painful emotional states and at worst disconnection can contribute to reduced physical and psychological health and wellbeing.

The 'Still Face Experiment' conducted in the 1970s by developmental psychologist Edward Tronick demonstrates the need for connection alongside the consequences of disconnection very early on in our life. Involving a baby

---

[1] Mindsight by Daniel Siegel presents a powerful way to explore and understand events and their effects on our mind and body. Siegel brings these to life through case studies to hit home the points!

and a parent, the experiment begins with the parent having fun while playing with their baby. The parent is smiling, talking, and responding to their baby's needs. During this first phase of the experiment, the baby is happy and engaging with their parent. The second phase of the experiment, known as the 'still face' phase, involves the parent turning away from their baby, then turning back for a period of two minutes with a still face. The parent avoids any communicative facial, vocal, or touch signals with their baby and ultimately ignoring any attempts from the baby to get their parent's attention to re-establish the happy connection: no smiles, laughs, or conversation, just stone-faced eye contact.[2] During this time, the baby is confused and distressed in their efforts to engage their parent, the longer they struggle to reconnect, the more distressed they become. After two minutes, the parent returns to interacting with their baby, they are once again smiling, listening, and responding to their needs. An immediate sense of relief and joy floods across the baby's face as connection is restored and the baby's needs are once again met. The research conducted from the 'Still Face Experiment' highlights the baby's response to socio-emotional disconnection. During the experience of disconnection, the baby searches for engagement, sending distress signals and re-connection requests to their parent. The movement from the mismatch of the still-face to the match of the mutual engagement between the baby and their parent highlights the importance of synchrony and finer adjustments based upon the perceived in-the-moment emotional signals. In doing so, the parent adjusts to their baby in a sympathetic, synchronous relationship. Since the initial experiment, research has expanded to the experience of connection and disconnection among couples, teachers, managers, and practitioner-client relationships. When nurturing growth among others in these wider contexts, research has demonstrated the role of being with another person in the moment, to be responsively open while retaining our own sense of self. It has begun to explore the impact of non-engagement and non-expressiveness by others (for example, a 'still face' manager or partner) on the experience of disconnection and it has highlighted the importance of listening, understanding, awareness, and mutual responsiveness for creating connection.

Our social interactions with others can often be characterised by a degree of messiness as we attempt to match those around, as we endeavour to tune in to their emotional needs and respond in a way which resonates with them. Responding to others in this way, allowing them to feel seen, heard, and

---

[2] If you are feeling brave you can find videos online demonstrating the experiment. The videos are not an easy watch, yet do show the power of warm, engaging, and responsive relationships between babies and caregivers.

understood, is known as attunement (Rowe & Mac Isaac, 2000). This process of attunement can be likened to dance-link sequences, as we carefully weave through a conversation, improvising in the moment based upon our emotions, cognitions, and the reciprocal attempts of attunement from those we are engaging in conversation with. When we attune, we shift our own internal state to resonate with the inner world of another. When you consider your relationships with coaches, colleagues, and clients, how have you experienced this process of attunement? Within a relationship, we inevitably move in and out of different intensities of closeness, connection, and distance with a client or colleague. At times we may feel a little distant, struggling to tune in to the moment with them, and then upon the discovery of a shared experience we feel drawn closer together. How might your experiences of attunement have changed over the course of a relationship with a client or colleague?

Building Relationships and Developing Connection as a Sport and Exercise Psychologist

Within the field of sport and exercise psychology, there is growing exploration of the 'person' and 'practitioner', with a focus upon how the personal qualities and characteristics a sport and exercise psychologist brings to a relationship can contribute to the success of a consultancy relationship (Woolway & Harwood, 2020). More specifically, how a sport and exercise psychologist's awareness of their own practice philosophy, beliefs, biases, views of themselves, others, and the world plays a part during these intimate interactions. With research largely focusing upon unpicking these dynamics within individual, one-to-one consultancy settings, it has predominately taken a top-down view of successful service delivery, emphasising the certain characteristics which help to build an effective relationship, including honesty, likeability, and psychotherapeutic counselling skills (Chandler et al., 2016). Nonetheless, applied sport psychology highlights that in addition to the qualities and characteristics held by the sport and exercise psychologist, working effectively in high-performance environments requires the development of contextual intelligence and cultural competency (Mellalieu, 2017; Wadsworth, 2021). Thus, this recognises that we do not consult in a vacuum, we are located in a cultural context. My experiences have highlighted that this cultural context is far more than a scenic backdrop for our development, it is an active agent in the relational processes that shape us as human beings. Take your own development, when you consider what factors have played influential roles, what comes to mind? When thinking about the critical moments that have contributed towards your development, what role does the environment(s) play?

In the current literature base, less attention has been placed on exploring how personal and professional attributes, in combination with the cultural context one finds oneself within, might contribute to fostering successful integration into an organisation. Within my professional roles, I have pondered how my skills, characteristics, beliefs, and values interact with the organisation within which I am entering. I have considered how they interact with the organisational culture I am becoming part of to influence my successful development and ability to thrive. In taking this perspective, this recognises the multidimensional nature of individuals, who are shaped by their life histories, identities, and identifications, (for example, sexual orientation, religious beliefs, gender, and race)[3] as well as the politics of their sport and the cultural narrative regarding what makes up good service delivery in a particular sociocultural context (for example, reactive, proactive, delivery styles, and delivery techniques).

Zooming out from individual development to take a wider view, sustained success of those in the 'team behind the team' is not solely based upon the embodied competence of the individual. It is further based upon how they function within a highly complex social and organisational environment. In light of this, practitioner success is dependent upon how they navigate the complex sociocultural construction of one's professional identity, both within and through, the cultural context of the high-performance environment they are working in. Underpinning the ability to thrive within their sphere of influence, is the integration of oneself into the environment, the sense of belonging to both the organisation as well as the people in and around them.

Understanding Belonging

The desire to belong is a deeply rooted human motivation, underpinned by our ancestral origins. It permeates our thoughts, feelings, and behaviours. In recent years, a distinction between trait and state belonging has been established, with trait belonging being a core psychological need, and state belonging being influenced by daily life events and stressors, much like our emotions. In this account, I refer to belonging as a unique and subjective experience that relates to a yearning for connection with others, the need for positive regard, and the desire for interpersonal connection (Rogers, 1951).

The broad conceptualisation of belonging as a fundamental need has been established across different theorists, from self-determination theorists, attachment theorists, social baseline theorists, systems theorists, and personality theorists; all have acknowledged the fundamental need to belong (Baumeister & Leary, 1995). In her book 'Belonging', Toko-pa Turner, describes that 'at the very heart of belonging is the word long. To belong to something is to stay with it for the long haul. It is an active choice we make to a relationship, to a place, to our body, to a life because we value it' (2017). Fundamentally, this highlights the connection between the concept of belonging and the need for autonomy, choice, and commitment, components we

---

[3] The (BPS) Sport & Exercise Psychology Review Vol. 17 No. 1 & 2 Special Issue on Equality, Diversity and Inclusion offers further reading from a diverse range of perspectives on topics such as racism in sport, disability inclusion in sport & exercise psychology, gender inequality, and inclusion of the LGBTQIA+ community in sport and physical activity.

highly value in our work-related activities. It is through belonging we find much of our meaning, identity, relevance, and satisfaction, thus making it something we ache to feel at work. When you think about belonging, what does it mean for you?

For me, belonging is in a constant state of flux, it is fluid, it is hard to articulate, you feel when it is present, and you feel when it is absent. It is not something external, that we can achieve and tick off like a goal on a spreadsheet. We carry belonging in our hearts, it is something we are ever seeking to find, and to maintain. My experience of belonging is much more than the passing feelings we feel hour by hour, from the turbulence of a challenging day at work or the nerves of an upcoming presentation, belonging for me, delves deep into the very essence of who we are. It gives us energy to drive forward, it gives us meaning to why we do what we do. In defining what we mean by belonging, it supports the subsequent deeper exploration of how to go about creating and developing our own sense of belonging.

The Case: Context

As a young female, a neophyte practitioner in a traditionally masculine sport, my experiences of belonging, of seeking connection, have gone through twists and turns. At the time of writing this case study, I am a trainee sport and exercise psychologist, completing a professional doctorate in Sport and Exercise Psychology, while finishing my third season as a psychologist in the academy of a professional football club. Having worked for the last four years in high-performance environments across both professional and Olympic sporting organisations, I felt I had a moderate cultural understanding of the environments within which I worked. My professional training encouraged engagement in reflective practice which helped develop my cultural understanding, increase my self-awareness, and harnessed my motivations for why I do what I do. Whilst our identity will always evolve, cast your mind back to your first few years as a practitioner, what was this like? How did you feel within the organisation you worked in?

When considering the context of psychology within UK professional football, it is only within the last decade that the role of a sport psychologist has begun to have a concrete and stable position. Progressing the governance over long-term youth development and introducing greater depth to the holistic support provided at certain football academies, the English Premier League introduced the Elite Player Performance Plan (EPPP) in 2011, commencing at the beginning of the 2012 season. With the introduction of the EPPP, this led to the formalisation of how sport psychology support is provided within certain football academies, alongside the wider multidisciplinary sport science and medicine team. As such, the opportunities to work within football in the UK have and continue to flourish. Despite the more recent formalisation of psychology support, the role of psychology within football has long been recognised, as once fittingly articulated by the Dutch football legend Johan Cruyff, 'you play football with your head and your legs are merely there to help you!'. In line with these progressions, so too have I experienced shifts in the perception and function of psychology in youth football. My experiences have highlighted a shift from reactive approaches to psychology, with a psychologist being there to fix problems, to proactive approaches encouraging learning, self-awareness, growth, and performance. The discipline itself is still evolving as to what it 'looks like' and how it's 'done', which of course will naturally differ consultant to consultant. For me, at this time, I was a young practitioner, in a relatively young discipline, as a gender minority, within a sport I had limited experience of.

Sensing the Difference

I found myself weaving carefully through the unwritten rules and social norms within the environment, trying to understand as quickly as possible the socially acceptable ways of interacting. Mindful of this, I began to tailor my language, conversation starters, general remarks, gestures, actions, and behaviours to ensure my ways of being were acceptable for the context I was within. From the weekend's results and the following week's score predictions, the latest rumblings of signings and transfers to the light-hearted, somewhat playful humour. This was my desire to fit in. It is natural. It is a normal part of human behaviour. As a psychologist, in effort to seek explanations for this behaviour, I turned to theories of evolution. Evolution theorists propose pursuing a sense of belonging in this way serves as a survival mechanism, as for our ancient ancestors being in a small group enabled the sharing of hunting and gathering, and thus an increase in their chances of survival. Take away the group and place one in a solitary environment, their chances of survival have substantially reduced. Without acceptance into the group, the chances of becoming immersed into an environment and having the platform to collaborate with the coaching team and wider support services to embed psychological principles would be more challenging. As I attempted to attune my attributes and abilities, so they did not deviate from the social norms, the gap between my real self and my authentic self was becoming larger and larger. The perceived pressure to fit it and conform, heightened by such a new and novel environment, led to my desire to reduce any individuality for fear of standing out and showing difference. This combination of experiences was a recipe for triggering the brain's evolutionary protection system to go into overdrive.

Once again, I found myself turning to explanations of human behaviour and seeking reason for the pursuit of conformity and comfort. Our complex, extraordinary brain is primed to keep us safe, focused on preservation while avoiding risks and threats. Novel situations which are unknown or uncertain, that can be both physical and psychological, can be appraised as a potential threat, triggering the body to move into safety. Today's modern day work stressors involve the fear of failing, the fear of judgement, the fear of not being or feeling good enough, and the fear of rejection. Examples of these may be the fear of messing up a workshop, the fear of others doubting your new idea, the fear of your work being *just average*, and the fear that if you show your true self, others may reject you. They can extend to simple behaviours such as unmuting yourself on a video call, walking into a room full of new faces, trying out a new idea in a workshop, keeping novel ideas to ourselves rather than risking the ridicule by sharing them. These fears drive us to self-protect. They drive us to put on our metaphorical armour, step back from a situation, and cover the areas which may expose our *perceived* weaker spots.

Brené Brown[4] talks about connection as 'the energy which exists between people when they feel seen, heard, and valued; when they can give and receive without judgement; and when they derive sustenance and strength from the relationship' (Brown, 2010). Looking at my early career experiences, I recognised my experience of connection in the aforementioned way, could never come without shearing away the judgement placed upon the self; the expectations, the should do's, the must do's, and the supposed to do's, while settling into a new role and a new environment. As I continued to try to be someone else, to fit in, to conform, I was shying away from my authentic self. I was inadvertently negating any possible growing sense of belonging and meaning within the present. Looking back, the difference provided an opportunity, it provided a platform to explore ideas in fresh ways and deliver psychology in a way which had not yet been incorporated into the club.

'Why diverse teams are smarter teams' (Rock & Grant, 2016). This is the title of a popular Harvard Business Review article expressing a plethora of advantages to having a varied workforce.[5] From new perspectives, increased decision-making capabilities, greater innovation, objectivity in analysis, and improved performance, the array of opportunities and advantages which diversity nurtures have become repeated conversations within occupational psychology. Alongside the advantages to the team of a varied workforce, are the challenges faced by the individual as they operate within the organisation. What is it like to be part of a minority in an organisation? What is it like to stand out? What is it like to bring your authentic self in an organisation where you are so visibly different?

Upon entering my role, I brought a fresh set of eyes, with different experiences in personal background, athletic training, professional experiences, educational training routes, and ultimately ways of looking at the world. The challenge which sat before me was how to find commonality with those around me, how to work together to push boundaries, and create an environment where all could thrive, while fundamentally bringing the uniqueness of my skills, and my difference, to the organisation. My challenge was to step up and step forward, to brave the wild.

Throughout this self-case study, I aim to encourage us to consider our own self in the co-constructed environment we find ourselves within, how our previous experiences, beliefs, and deep-rooted values interact with the culture to help or hinder our integration into the organisation and the cultivation of our own sense of belonging. In doing so, it provides us, as individuals, with the foundations to influence our own sense of connection. It equips us with the tools and the

---

[4] Brené's podcast 'Unlocking Us', contains a variety of honest conversations linking together her research and her own experiences.

[5] You can find the full article on The Harvard Business Review website: https://hbr.org/2016/11/why-diverse-teams-are-smarter

techniques to be able to make changes and take responsibility for our own sense of belonging in the workplace.

Taking Responsibility for Belonging

For so long I looked for answers in books, journals, blogs, and Ted talks on how to navigate the environment I found myself within. Until I came across a quote from Joseph Campbell expressing 'if you can see your path laid out in front of you step by step, you know it's not your path. Your own path you make with every step you take. That's why it's your path'. And so, I stepped into the adventure of paving my own pathway, of finding my own answers from my personal experiences.

Belonging as a Framework

Below I share with you a framework from research into the psychology of belonging. I incorporated this framework to support my thinking and explore different ways of viewing events and experiences. Ultimately, this is a framework which we may all find useful to help us make sense of the cultural co-created landscape in which we work (Allen et al., 2021). Authenticity is a choice which requires courage. Seldom do we wake up and believe we can do something, and we need more than manifestations of 'I am worthy, I am different'. What gives us the courage to step forward? What has given you the courage to stand out and be you? Exploring the components covered in this framework gives us a platform to begin to bring our authentic selves. The framework contains four interrelated components: competencies for belonging, opportunities for belonging, motivations for belonging, and perceptions of belonging.

Competencies for Belonging: What Are My Skills and Abilities That I Can Draw upon to Connect?

Competencies for belonging is referring to the skills, abilities, and aptitude one has, to connect with people, things, and places, to experience a sense of belonging. These competencies may be both subjective and objective, and can include emotional, social, and cultural skills. As we begin to unpick these competencies, it becomes clear how they complement and reinforce each other, as well as contribute to, and are further reinforced by a sense of belonging.

For me, at the centre of exploring and expanding the competencies for belonging is curiosity in yourself, in others, and in the world. The connection to ourselves provides the foundation to connect with those around us. In this instance, I am not just talking about our values, beliefs, worldly perspectives, but our nervous system, the understanding of how our autonomic nervous system responds during moments of challenge, excitement, and novelty, for example. In consideration of the emotional competencies for belonging, as psychologists we often talk about understanding the specificity of our emotional experiences and expanding our emotional literacy to better describe what we feel, a term coined by Lisa Feldman Barrett known as emotional granularity.[6] Emotional granularity enables us to better articulate the precise experience of our inner world. In making sense of our inner world, our response to our arising emotions have the potential to be more helpful, more appropriate to what we are sensing. Strengthening my own skill of curiosity through greater emotional awareness has brought about a greater appreciation for the *potential* of our emotional experience as human beings, recognising the ease of oversimplifying such experiences and the vibrancy of the nuances should we choose to open up. For me, being connected to and aware of myself is about being with things as they are, having the skills to remain with the uncertain, to stay open to the different, to explore the unknown, to fully inhabit each moment. A busy meeting room filled with new faces, an opportunity to raise a new idea among colleagues, giving feedback to a coach on a session, walking into the canteen as the only female. These experiences have required me to sit with the uncomfortable, to look beneath the initial sensations as to why I was feeling nervous or unsettled and make sense of what was going on. Becoming more observant and open increases the capacity to remain receptive to our inner world, monitoring with greater clarity, objectivity, and depth, to subsequently respond to and modify our interpersonal world. To modify our interpersonal world from a place of reflective awareness. For me, curiosity with my emotional experiences has given me different ways to look at challenging situations. Take a moment of nervousness, rather than jumping to the end, or an outcome, what happens if we replace assumptions, expectations, or judgements with curiosity? What happens if we use our skills to delve deeper into what a feeling may mean or the function of the behaviour we are drawn to execute?

Increased understanding of our emotional experiences, and subsequent emotional and behavioural regulation enables us to be in the present with those around us, to be able to empathise with people, hear people for what they are saying, rather than occupied by our own emotional experiences. Not only do emotions allow us to navigate the world, they also enable us to connect with others.

Opportunities to Belong: Where Are the Places, Times, Spaces, and Groups That Facilitate Belonging?

Opportunities to belong is referring to the availability of places, times, physical spaces, and social groups or networks which enable connections to take place. We may have the capability and motivation to connect, yet without the platform to do so, this may limit the opportunities to foster belonging. Opportunities will undoubtedly change organisation to organisation yet spending time identifying

---

[6] How Emotions are Made: The Secret Life of the Brain by Dr Lisa Feldman Barret investigates the link between neuroscience and emotions while ironing out myths surrounding emotions. You can also find some great videos on Youtube should you wish to listen to Dr Barret!

what physical and social features exist within an organisation may enhance the possibilities to connect.

I consider exploring opportunities for connection rather like painting a picture, in which you gradually add more depth and more colour. Beginning at the base, fundamentally the nature of your role, whether that be part time or full time, determines the time you can commit to physically being in the environment. From here, we can add depth with additional role related factors to provide a rich depiction of *what* you can consider and *how* you can operate.

When first adding depth to the opportunities available, I have found value in considering *what* is expected of you in your role, for example key objectives and project areas. Gaining initial clarity on role expectations and responsibilities around training schedules and season calendars, provides a foundation to create a working week, month, quarter, and block that contains a variety of experiences that help develop connection with those that you work with. The clarity provided regarding expectations presents a canvas to work with moving forward to thus consider *how* you can operate within the environment.

When working in sport, the environments within which we work across can be hugely varied. At times, the frequency at which we are required to change 'hats' and operate in different settings can be somewhat daunting. Nonetheless, these environments provide opportunities to connect with different people, in different ways. Below I present some of the opportunities available to connect across different settings within an academy environment.

Training.
On the pitch, off the pitch, athletic development sessions, analysis sessions, group workshops from external providers, group workshops from internal members of staff, free play time.

Games.
Friendlies at home and away, games as part of a larger league both at home and away, tournaments.

Tours.
Domestic training camps, international trips.

Additional Settings.
Permanent desk, 'hot-desk', informal coffee machine conversations, set mealtimes, informal social events, travelling, support networks within the organisation (for example, Women's Network), peer support networks outside of the organisation (for example, the Football Exchange Women's Network[7]).

---

[7] Liverpool John Moores University has developed a Football Exchange Women's Network which aims to connect women working in the football industry from across the world. With members from across psychology, nutrition, analysis, physiology, and coaching, the network offers opportunities to engage in activities such as peer learning, mentoring, and research collaborations.

The settings provide an opportunity for you to connect with players, coaches, and staff in different ways, and thus as a result, foster an understanding of who they are on different levels. In approaching opportunities that foster connection and belonging in this way, it opens the door to approaching the construction of a working week in a creative, varied manner. How do you add depth to your picture? What environments could you use to create your working week? In being mindful of the potential array of opportunities, we have to connect; we are consciously choosing to increase the frequency at which the doors will open to foster a sense of belonging.

Motivations to Belong: What Are My Desires and Drivers for Connecting?

Motivations to belong is referring to drivers for seeking social interactions and connections with others. Motivation is something which gives us a reason to act, a reason to move forward. My experiences in unpicking reasons that drive connection, have been focused upon greater exploration of my personal values and the wider organisational purpose.

Personal Values: Tiny Steps Over Big Leaps

Values are what we really care about deep in our hearts. They are what we hold important as we navigate the sometimes messy, sometimes complex, and often remarkable world we live in. As such, values provide us with principles by which we live our life. They provide directions for the journey we are on and can help clear the haze to illuminate a pathway in times of ambiguity, during difficult decisions, or challenging conversations. For me, value-driven thoughts and behaviours have become particularly important in guiding myself through the twists and turns of integrating into an organisation. Upon entering an organisation, there are many voices to listen to and many approaches to ways of working. As such, being able to be clear on what you stand for has guided decisions on my own course of action and supported a deeper understanding of my own responses to certain situations. For example, why particular behaviours trigger a response in yourself, or why certain staff members are harder to connect with. Spend time getting to know what really drives why you do what you do. Pose questions to get to know yourself better. What do you want to stand for as a psychologist? What do you believe in? What do you want to be known for? Break down these values into smaller day to day actions which align with the overarching values, ultimately, moving you towards the type of person *and* practitioner you want to be.

Organisational Purpose: Top Down, Inside Out, and Bottom Up

While the focus of the chapter thus far has been on how developing connection can be influenced by the people and the settings within a place of work, the drive to link personal values and career goals to the wider organisational purpose has become more common over recent years. With this in mind, a sense of belonging extends further, to connection with the organisational principles within which an individual works. As a result, I have found understanding the wider strategic goals and vision of the organisation, and specifically how the goals of my team fit within this vision, a powerful component in fostering a sense of belonging. It helps highlight meaning to my day-to-day work-related actions and behaviours which contribute to the wider goals. It shines a light on how my jigsaw piece fits into the wonderfully complex inner workings of an organisation. With greater understanding of the strategic goals, it helps join the dots to enable alignment between my personal values and my role. At times, the connection between your values and goals to the strategic-level goals may feel faint, requiring greater exploration and time to discover the alignment. Reflection upon and recognition of the critical moments in one's journey can add depth to the motivations for why you do what you do, while discovering possible ways to move forwards with your values-driven actions.

Perceptions of Belonging: How Do My Subjective Feelings and Cognitions about This Experience Support Connection?

Perceptions of belonging refers to our beliefs, our self-confidence, and our desire for connection. Our perceptions are undoubtedly informed and shaped by our previous experiences and encounters in previous jobs or academic institutions. In this way, perceptions of belonging within an organisation can be complex and are often multi-layered, involving views about our interpersonal relationships, the organisation as a community, and the workplace facilities themselves.

There is a plethora of questions, which in asking oneself before entering a role can clarify how our past experiences may shape the experience we are having, or are about to have, in the organisation. Take a moment to pause. What was your experience of connection and belonging in your previous role or with a previous team? What views and beliefs about the sport or team itself were you carrying into your role? How might these have influenced your initial behaviours when connecting with others? For me, I have found my knowledge of, and previous experience in playing or participating in certain sports, has influenced my sense of belonging when stepping into a new role. More specifically, the less knowledge and experience I felt I had, the less belonging I felt upon first entering the organisation. In understanding the drivers behind my behaviours, coupled with the beliefs underpinning them, I was able to sit with my feelings of uncertainty and the nervousness. In moving forward from the awareness of my perceptions of belonging to actioning the development of a greater sense of belonging, I used the earlier explored components outlined in the framework (competencies, opportunities, and motivations) to foster deeper connections with coaches, staff, and players.

Conclusion

We are social beings with a fundamental need to feel accepted and connected to groups to optimally function. A sense of belonging. A sense that we are part of something. This shapes how our relationships with others develop. When we feel a sense of belonging, we can more effectively engage with others, we are more able to use our strengths, and bring our best selves to work. Being around other people does not guarantee a sense of belonging. It is all too easy to place expectation and responsibility for creating a sense of belonging on those around us, and believe that others must reach out to us. For me, it is quite the contrary. It is the interactions and experiences we co-create and the work we can undertake as individuals that helps create a sense of belonging for both ourselves and for others.

As the 1980s film 'The Breakfast Club'[8] reminds us, being yourself is your only real option. I have shared my own pathway to exploring and making sense of my experiences within the cultural backdrop I was working within. Some of this may resonate and you may be able to draw from your own experiences to understand the nuances of developing connection and fostering belonging. Irrespective of our level within an organisation, belonging is something we can all affect and influence if we take the time to explore our skills, motivations, opportunities, and perceptions surrounding connection. Although this is a reflective account of a young practitioner, a sense of belonging and connection is an important aspect for any individual stepping into a new role. I hope this self-case study inspires thoughts, new perspectives, and encourages reflections about yourself and those you work with.

REFLECTIVE QUESTIONS

- What could you do to commit to building positive connections among those you work with?
- What actions would help foster a greater sense of belonging, either for yourself or for a colleague who may be new into the organisation?
- Reflecting on your own experiences, have you ever felt a lack of connection in a role? If so, spend some time reflecting on why that may have been the case.

---

[8] The Breakfast Club is a comical, coming of age film directed by John Hughes in 1985. Well worth a watch to see the journey of how the five key characters move from seeing themselves for how they are socially presented, through to how they truly are.

References

Allen, K. A., Kern, M. L., Rozek, C. S., McInerney, D. M., & Slavich, G. M. (2021). Belonging: A review of conceptual issues, an integrative framework, and directions for future research. *Australian Journal of Psychology*, *73*(1), 87–102.

Baumeister, R. F., & Leary, M. R. (1995). The need to belong: Desire for interpersonal attachments as a fundamental human motivation. *Psychological Bulletin*, *117*(3), 497–529.

Brown, B. (2010). *The Gifts of Imperfection: Let Go of Who You Think You Are Supposed to Be and Embrace Who You Are*. Center City, MN: Hazeldon Publishing.

Brown, B. (2017). *Braving the Wilderness: The Quest for True Belonging and the Courage to Stand Alone*. New York: Random House.

Chandler, C., Eubank, M., Nesti, M., Tod, D., & Cable, T. (2016). Personal qualities of effective Sport Psychologists: Coping with organisational demands in high performance sport. *International Journal of Sport Psychology*, *47*(4) 297–317.

Fraser, N., & Wilson, J. (2010). Self-case study as a catalyst for personal development in cognitive therapy training. *The Cognitive Behaviour Therapist*, *3*(3), 107–116.

Goleman, D. (2007). *Social Intelligence*. New York: Random house.

Lafferty, M. E., Coyle, M., Prince, H. R., & Szabadics, A. (2022). "It's not just a man's world"–Helping female sport psychologists to thrive not just survive. Lessons for supervisors, trainees, practitioners and mentors. The British Psychological Society.

Mellalieu, S. D. (2017). Sport psychology consulting in professional rugby union in the United Kingdom. *Journal of Sport Psychology in Action*, *8*(2), 109–120.

Porges, S. W. (2001). The polyvagal theory: Phylogenetic substrates of a social nervous system. *International Journal of Psychophysiology*, *42*(2), 123–146.

Rock, D., & Grant, H. (2016, November 4). *Why Diverse Teams Are Smarter*. Harvard Business Review. https://hbr.org/2016/11/why-diverse-teams-are-smarter.

Rogers, C. R. (1965). The therapeutic relationship: Recent theory and research. *Australian Journal of Psychology*, *17*(2), 95–108.

Rogers, C. R. (1951). *Client-Centered Therapy: Its Current Practice, Implications, and Theory*. Oxford: Houghton Mifflin.

Rowe Jr, C., & Mac Isaac, D. (2000). *Empathic Attunement: The 'Technique' of Psychoanalytic Self Psychology*. Maryland: Jason Aronson.

Siegel, D. J. (2001). Toward an interpersonal neurobiology of the developing mind: Attachment relationships, "mindsight," and neural integration. *Infant Mental Health Journal: Official Publication of the World Association for Infant Mental Health*, *22*(1-2), 67–94.

Turner, T. P. (2017). *Belonging: Remembering Ourselves Home*. Salt Spring Island, BC: Her Own Room Press.

Wadsworth, N., McEwan, H., Lafferty, M., Eubank, M., & Tod, D. (2021). A systematic review exploring the reflective accounts of applied sport psychology practitioners. *International Review of Sport and Exercise Psychology*, 1–27.

Woolway, T., & Harwood, C. G. (2020). Consultant characteristics in sport psychology service provision: A critical review and future research directions. *International Journal of Sport and Exercise Psychology*, *18*(1), 46–63.

2

PLAYING WITH HEART: A CASE STUDY ON SUPPORTING VARSITY MENTAL HEALTH

Anna Abraham

Introduction

This chapter provides an in-depth analysis into why and how a graduate student-intern became one of, if not the first full-time mental health counsellor for a Canadian university athletic department. The case study will thoroughly examine my timeline of crusading, designing, piloting, and eventually cementing a fixed position with the University of Ottawa Gee-Gees' varsity sport programmes. Pushing through plenty of uncertainty over the past few years while gripping the reigns of passion for normalising mental health care in high-performance sport, I found an immensely fulfilling role. Getting here involved navigating quite a variety of challenges for the first time in addition to my duties as a practitioner. Throughout the chapter, client vignettes highlight therapeutic experiences with this special demographic. Looking back, I can now offer my younger self some solace. I can tell her that even though she does not know where her path will lead, she is paving the way for something very much deserving of her efforts.

Background

I can still remember facing the doubt in my father's voice as he walked away from me asking, 'How are you going to find a job in sports *and* mental health?' I did not have an answer for him back then, but I figured if I truly felt this passionately about something, it must be worth at least trying. I was a graduate student completing my master's in counselling at Saint Paul University still deciding on a specialty to pursue like the rest of my peers. Some were choosing to work with addictions, couples, grief, recent immigrants, trauma, and/or youth. I recognised the value in picking an area that would remain personally challenging yet rewarding. It seemed like the only way to avoid the burnout our professors kept warning us about. Problem was, the only constant love in my life was sport and by

DOI: 10.4324/9781003263890-4

that point in 2013, there had not been much dialogue yet around mental health.[1] And so, the real adventure began. One filled with many obstacles where I would have to advocate for others, believe in myself, convince a lot of people, and create my own opportunities.

An example of creating my own opportunities was being the first student in my counselling master's programme to ever seek an external internship placement in the world of high performance. After navigating through some red tape due to the novelty of the request, I was lucky enough to find a supervisor approved by my administration who was teaching at the School of Dance and was willing to take me on as a mental performance intern. I ended up inheriting her position when she retired a few years later and still teach Performance Psychology courses there today. You never really know where any given experience may lead. Graduate school may be the perfect time to pursue any number of paths without putting pressure on any one direction. Even the smallest interaction can be a chance to learn and create connection. This became apparent to me as I taught in a contemporary dance diploma programme without a background in the performing arts. If I had chosen to solely stay in my comfort zone of team sports, I may have never been able to gain so much from my student-dancers each year. That environment continuously expands my understanding of mental training and humbly allows me to remain a life-long pupil of the field. It is worthwhile to explore contexts and serve populations outside of what may be personally relatable. In this way, you can be challenged to grow as a professional and you may even stumble upon something rather meaningful.

Through courses and internships, my graduate degrees set me up for eventual dual certification as a mental health counsellor in the province (through the College of Registered Psychotherapists of Ontario) and a Mental Performance Consultant (MPC) in the country (through the Canadian Sport Psychology Association). This would allow me to reach the ultimate goal of becoming a sport and performance-informed psychotherapist. By the time I was completing my second master's in health and performance psychology at the University of Ottawa, I was also qualifying to be a counsellor. I was honoured to have an internship as the MPC for their Women's Basketball programme. It became evident that their athletes' needs would fluctuate between mental health and mental performance. Thankfully, I was equipped to support both. It was an incredibly rewarding season with the team and reinforced my desire to work in sport. I asked my internship director if I could speak to the mental health representatives for the school's varsity sport programmes. I assumed it would be a solid place to ask questions about their exclusive work and maybe even score a job. Unfortunately, there was no such sector. The student-

---

[1]   Thankfully, at the time of writing, the conversation surrounding mental health and mental illness has grown, with athletes sharing their stories. 'The Players Tribune' offers a collection of mental health stories by professional athletes (https://www. theplayerstribune.com/collections/mental-health-awareness) with an accompanying podcast called 'Blindsided' with Corey Hirsch and Dr Diane McIntosh.

athletes of my alma mater did not have access to specialised mental health care. I was shocked but soon found out it was standard practice across Canadian universities. Sport-specific support may first be made available in many other areas such as medical health, nutrition, and strength training. I thought to myself that somebody should really do something about this. I even wrote about it in one of my essays for the performance psychology master's programme stating, 'I would like to see counselling being a regularly offered service for varsity athletes at the University of Ottawa'. Talk about manifesting!

Returning for a second season as the MPC for Gee-Gees' Women's Basketball on an Honorarium basis, I reached out to the newly appointed Athletic Director and booked a meeting to discuss the lack of mental health support on campus for their teams. I am unsure where I found the courage to even approach upper management as a recent post-grad, but it seemed unfair that their student-athletes were often left on their own to deal with mental health struggles. I wanted to be a part of the solution and not the problem. Learning stories of student-athletes in mental health crises around the world, including my own friends, and knowing I could now be of qualified service all added to a feeling of betrayal if I walked away. I witnessed the difference an available practitioner made after my year with the basketball team but there were still nine other varsity programmes without that access. I could have never guessed a cold email to the Athletic Director back in 2016 would lead me to where I am now in 2022.

Focus on the Controllables

Maintaining Faith When Facing Mass Uncertainty

One of the toughest challenges from the last few years was the lack of job security. After many emails and even more meetings with different levels of management about my work with Women's Basketball and the requests now coming in from other teams, I was given a small Service Agreement to start a pilot project where I would be available to offer counselling services to all varsity sport teams for a few hours a week. It was very exciting to have my foot in the door even if I was unaware at the time for how long I would remain teetering that line.

Living with different employee contract models and navigating the Human Resources' (HR) demands of a large educational institution proved frustrating and stressful. As time passed, I received increasing pressure from family and friends to at least consider seeking opportunities outside the University of Ottawa. I juggled appreciation for my loved ones' concerns with trying to remain steadfast in my mission. I really wanted to make them proud, but I could sense their annoyance and worry for me growing. I even turned down some random full-time job offers because my heart would not be in it. If I was not fortunate enough to be living with my parents while working part-time, I may have not even had the choice of rejecting those openings. I knew my cause at the university was immensely valuable, but it came at an expense I had to be willing to accept. For example, I remained living at home until my contract provided me enough protection to qualify for a decent mortgage and purchase my own place. That process alone took about five years through different honorariums (2015–2017), part-time service agreements (2017–2018), full-time term positions (2018–2021) until finally earning a full-time fixed position (2021 to present). I could not control the circumstances or duration of each step but I could keep investing in the factors I could control such as: being authentic and compassionate with my clients, being financially responsible, building relationships with coaches and support staff, developing connections with campus counselling staff, presenting accurate service-related statistics, regularly campaigning to upper management, seeking guidance from real-estate professionals, practicing self-care, preparing and completing any HR-related requests such as job interview processes, and demonstrating patience with the whole process. Using all my internal resources to do what I could with the external circumstances out of my hands would really require me to practice what I so often preach to clients. I believed in the deepest pockets of my soul that what I was doing was making a difference. I let that faith fuel me. It was helpful that the work itself was remarkably gratifying. My Athletic Director still checks in with me to this day asking, 'Are you good, Anna? Are you still enjoying it?' Every time, I respond wholeheartedly, 'Of course, I love what I do!'

Pick Your Battles

In those initial years at the university, I enjoyed what I did so much that I was willing to carry the anxiety and disappointment of contract work. I was also just grateful to actually be doing what I had worked so hard to create. I was the mental health counsellor for all varsity sport programmes at the university. Gee-Gees' student-athletes finally had access to free and confidential counselling support. I was fully welcomed into the Varsity Integrated Support Team and was also receiving clinical support from supervisors at the university Counselling Services. Even still, I found it arduous to decide which issues beyond therapy services to fight for and which to either postpone or let go indefinitely. It felt like the weight of this new wonderfully accessible service was now on my shoulders and if I messed up in any way, a lot of vulnerable young people would suffer the loss. I learned that in this sort of position of developmental responsibility, it is important to be intentional with the actions you do take while ensuring the purpose that drives you is still worth the cost of your periodic inaction. In my case, it was. I quietly advocated for increased job security when I had opportunities like check-ins with supervisors and performance reviews but for the most part, I focused on what I could do with the scope that was given to me. I knew that if I poured myself into that no matter how incremental it was, I could at least make a purposeful change and I hoped it would then speak for itself. I should note that during these times, it was extremely helpful to seek support from my family and friends. Although they would often become frustrated for me, they were also generous listeners who validated my personal attachments to my work.

I imagine it is quite a relief for them to see where I am today given they were by my side as I took every initial unsteady step.

One of the first requests asked of me outside counselling services was to conduct an environmental analysis and determine a pathway for our department towards best practices. I recognised the value in this to ensure we followed efficient steps going forward and as my Assistant Athletic Director illustrated, to avoid 'reinventing the wheel'. I met with all the varsity Head Coaches to get a feel for their team's needs and their current contacts for mental health or mental performance support. I also connected with numerous other individuals around campus to identify their student resources, referral networks and relationships with the athletic department. I reached out to other universities across North America to learn about their own mental health care models, paying particular attention to any who were sport-informed. I spent a lot of time analysing the relevant research on varsity mental health and comparing it to the compiled data I was simultaneously gathering on the ground. The more I read, the more confident I became in my call to action. It was clear student-athletes usually faced numerous barriers in accessing general campus counselling services and would benefit from receiving specialised care from practitioners who understood their unique circumstances. I determined the most advantageous battles to pick outside of being a mental health counsellor included researching the barriers and needs of my target population, offering my department evidence-based recommendations, and providing educational resources.[2,3] These each came with their own learning curve which further added to the foundation I was building.

Research Target Population

Throughout history, the perception has been that student-athletes are better adjusted and less likely to struggle with mental health challenges than their non-athlete peers (Chew & Thompson, 2014; Van Slingerland, 2020). They are often praised and glorified for their ability to display mental toughness (DeLenardo, 2014). Although sport participation has shown to encourage pro-social behaviour in high school, post-secondary student-athletes are at increased risk for difficulties related to alcohol abuse,[4] aggression, and injuries. They may be just as or even more likely to deal with overall mental health challenges because they have the same risk factors as non-athletes in addition to the stressors of high-performance sport (DeLenardo, 2014; Van Slingerland, 2020). Contributing factors to their specific issues may be from: their age,

---

[2] 'Believe Perform' shares a range of educational resources related to sport psychology and mental health.

[3] *'Mindfulness for Student Athletes: A Workbook to Help Teens Reduce Stress and Enhance Performance'* is a great workbook by Gina M. Biegel and Todd H. Corbin.

[4] To understand more about addiction and childhood trauma, see *'Playing with Fire: The Highest Highs and Lowest Lows of Theo Fleury'* a memoir by former National Hockey League player Theo Fleury.

being body shamed, circadian dysregulation due to travel, concussions, their current period of transition, decreased athletic performance, discrimination, environmental or organisational stressors, gender stereotyping, genetics, high levels of athletic identity, intense training, limited coping resources, the marginalising use of binary terms in sport, normative beliefs about heavy peer alcohol drinking, overtraining, pain or injury, poor sleep, the pressure to win, public performances, recovering from surgery, retirement, significant time demands, sport-specific training before their bodies are fully mature, their stressful lifestyle, suffering non-accidental violence such as psychological abuse, team weigh-ins, the tendency towards maladaptive perfectionism, tough competitions, triggering pressures, tumultuous acculturation, and weight sensitive sports (Carr & Davidson, 2014; Henriksen, 2019; Moesch et al., 2018; National Collegiate Athletic Association [NCAA], 2007; Reardon et al., 2019; Schinke, Stambulova, Si, & Moore, 2017; Van Slingerland, 2020). The expectation of perseverance, strength and stability in sport may create a stigma that prevents certain individuals from disclosing any personal struggles (Carr & Davidson, 2014; Chew & Thompson, 2014).

Having accessible mental health services for all students may lead to several benefits including better grades, higher retention rates, higher graduation rates, and limited risks of behavioural issues or suicide[5] (Chew & Thompson, 2014). Unfortunately, student-athletes in particular do not often accept referrals and continue to use these services at a lower rate than their non-athlete peers (Chew & Thompson, 2014; NCAA, 2007). Barriers to their particular access may include confusion over what counselling is, cost of services, embarrassment, fear of being considered weak, fear of being excluded or not allowed to compete, fear of change, fear of teammates finding out they are in treatment, feeling obligated to attend, having learned early on to push through pain or win at all costs, hyper-masculine environments, lack of mental health literacy, lack of privacy at campus counselling centres, lack of understanding about sport from campus counsellors, limited free time, negative past experiences with mental help-seeking, preferring a quick fix, restricted availability of campus counsellors, stigma surrounding seeking help, and uncertainty of why they are being referred (Chew & Thompson, 2014; DeLenardo, 2014; Moesch, 2018; Reardon et al., 2019; Schinke et al., 2017; Van Slingerland, 2020). For example, Delenardo (2014) discusses the specific impact of stigma on Canadian University football players and the role it plays as a deterrent to seeking assistance with mental ill health.

Athletic programmes may be strengthened in numerous ways if the barriers that prevent student-athletes from receiving mental health services are reduced. Results may include eliminating significant drops in academic or athletic performance, helping student-athletes enhance functioning in multiple areas of their lives, improving overall student wellness, reducing behavioural concerns that may impact

---

[5] For more context surrounding suicide in student-athletes, see '*What Made Maddy Run: The Secret Struggles and Tragic Death of an All-American Teen*' by Kate Fagan.

team dynamics, reducing risks and liabilities associated with mental health concerns, serving as additional support for students in need, and taking pressure off coaches or other support staff members in working with student-athletes who may be in distress. This was already apparent when I first spoke with my own varsity colleagues. Many of them talked about experiences where they needed to support student-athletes in a mental health crisis because there was not a designated professional in their referral network. Keeping all these researched needs and barriers in mind, I felt more equipped to outline specific recommendations for best practices and narrow down those particularly worthy of prioritisation.

Offer Recommendations

Dual Competency

An immersed and well-trained mental health care provider with competency in sport psychology is the ideal resource to provide services to student-athletes although few campus counselling centres employ someone with this expertise (Carr & Davidson, 2014; Henriksen et al., 2019; NCAA, 2017; USPORTS, 2019). This competency should be demonstrated in the practitioner's training background and involve the understanding of athletic culture with its related interpersonal dynamics, external stressors, motivations, and performance needs (Carr & Davidson, 2014). I remember telling my Athletic Director in one of our earliest meetings that the specialised mental health support for their student-athletes did not even have to be me, but it did need to be someone who was also qualified to serve this population. The dual knowledge base of treating mental health in a clinical setting and understanding the demands of high-performance sport is a combination that is not common in Canada (Carr & Davidson, 2014; Van Slingerland, 2020). Athletes often prefer counsellors who are familiar with their sport, are in close proximity to the sport facility, are older but close enough in age to understand their lives, are the same gender and/or who have participated in sport (Reardon et al., 2019; Van Slingerland, 2020). I spent most of the first year during the pilot project working out of the graduate student meeting rooms thanks to the generosity of my performance psychology master's programme administration. Once my contract grew and new office space became a point of discussion, I was adamant to be located within a sport building on campus which could remain both accessible and confidential for clients. This served practical purposes to be closer to training facilities but also a symbolic gesture of normalising varsity mental health care. I took time to decorate my office meaningfully in hopes of providing a comfortable room for therapy with my undeniable love of sports displayed around every wall.

Accessibility

The NCAA (2017) specifically recommends that every institution have a licensed practitioner providing mental health care who is accessible for their student-athletes.

A clearly defined referral process is also suggested. This process should not operate through the coaching staff as this would create additional barriers to accessing care. Every member of the athletic staff who works directly with student-athletes should be aware of this referral process. Henriksen et al. (2019) also note the benefit of a support staff member who manages, monitors, and evaluates the structure of athlete mental health care within an organisation. Integrating mental health services within the athletic department's support staff may be advantageous in ensuring athlete confidentiality on campus, increasing availability of the practitioner to consult with coaching and administrative staff members, maintaining consistency in treatment from the sport medicine team, normalising mental health challenges, reducing stigma of seeking help, and strengthening the prevention and intervention of any issues (Carr & Davidson, 2014; Chew & Thompson, 2014). The likelihood of a successful referral may increase if there is some personal knowledge of the recommended practitioner/ agency and even better if it is made to a specific person (NCAA, 2007). Being a counsellor can be a rather isolating job and building relationships with all points of contact for potential clients increase the ease and efficiency of referrals. I receive many self-referrals, but a large percentage of new clients also come from being told about me through their athletic therapists, coaches, physicians, and teammates. Word-of-mouth referrals can create a sense of comfort which may not be there if I am just an email address someone finds online.

It is encouraged that practitioners working with elite athletes should: avoid experimental treatments that may give clients false hope, be flexible about the timing of sessions, insist clients undergo substance use disorder treatment if needed, obtain information from close informants with consent for clients with severe mental health symptoms or disorders, recommend psychotherapy with pharmacological therapy when indicated for cases of moderate to severe mental health symptoms or disorders, and urge couples or family therapy when relational issues impact functioning or performance (Reardon et al., 2019). These practitioners should also agree not to see surrogates such as coaches for psychotherapy sessions. This was something that was initially on the table in my first few semesters before I foresaw how messy it could get. To avoid potential conflict of interests and damage to client therapeutic safety, we created boundaries in my duties that narrowed my counselling services just to student-athletes and excluded members of staff.

Provide Educational Resources

Another one of my earliest priorities outside counselling responsibilities was to create Mental Health Emergency Actions Plans that would be specific for our athletic department. I recognised there was a lack of sport-informed resources that could serve as relatable guidelines for our staff. I created colourful and printable resources related to, for example, supporting student-athletes in distress and what to do when student-athletes returned from the hospital. These have since been requested and shared with numerous other schools and organisations. As I continue to build these tools today, I also hope to increase mental health training among our varsity coaches and support staff. For example, I have tried bringing in suicide prevention training every few years to ensure at least some full-time staff members from each team feel confident in having those hard conversations with their student-athletes. This is even more vital given I cannot be everywhere and do not usually travel with teams. Developing these sorts of resources and training opportunities requires expanding my scope of duties past mental health counselling. This has proven helpful for me to tap into different skill sets while regularly resting my therapist hat and hopefully in the long run, promoting resilience over compassion fatigue. Sometimes, there may be tasks outside your main priority which promote its very sustainability. For example, I recognise being able to educate coaching and support staff contributes to the experiences and well-being of their student-athletes. And is that not my mission after all?

Know Your Why

This one is easy. It is for them: every past, present, and future client. It is for every student-athlete who may be carrying the weight of the world on their shoulders and just needs someone to talk to.

It is for those like Athlete A,[6] who comes to see me while awaiting their second Anterior Cruciate Ligament (ACL) reconstruction surgery. We explore the grief over lost time, the frustration over the initial misdiagnosis and the worry over whether they will ever perform the same way again. I normalise their feelings and share my own experiences with two ACL reconstructions. I rarely discuss anything about my personal life, but I often choose to bring up those specific injury experiences if it has the potential to connect with clients who may be going through something similar. I try alleviating any shame by stating that injuries can have a profound impact on who we are by stripping us raw of what made us feel like athletes. If deliberate and meaningful, self-disclosure can nurture the therapeutic alliance and model the vulnerability of honesty (Bray, 2019). I share the vivid memory of how daunting it felt after my second diagnosis in particular with the knowledge I needed to somehow rebuild myself all over again. There was a cruel agony without the blinders of ignorance I was afforded the first time.

Athlete A seems to agree. They recognise their proven strengths in resilience as we discuss their recovery after the first surgery. Their own experience provides evidence it is possible to return to play after tearing your ACL. We talk about the anticipated phases ahead for them as chapters in their life such as rest, rehab and return to play. They create a goal sheet we agree to keep in my office

---

[6] Each vignette is based on a mixture of similar stories from various cases. No one vignette is that of an individual client. All identifying information has been either changed or omitted.

where they decide certain points for each chapter such as known factors in their control, primary objectives, probable timeline, possible challenges, and overall keywords to keep in mind. We explore identity and debate how they can still be a hard-working athlete even while sidelined. They recognise these cherished qualities of determination and work ethic hold true regardless of their ability to participate and perform. We establish and regularly modify strategies related to being in the present, celebrating small wins, process-based goal-setting, realistic expectations, self-compassion, exploring other joys such as creating art, using visualisation to reinforce learning and executing physical feats, and an over-arching focus on the controllables. Using visualisation, for example, involves immersion into their inner vision where they could work on seeing themselves successfully complete certain skills and exercises. Benefits of this mental tool include building their self-efficacy in re-trusting their bodies and getting in another mental rep of the desired action.

This case demonstrates when client interventions can endlessly mingle between performance psychology and mental well-being. Precise separation between the two appears unlikely in my line of work. As Athlete A surpasses each chapter, we pause to reflect on any lessons learned. By the time they are ready to return to play, they are overcome with both nerves and excitement. They express pride as they revel in the long-awaited realisation of their comeback story. Working with clients like Athlete A is a reminder that although I may have experienced similar situations, their circumstances and responses are unique to them. It is ideal to enter each session without any assumptions I may know what clients are going through. I prefer they feel like the experts of their own lives – because they are!

It is for those like Athlete B, who comes to see me after their rookie season where they report experiencing crippling performance anxiety in both school and sport. They describe themselves as being a life-long perfectionist which has usually served them quite well. They were almost always rewarded for their high efforts with great results – until university. They were no longer the A+ student or star athlete on their team. They felt mediocre for the first time, and it was devastating. They were bombarded with the pressures of independent learning and time management. They became increasingly worried before exams and competitions, ruminating over the possible worst-case scenarios. They questioned whether they would ever be able to get into medical school as they always imagined and doubted if their race times would ever grant them a spot at Nationals. We talk about the cost of a results-based focus. We identify their dream goals and separate those from the process goals they would need to reach to them. Simões et al. (2012) reiterate the effectiveness of this type of goal-setting strategy in their study of swimmers who showed significant improvement to their chronometric per-formance during the season they received mental training where short-term ob-jectives were pre-determined and regularly modified in pursuit of long-term goals. Athlete B gradually recognises the destructive connection they were making between their performance and self-worth.

We explore possible contributing factors to this core belief such as growing up with demanding parents and coaches. Even still, they feel it was their own internal expectations that were the heaviest to carry. They are willing to acknowledge that their previous worldview may have been skewed by their experiences as they admit effort does not always equal results. Over time, they are able to focus on simply working hard and finding pride in their actions more than their evaluations. They realise that no test score or race time is truly defining of who they are as a student, athlete, or human being. We also establish specific strategies to manage anxiety before, during, and after performance tasks. This included a re-focus plan for whenever they would inevitably be hit with intrusive thoughts such as taking a deep breath and acknowledging their preparation. We modify their strategies over time to better serve them as they figure out what works and what does not. They note the helpfulness of writing about the worries that feel particularly overwhelming before going to sleep. This allows them to express their fears while symbolically putting them away. They learn to challenge their negative thoughts and seek evidence against those that are irrational. They more appropriately measure upcoming exams or races for what they really are, just a test of performance in a moment of time. Neither all-encompassing nor world-ending. Just a moment in time. These are similar lessons I can find in my own career. I had to focus on the process goals I could control on my way to the outcome goals I desired. I often tell clients that I hope life is not just about reaching those checkpoints of achievement. I explain that it would be most meaningful if we recognised life for what it seems to be more about, all the time we spend in between.

It is for those like Athlete C, who comes to see me after almost a decade of struggling with low mood. We go through their personal and family history of mental health. They reflect on their previous experience with a therapist as a young teenager at the push of their parents after many days of missing school and many years of not being the seemingly happy child they once were. They remember not quite clicking with that practitioner and only attending for a few sessions. I commend their perseverance to the process since they tried again once they were truly ready to do so. We explore the possible contributing factors to their current mood baseline which often includes indifference or sadness. They question whether it may have been their parents' messy divorce around age 7, the limited relationship with their father after he moved out, the bullying in middle school from former friends, the first heartbreak in high school, or the difficulties with concussions throughout their athletic career. We agree that we cannot know for sure what may have been a catalyst but acknowledge the varying impacts these events have on who they were and are today. I validate the difficulties of these circumstances and the resilience shown to overcome them. We talk about the past semester and the drag of some days of getting out of bed or staying on top of the school. We spend most of our first sessions together talking about the past week or two since the last checking-in. We often talk about challenges related to emotional management, energy management, interpersonal relationships, motivation, self-image, self-talk, and time management. They often describe themselves as weak but all I notice is strength.

After about a year of on-and-off therapy, they are more consistently displaying acceptance and self-compassion. They gradually open up to a few friends and alleviate their previous isolation. They develop further self-awareness and apply our established healthy coping strategies during their lows. Even still, they continue reporting impairment from some symptoms and we discuss the possibility of seeking a further assessment. They agree to speak to the Team Doctor and are eventually diagnosed with Major Depression.[7] They start on anti-depressants but hesitate to fully embrace the diagnosis. They explain both its validation in conceptualising their experiences but the dissonance of lacking cultural understanding from their community. They do not feel comfortable talking to their parents for fear of dismissal and judgement. After trying different dosages and medications, they seem to find one that decreases much of the previously persistent brain fog and chronic fatigue.

With their tank more regularly full, they suddenly open up about the suicidal thoughts they used to have in high school. They describe not having felt that down in a long time but knowing it was an important part of their story they were previously ashamed of sharing. I thank them for their courage and honesty as we take some time to reflect on those darker days. They are grateful for being where they are today and empathise with their younger self who often dreamed of non-existence. They know they now have the tools to manage their bouts of low mood even if it may persist for years to come. They are no longer as afraid of depression and choose to live as fully as possible despite it. Working with clients like Athlete C is a reminder that sometimes the best you can offer is to simply stand alongside them. Battles as potentially chronic and debilitating as depression may not be overcome after just a few chats, if ever at all. Hopefully, over time, the consistent sincerity and support illustrated in counselling lessens the intensity of their symptoms and provides light in the bleakest of hours. One of the most powerful beliefs we can hold for them as practitioners is that they are worth it. Their life and well-being matter. We may especially need to be the loyal bearers of these notions for the clients who have yet to believe it about themselves.

It is for those like Athlete D, who comes to see me during their last year of school. They describe feeling more adrift as their career comes to a close. They decided not to pursue sport professionally which meant this season was their last as a high-performance athlete. They talk about the difficulty of coming to that conclusion but knowing it was right for them after enduring several serious injuries and concussions. They try to look forward to the future but hesitate to be confident without the previously provided certainties of carefully laid plans and very transparent timelines. We explore the security of the student-athlete identity

---

[7] Canadian Olympian, Clara Hughes shares her experience of depression in her memoir 'Open Heart, Open Mind'.

which has served them and saw them thrive in for almost two decades. They admit it holds much pride and responsibility. They wonder who they really are without it. I normalise the fears of the unknown and the significance of this upcoming life transition.

We discuss the factors of sport that have been beneficial to their quality of life, and they easily list several including the busy schedule that facilitated time management, challenge and gratification of improving their skills, close relationships they built with teammates, competitive environment they could excel in, focus on an active lifestyle, and the teamwork they experienced. I explain that it may be an unrealistic expectation to assume all these beloved factors would be found again in one area. That is what made their primary sport so special for so many years. Instead, it may be easier in retirement to seek out those factors in multiple areas of life while allowing themselves the time to process the grief that may come in waves. Athlete D hypothesise they may be able to, for example, find fulfilment in self-growth and teamwork via their business career. They are also excited to invest more time in their friendships back home. We explore different possible scenarios and their ideal reactions to them. Even the less-than-ideal hypotheticals end with them figuring it out. They acknowledge the strengths they have built over time such as adaptability, determination, and resilience. They know these are not sport-specific and will remain long after they hang up their cleats. Their hesitation about life after sport lingers but they know they have the means to find their way through.

I often try and bring up retirement with clients when the opportunity presents such as over-identification with their athletic identities or 'trial runs' without training when sidelined with injuries. I figure the least I can do is help them start facing that tough topic of the inevitable end of their playing careers. This mental acceptance and preparation may be helpful given that approximately 20% of athletes experience a crisis in the transition out of sport including emotional distress, decreased mental health, difficulties adjusting and struggles coping (Hoffart, 2020). Effects of sport retirement may include decreased feelings of self-worth outside athletics, feelings of being inadequate, lack of purpose and identity, loss of daily routine, and a sense of boredom. Hoffart (2020) emphasises the normalisation of difficulties during transition out-of-sport can promote emotional awareness and positive coping strategies as individuals may recognise their challenges, process their experiences and access needed resources. Even better, preparation prior to retirement can aid athletes in greater self-efficacy and ensure a plan for what is to come.

Summary

There was not a set path for me to take in my career. There was not even one graduate programme in the country at the time that would have made me appropriately qualified to do what I wanted to do! Instead, I could only seek the most favourable options out of the available opportunities and mould myself a professional life I could be proud of. This included almost a decade of university learning to achieve the credentials necessary to advocate for the services I believed in: mental health care in sport. The adversity I then faced for years in immense job uncertainty was worth it because I trusted this greater purpose which eventually zoomed into the creation of specialised varsity mental health care at the University of Ottawa. The meaningfulness of seeing it through overcame any internal doubt or external pressure that crossed my path. As I slowly gained space and leverage in my position at the university, prioritisation beyond mental health services included conducting research, offering recommendations, and providing resources. Although these projects were outside the duties of a practitioner, they ensured a steady foundation of evidence-based strategies to best understand and serve our unique demographic. Even through long days and longer session notes left to write, supporting my clients continues to reinforce my joy of this work and that long-shot mission I took up so many years ago. I am so blessed to do something I love – to keep playing with heart every day. What a ride to reflect on.

In honour of my clients, who offered me the privilege of sharing their space and hearing their stories. With special thanks to those at the table who listened and supported, including the teams at the University of Ottawa Varsity Athletics and Counselling Services.

REFLECTIVE QUESTIONS

- Are there particular specialties and/or populations you could work with that may be both challenging and rewarding?
- What would you consider worthy collateral while waiting to achieve your dream goals?
- Do you have access to positive supports who you can lean on through the inevitable ups and downs of your career? If not, are there resources you can access in your community that may serve this purpose (e.g., peer support groups, clinical supervision, etc.)?
- Do you currently recognise a gap in your desired career of choice where your interests and expertise may fulfil? This may be in a specific organisation or in the field as a whole.
- Which personal experiences and values shape who you may become as a professional?

References

Biegel, G. M., & Corbin, T. H. (2018). Mindfulness for Student Athletes: A Workbook to Help Teens Reduce Stress and Enhance Performance. Oakland, California: Instant Help Books.

Bray, B. (2019, January 29). *Counselor Self-disclosure: Encouragement or Impediment to Client Growth?* Counseling Today. https://ct.counseling.org/2019/01/counselor-self-disclosure-encouragement-or-impediment-to-client-growth/#.

Carr, C., & Davidson, J. (2014). The psychologist perspective. *Mind, Body and Sport: Understanding and Supporting Student-Athlete Mental Wellness*, 17–20 [PDF file]. Retrieved from http:// www.ncaa.org/sport-science-institute/mental-health-educational-resources.

Chew, K., & Thompson R. (2014). Potential barriers to accessing mental health services. *Mind, Body and Sport: Understanding and Supporting Student-Athlete Mental Wellness*, 96–99 [PDF file]. Retrieved from http://www.ncaa.org/sport-science-institute/mental-health-educational-resources.

DeLenardo, S., & Terrion, J. L. (2014). Suck it up: Opinions and attitudes about mental illness stigma and help-seeking behaviour of male varsity football players. *Canadian Journal of Community Mental Health, 33*(3), 1–14.

Fagan, K. (2017). *What Made Maddy Run: The Secret Struggles and Tragic Death of an All-American Teen.* USA: Little, Brown and Company.

Fleury, T. (2010). *Playing with Fire: The Highest Highs and the Lowest Lows of Theo Fleury.* Canada: HarperCollins Publishers.

Henriksen, K., Schinke, R., Moesch, K., McCann, S., Parham, W. D., Lasen, C. H., & Terry, P. (2019). Consensus statement on improving the mental health of high performance athletes. *International Journal of Sport and Exercise Psychology. 18*, 553–560.

Hoffart, L. (2020, October 21). *Mental Health Considerations of the Athlete Transition Out of Sport.* SIRC. https://sirc.ca/blog/athlete-transition-out-of-sport/.

Hughes, C. (2015). *Open Heart, Open Mind.* Canada: Touchstone.

Moesch, K., Kenttä, G., Kleinert, J., Quignon-Fleuret, C., Cecil, S., & Bertollo, M. (2018). FEPSAC position statement: Mental health disorders in elite athletes and models of service provision. *Psychology of Sport & Exercise*, 61–71.

National Collegiate Athletic Association (2007). Managing student-athletes' mental health issues [PDF file]. Retrieved from http://www.ncaa.org/sport-science-institute/mental-health-educational-resources.

NCAA Sport Science Institute (2017). Mental health best practices: Understanding and supporting student athlete mental wellness. Retrieved from http://www.ncaa.org/sites/default/files/SSI_MentalHealthBestPractices_Web_20170921.pdf.

Reardon, C. L., Hainline, B., Aron C. M., Baron, D., Baum, A. L., Bindra, A., ... Engebretsen, L. (2019, May). Mental health in elite athletes: International Olympic Committee consensus statement (2019). *British Journal of Sports Medicine, 53*, 667–699.

Schinke, R. J., Stambulova, N. B., Si, G., & Moore, Z. (2017). International society of sport psychology position stand: Athletes' mental health, performance, and development. *International Journal of Sport and Exercise Psychology.16*(6),622–639.

Simões, P., Vasconcelos-Raposo, J., Silva, A., & Fernandes, H. M. (2012). Effects of a process-oriented goal-setting model on swimmer's performance. *Journal of Human Kinetics, 32*, 65–76. https://www.ncbi.nlm.nih.gov/pmc/articles/PMC3590857/.

USPORTS. (2019). Mental health best practices. *Sport Medicine & Research Science Committee Mental Health Guideline January 2019.*

Van Slingerland, K., Durand-Bush, N., Bradley, L., Goldfield, G., Archambault, R., Smith, D., Edwards, C., Delenardo, S., Taylor, S., Werthner, P., & Kenttä, G. (2020). Canadian Centre for Mental Health and Sport (CCMHS) position statement: Principles of mental health in competitive and high-performance sport.*Clinical Journal of Sport Medicine29*(3),173-180.

3

PARENTAL INVOLVEMENT AND ONLINE CONSULTANCY DELIVERY: A CASE STUDY OF A PSYCHOLOGICAL INTERVENTION WITH A 9-YEAR-OLD TENNIS PLAYER

Beth Yeoman

Introduction

Enjoyment of sport for children is a vital contributing factor in sport retention (Bailey et al., 2013) but also performance (Snyder, 2014). Introducing a child to sport psychology concepts can help enhance this enjoyment (Knight, Harwood & Gould, 2018; Orlick & Zitzelsberger, 1996) as well as enhance their well-being and performance (Knight et al., 2018). However, how sport psychology is introduced to children is not a one-size-fits-all approach and should vary to suit the age of the child. For example, when working with children during mid childhood years (6–11 years) there are some important developmental features that may affect methods of applying psychology (Visek, Harris & Blom, 2009). For example, at this age, children are logical thinkers, have a limited attention span, and they begin to become more sensitive. Practitioners working with a child of this age therefore may want to consider how they can make their practice simple enough for the child to understand, but also engaging to hold their attention. Also at this age, to safeguard the client and the practitioner, parents are recommended to be present within one-to-one consultancy sessions. This adds another level of consideration for practitioners working within youth sport. Within youth tennis, Gould et al. (2006) found some actions of parents to be helpful (e.g., financial and social-emotional support) and some to be unhelpful (e.g., over-emphasising winning and criticism) within tennis coaching. These helpful and unhelpful factors may also be applicable to sport psychology specific sessions, but practitioners may want to consider within their individual contexts what parental behaviour would be helpful and what behaviour would be unhelpful for the consultancy. From the outset, sport psychologists should outline these expectations.

Within the sport psychology literature, the challenges and benefits of involving parents within consultancy are discussed (Visek et al., 2009). A potential challenge

DOI: 10.4324/9781003263890-5

is how the presence of the parent may affect the openness and honesty of the client (Peterson, 2004). For example, the child may not feel comfortable in fully opening-up with their parent present. This could affect the trust developed between the practitioner and the client and as a result the effectiveness of the consultancy. It is therefore important for sport psychologists to consider what they can do to lessen the potential negative effects. However, there are some benefits to parental involvement to also be considered. Firstly, during the session it is likely that the parent is also receiving some education on psychological concepts (Visek et al., 2009). Secondly, Bergin (2004) suggests that children may not yet have the maturity or self-awareness to recognise their own behaviours and make choices. If parents are involved, they can assist their child in making these choices while at home, training, or competitions.[1]

On top of these challenges, over recent years the COVID-19 pandemic has in some ways restricted practitioners in their methods of delivery, but in other ways benefited practitioners by offering new and innovative ways of practicing (Price, Wagstaff, & Thelwell, 2021). Whether a barrier or a benefit to practice, the impact of working virtually is another factor that psychologists have had to consider when working with youth athletes. One consideration for practitioners is how to keep a child engaged over video call. For example, when at home, the child may have more distractions than they would in a face-to-face session. Keeping their attention on the screen and content of the session may therefore be tricky. In addition, non-verbal cues can be the most important factors for practitioners with children who may have a limited vocabulary. Research shows that picking up on these non-verbal cues such as body language and eye contact is more difficult during online consultancy (Bambling et al., 2008; Price et al., 2021).

This chapter is therefore going to provide an example of an intervention that was developed for a 9-year-old tennis player, delivered online, and successfully engaged the parents throughout the intervention. Throughout, examples are given of the tasks created and adaptations made to suit both the age of the client and the online service delivery. The important role the parent played during the process is also discussed.

Professional Philosophy

When considering which methods would be most appropriate to use with a 9-year-old athlete, it is clear my underlying beliefs played a significant role. At 9 years old, I believe that enjoyment should be the number one priority in sport. Children should be encouraged to embrace their differences, be proud of what sets them apart from others, and be praised for what they are good at. The theoretical paradigm that was congruent with these beliefs and was used to underpin the

---

[1] Podcasts such as 'The Sport Psych Show' episode 157 with Dr Camilla Knight entitled 'Creating a Parent-Positive Environment' and 'Eighty Percent Mental' with Dr Camilla Knight & Andy Bradshaw entitled 'How to work with/be a good sports parent' offer further considerations when working with parents in youth sport.

current case was a strength-based theoretical approach, which is often referred to in a sporting context as super-strengths (Ludlam et al., 2016). I believe that helping an athlete to recognise and focus on what they are good at and not just 'problems' is valuable in enhancing sporting performance, but also building confidence (Ludlam et al., 2017). With a 9-year-old, it is even more important to employ an approach that includes a strength focus as it is suggested that over criticism in early life affects confidence in adulthood (Bailey et al., 2013).

Ethical Consideration

One important ethical consideration within this case was the involvement of the client's parent, how this affects confidentiality, and the impact of this on consultancy effectiveness. To navigate this, it was firstly explained to both the client and the parent the parameters of confidentiality as outlined by the British Psychological Society (2017). Namely, anything shared in consultancy will not be shared by the practitioner, unless the practitioner feels that the client is a danger to themselves or others. To help the client feel more comfortable in being open, the parent was also asked to abide by these rules and not share anything without the client's consent. Secondly, it was explained that the child is the client in the relationship and that the focus will be on the child and what is best for them (Andersen, Van Raalte, & Brewer, 2001). For example, the child may wish to discuss something that the parent does not feel comfortable with and in this situation the child's decision should be respected. Thirdly, detailed informed consent was gained from both the client and the parent at the outset. To suit the age of the client, I chose to explain informed consent verbally and follow this up with an email for written informed consent (British Psychological Society, 2017).

The Case

Nature of the Consultancy

The client will be referred to throughout as Emily (pseudonym). Emily is a 9-year-old tennis player who competes in intra club matches and tournaments more widely across the county. I worked with Emily for approximately nine months, with sessions occurring every two weeks and each session lasting approximately 30 minutes. 30 minutes were chosen as an appropriate length of time to suit the attention span of a 9-year-old (Visek et al., 2009). Consultancy sessions were conducted using an online platform. This method was first chosen due to the COVID-19 pandemic; however, due to flexibility and ease of access (Price et al., 2021), this method continued for the duration of the consultancy. Working online allowed the sessions to remain frequent throughout the consultancy process, allowing the relationship with the client to gradually develop over time. This was evidenced by the parent expressing her thanks for being able to run the sessions online as it meant they could fit them around their busy schedules. Secondly, online delivery allowed the client to complete the sessions in her own house, an environment where she feels comfortable. Literature suggests that this aspect of online consultancy can increase feelings of safety, diminish a client's sense of vulnerability, and play a facilitative role in disclosure, which in turn assists the working alliance (Harris & Birnbaum, 2015).

Parental Involvement

Consultancy was initiated through Emily's mother whose initial request was to introduce Emily to sport psychology with the aim of performance enhancement. Emily's mother was always present in the sessions. To ensure this involvement was helpful for the consultancy, expectations were outlined to Emily's mother during the initial introductions. Key points outlined include: 1) for Emily to get the most out of the consultancy, Emily should take the lead on responses, tasks, and questions. 2) Supporting Emily with tasks away from the sessions is encouraged and will be helpful. 3) Being 'within earshot' of sessions will be helpful for you to understand what we are discussing and help to continue conversations following sessions. Finally, it was explained to Emily's mother that we may not put much emphasis on the overall outcome of winning during sessions but focus more on enjoyment and process goals. She was encouraged to take the same approach away from sessions.

Within the first few sessions the parent was on screen and helping Emily with her responses. This was a challenging dynamic as it made it difficult for me to build a rapport with Emily. I felt as though Emily was holding back on engaging in conversation as she knew that her mother would take over and answer on her behalf if needed. I did however recognise that at this stage it was likely that Emily's mother was a bit wary of the situation and wanted to build her own trust with me. To manage this challenge, I continued to let the parent engage within the conversations as this was also an important relationship to build. However, I also included questions that were directly aimed at Emily. For example, 'Emily, could you tell me how that was for you … .' After the first few sessions, Emily's mother naturally shifted to taking a back seat, was out of view of the screen and allowed Emily to take the lead.

Needs Analysis

One-to-One Sessions

Most of the information was gathered through one-to-one sessions. These were practitioner-led due to the age of the client. Key points revealed were:

- Most enjoys tennis when she is with her friends.
- Gets nervous before games.
- Feels sad when she doesn't do well.
- Likes to talk about other hobbies when at tennis.
- Mum goes to every game – Enjoys her mum being there.

Parental Input

The parent provided information during sessions with Emily. She also provided information via email between sessions. Key information shared was:

- A recent game, Emily was not expected to win as the girl she was playing against was much better, but Emily beat her.
- Tournaments are more frequent now than they used to be.
- The children in Emily's group are all very competitive and so are their parents.
- Emily cried at her last tournament – this is not uncommon.
- Emily would say the night before a tournament that she doesn't want to play but is normally ok when she gets there.
- Emily appears to be dissatisfied with her tennis at the moment.

Tennis Profile

As the aim of the intervention was not performance focused, the word performance profile became a 'tennis profile' to give a more holistic view of Emily's tennis. Emily drew a stick person tennis player. Around the outside she wrote all the things she thought the tennis player needed to be good at. To rate herself, Emily highlighted the three things she thought she was best at and gave them a rating with smiley face stickers (5 stickers = the best she could be, 1 sticker = not very good). She then highlighted with a different colour the three things she thought she needed to improve the most, followed by rating these with the same process.

Top three:
- Speed
- Backhand
- Concentration

Bottom three:
- Serving
- Being calm before a game
- Power in shots

Case Formulation

The case formulation approach used to summarise and organise the information was the Five P's Model (Johnstone & Dallos, 2013), which consists of five dimensions: 'presenting issues' (adapted to issues and strengths), 'predisposing factors', 'precipitating factors', 'perpetuating factors', and 'protective factors'. This is followed by an intervention plan decision-making process. Table 3.1 shows the key points considered in each dimension.

TABLE 3.1 An overview of the case formulation of Emily

Case Formulation Using the Five P's

Presenting issues and strengths

Issues

- Not enjoying tournaments
- Getting upset at tournaments when things are not going well
- Difficulty with coping with nerves before a game, effects how she feels and how she plays
- Dissatisfied with tennis

Strengths

- Concentration during a game
- Decision-making during a game
- Technically and physically skilful
- Does not get 'put off' by her opponent

Predisposing Factors

- Younger sister – parents think she is better than her brother. Increased pressure here to live up to these expectations
- Started playing tennis because it was fun – used to enjoy playing games
- Parents highly involved in her tennis – Emily enjoys her mum's involvement therefore mum could be involved within the intervention

Precipitating Factors

- Moved up an age group last year – the tennis has become more competitive and focused on winning and losing. More pressure on Emily to win
- She could get a spot in the county squad next year – focus again placed on performance
- Tournaments have become more frequent – not much time between tournaments to play for fun with friends

Perpetuation Factors

- She is getting further through the season – getting closer to the decision of whether she makes the county team
- She has a regular coach which is helping her strengths to continue
- Her focus is on performance outcomes
- Her parents' focus is on performance outcomes

Protective Factors

- Has supportive parents – willing to be a part of Emily's tennis journey
- Has a supportive brother – they get on well and have a good relationship
- She has the love of tennis as why she started playing and still sees this as an important part
- She is young
- Open and engaged with sport psychology support so far

Intervention Plan Decision-Making

- Presenting issues/strengths – increase Emily's self-awareness of her strengths. Ensure sessions are balanced and not issue focused to do this. Not wanting to go to tournaments and not enjoying them when she is there are key issues.
- Predisposing factors – Emily appears to have lost sight of why she started playing tennis in the first place. The enjoyment and love for tennis was there in the first place. Focus on bringing this back.
- Precipitating Factors – tennis has got harder this year and more competitive which Emily appears to be struggling with. Remind Emily of her strengths (E.g., speed, concentration and backhand)
- Perpetuation Factors – resulting in her enjoyment of tennis decreasing further. Focus on performance outcomes and parental focus on performance outcomes.

(*Continued*)

TABLE 3.1 *(Continued)*

Case Formulation Using the Five P's

- Protective Factors – supportive parents who are willing to be a part of Emily's tennis journey. Emily also enjoys the involvement of her parents. Parents can therefore be used to help with the implementation and maintenance of the intervention.

Talked through Case Formulation with Emily and Mum
- Emily says she wants to feel happier when she is at tournaments and wants to feel excited about going. She says she still wants to play well as this makes her happy. Feeling happy and not upset on a game day is the main part for her. She is rarely asked by her coach to practice what she is good at, so she is also excited to do this. Emily would like to have her mum involved in the plan.
- Mum says she wants Emily to be happy. If playing tennis makes her happy then that is great, but if it does not then she will not force her to play in tournaments. She knows that Emily used to love going to games and playing, so wants to get this back. I explained the link between enjoyment and playing well and she understood this. Performance focus is no longer number one priority for mum

Intervention Plan

1. Help Emily to explore her values in tennis and why she started
2. Increase self-awareness of Emily's strengths
3. Create a plan for a tournament day that makes it more enjoyable

Intervention

An individualised approach to intervention development was adopted where methods used where designed with the client and online nature of the delivery in mind (Collins, Evans-Jones & O'Connor, 2013; Sharp & Hodge, 2011; Van Raalte, 2003; Winter & Collins, 2015). The intervention was split into four main parts: values, strengths building, game day plan, and evaluation (see Table 3.2 for an overview of the intervention).

TABLE 3.2 Overview of the intervention

Intervention Step	Intervention Session Number	Topic
Values	1	Listing what's important
	2	Ranking order of importance
	3	Adding the detail (what, how, why, when)
Building Strengths	4	Listing strengths
	5	Mapping strengths on a timeline
	6	Using at a game

(Continued)

TABLE 3.2 (*Continued*)

Intervention Step	Intervention Session Number	Topic
Game Day Plan	7	What's in the game day bubble
	8	The bubble is not fixed
	9	Putting into practice
Evaluation	10	Revising the plan
	11	Revisiting the values list and tennis profile
	12	Reflection

Values

Helping Emily recognise what is important to her in tennis was the first step in the intervention. This was to remind Emily what she likes about tennis and why she started playing. An adapted version of values mapping that is outlined by Perry (2019) was used with Emily.

Session 1

Due to the age of the client, a list of words was shown that may help Emily to think of what is important to her. Using the 'shared screen' feature on the online platform, I displayed the words on the screen. Using the list of words on the screen to help, Emily listed everything she enjoys about tennis, things that make her happy and why she started playing tennis. Values listed were having fun, being with friends, having mummy there, smiling, playing well, winning, beating the other person, having brother there, practising what I have been taught and being nice to the other person.

• After session task: Look over the words, think about why you wrote them, and how important they are to you. Emily's mum was asked to help with the task and ask the questions of 'why did you write this word?' and 'on a scale of 1 (not at all important) – 10 (very important) how important is this word to you?'

Session 2

Emily ranked her words in order of importance. Based on discussion from the previous after session task, Emily's mum was able to help remind Emily of what she had previously said. I typed these onto the screen for all parties to see. Emily then wrote the top five most important things on her list on a tennis ball. The words fun, friends, mummy, smile, and playing well were written on the ball.

Session 3

Emily threw the ball back and forth with her mum. Every time she caught the ball, she looked at the word she had written that was facing her and read it aloud. For example, 'fun'. We then discussed why she had written fun, what can she do to make tennis more fun and how it makes her feel when she is having fun. We continued this until every word was discussed.

- After session task 1: Play this game with her mum or brother. Try and say something different about the word each time. Mum to ask the questions about the word.
- After session task 2: Take this ball to training and play with it before you start. Mum to ask Emily how she feels when she looks at the words on the ball.
- Emily kept this tennis ball with her and took it to tournaments. Before a game Emily played with the ball by throwing to back and forth with her brother.

Building strengths

The next step of the intervention was helping Emily to recognise her strengths, learn how they set her apart from others, when they are important, and how she can build on these. As mentioned, children of this age are starting to become more sensitive and over criticism can have a negative impact later in life. Therefore, a clear focus on exploring Emily's strengths was important. The approach taken was similar to the strengths audit outlined by Perry (2019).

Session 4

Emily created a superhero poster. This was a similar style to the tennis profile, but solely focused on Emily's strengths. In the middle Emily drew a picture of a superhero tennis player, coloured her in and gave her superhero a name. Around the outside of her superhero, she wrote all the things that Emily was good at in tennis and in general life. These were the superhero's superpowers. Mum gave important input in this part of the session in helping to remind Emily of times when she had done well. To initiate this, I printed a picture of a superhero in the middle of a page. I wrote two examples of 'superpowers' to get Emily started. I held this up to the camera to show Emily what the task would look like.

- After session task: Emily transferred each of her superpowers onto separate pieces of small card and folded them in half. She put the folded pieces of card into a small box that she had with a padlock on and labelled it 'Emily's Magic Box'. She chose to laminate her poster and put it on her bedroom wall. Emily's mum helped her complete this task at home.

Session 5

We mapped out Emily's strengths. Ludlam et al. (2016) highlighted that it is important for athletes to understand when, where and how their super-strengths give them a competitive edge. One by one Emily pulled a strength out of the box and placed it on a timeline of pre-game, during game and after game to represent when that strength was most helpful. Her mum aided with this process and provided specific examples. To brings this to life online, before the session I created an example of the task. I cut out the two superpower examples, stuck them on a timeline and showed it up to the camera.

- After session task: Just before going to training, Emily's mum to ask her to pull a card out of the box and read it to herself.

Session 6

We talked about how Emily could use this box on the day of a game. When Emily was finding it difficult to remember her strengths (e.g., when feeling nervous before a game or after a poor performance), Emily pulled a card out of the box. Her mum was encouraged to be involved in this process and ask Emily questions such as, 'when is that strength important?'.

Game Day Plan

The third step of the intervention was to put steps one and two of the intervention together into a game day plan. This was so Emily could create an environment ('bubble') on a game day that was enjoyable.

Session 7

Emily created her own game day bubble. To make the concept more tangible, a balloon was used to represent her bubble, which Emily's mum had ready for the session and blew up for her. Emily wrote on the balloon everything she likes to do on the day of a game that makes her happy. This included people around her, topics she likes to talk about and food she likes to eat. It also included playing with her tennis ball she had written on and looking in her magic box.

- After session task: Emily was asked to keep adding to her bubble with anything new that came to mind outside of the session.

Session 8

Emily brought her balloon to the session. The use of the balloon helped to demonstrate to Emily that what she likes in her bubble could change over time. By the time of this session Emily's balloon had naturally deflated. We talked about how this represented how her bubble can be ever changing and doesn't have to stay the same. We talk about the key parts that were likely to remain stable for Emily and the parts that may change.

Session 9

With the help of Emily's mum, we devised a plan of how she can put this into practice on the day of a game. Using the 'shared screen' function, I wrote the plan as we were discussing. The plan included four sections with approximately six actions under each section. The sections were: Night Before, Game Morning, At Game, and After Game.

- After session task 1: Emily and mum were asked to do a role play of the game day plan on a Saturday when there was no game or training. This was to see if without any game or training day pressures this was manageable. At this point, no revisions were made.
- After session task 2: Emily and mum to put the game day plan into practice on the day of training.

Evaluation

The final step was to evaluate the intervention. This involved discussions of how the intervention was going, repeating pre-intervention tasks and self-reflection for the client.

Session 10

This was a conversational session where we talked through how the game day plan went. As this session was conversational, I was aware that the virtual nature of the consultancy could have a negative impact if not considered. To keep Emily engaged, I used an 'emoji' feature on the online platform. At each aspect of the game plan, I asked Emily to pick an emoji that represented how she felt about doing this part of the plan. Parts of the plan were then revised to suit Emily. For example, under Night Before was 'do not talk about the tournament'. This was difficult to avoid with Emily's brother also playing. This was changed to a set time limit of a maximum of 20 minutes talk about the tournament and it must be before dinner.

- After session task: Emily used the game day plan at her next tournament.

Session 11

Revisited the values map that Emily created prior to the intervention. She created another list of 10 words and ranked these in order of importance. I used the 'shared screen' feature to show the list of words from before. Next Emily rated herself again on her tennis profile.

- After session task: Emily was asked to look at the new values map and create a new tennis ball to reflect these words. This ball replaced the old one within the 'Game Day Plan'.

Session 12

This session was focused on self-reflection. Emily described what she had improved on over the last few months. She described how she felt about going to tennis tournaments now and compared this to previously. Emily's mum was involved with helping with this part of the session and inputting on what improvements she had seen Emily make. The emoji's icon was used to help Emily represent her feelings.

Monitoring and Evaluation

Anderson et al. (2002)'s effectiveness indicators were used to guide what was evaluated throughout the intervention.

Consultant Effectiveness

Consultant effectiveness was evaluated on an ongoing basis (Henriksen et al., 2019). One method used was personal reflections (Poczwardowski, Sherman, & Henschen, 1998). As working with a client as young as 9-years old and via online services was unfamiliar, I chose to reflect after each session with Emily. An example of a reflection regarding working online is shared later in this chapter. Secondly, verbal feedback was gained from the client through informal questioning within consultancy sessions. Due to Emily's age, this was chosen over formal written responses (e.g., Consultant Effectiveness Form; Partington & Orlick, 1987). I asked Emily questions such as, 'how do you find the drawing tasks we are doing?' and 'is there anything that would make these sessions more fun?' From this feedback paired with self-reflections, I learnt that Emily found it easier to know what to do with tasks when I did the task alongside her and held it up to the camera. This was valuable information as it gave me direction of how to remain effective while delivering online.

Psychological Skill and Well-Being

The focus of this part of the evaluation was on comparing Emily's enjoyment and happiness at tennis before and after the intervention. Firstly, feedback from Emily's mother was used as a tool for evaluation. For example, she reported before the intervention that Emily frequently cried at tournaments. At the end of the intervention, I asked 'how has Emily appeared at tournaments recently?'. Among the feedback was that 'Emily hasn't cried at a tournament in a couple of months'. Secondly, her mum shared feedback from Emily's coach. Her coach had been really impressed with Emily, specifically noticing a positive change in her mood and enthusiasm for sessions. Finally, at the end of the intervention, Emily rated herself again on her tennis profile and completed another values map. Emily's strongest skills (i.e., backhand, speed, and concentration) had remained the same on her tennis profile. This indicated that she is recognising her strengths and continuing to focus on them. Within the values map, there was a key change in that Emily added 'game day plan' to her list. This indicated that she saw value in the intervention that was developed as this was now an important part of her tennis. Another key change was 'winning' moved from 6th to 9th in the importance ranking. Reflections allowed me to make sense of these evaluations and consider how Emily's psychological skills and well-being had progressed over time.

Response to Support

In addition to feedback from conversations, Emily's adherence to tasks outside of the sessions was used as an indicator of response to support (Anderson et al., 2002). For example, at the start of each session we would begin by talking about the task. The detail in her response provided an indication of whether she had engaged well with the task or not. Furthermore, Emily's mum would often communicate with me over email about how Emily had engaged with the task that week. Secondly, during sessions with Emily I could gauge how she was responding to the support from her non-verbal cues such as eye contact with the screen and her body language. For example, whether she was sat up and leaning forward or was she sat back and sinking into her chair. From these observations I started to see a pattern and learn when she was responding well to a task or whether it needed adapting to be more engaging.

Performance

As the aim of the consultancy was to move Emily away from performance-focused thinking and towards enjoyment, performance was the least important indicator to evaluate effectiveness. The decision was therefore made to not include performance as an indicator of effectiveness of the consultancy.

Discussion

Most literature on sport psychology interventions focuses on senior athletes (e.g., Andersen, 2005; Gould & Maynard, 2009; Vealey, 2007), with limited literature discussing how to design an intervention for a youth athlete. Moreover, how to positively include a parent within this intervention design and deliver this virtually is a gap within the literature. However, Henriksen et al.

(2019) do provide some suggestions of how to successfully implement an intervention with youth athletes. They suggest that interventions need to be flexible to meet the need of the client's age and the client's sport and do not need to follow a pre-determined curriculum. Additionally, they found that involving significant others such as parents and coaches in the delivery increased the success of the intervention. The current case firstly supports the need for a flexible approach when designing an intervention. For example, the intervention had to be built so that the tasks were appropriate and engaging for a 9-year-old, but also could be delivered online. Secondly, the current case supports the suggestion that significant others involvement enhances the success of an intervention. For example, Emily's mum helped Emily with tasks away from sessions ensuring that the momentum of the consultancy process was continuing. The current case demonstrates that the parent can play a pivotal role throughout the intervention in its design, implementation, and evaluation.

Reflections

An important area for reflection during this case was the process of working with a client as young as 9 years old. This was my youngest client and an experience that was unfamiliar. When first approached to work with the client I felt uneasy about the request. On reflection, this was due to my beliefs that a child of this age should be playing sport for enjoyment and not putting great emphasis on improving performance. The initial requests from the parent of wanting performance enhancement support for her daughter therefore did not align with these beliefs. This led to the perception that there was likely to be incongruence between my beliefs and my practice, which is suggested to have a negative effect on my professional growth and development (Lindsay et al., 2007; Poczwardowski et al., 1998), authenticity (Rogers, 1961), and effectiveness as a practitioner (Lindsay et al., 2007). However, during the first session I felt those uneasy feelings disappear as I could see the client enjoying the tasks and her love for tennis shining through. This highlighted to me that the child's primary experience of sport was enjoyment. As sessions progressed it became clear that Emily's early experiences of tennis were positive, but this had become lost along the way. A focus on performance and winning had taken over and was leading to her losing enjoyment for the game. Therefore, helping her to find ways to love tennis again aligned with the client's needs and with my core beliefs.

Upon making decisions throughout this case, another significant consideration was parental involvement. Firstly, I needed Emily's mum to buy in to an intervention focusing on enjoyment rather than performance, which conflicted with her initial requests. For her to play a helpful role within the intervention, I knew that resolving this potential conflict of interest was an important starting point. To do this, I ensured that I was upfront and honest with Emily's mum from the start about my plans for the intervention. Andersen et al. (2001) suggest that when working with athletes it is best to keep interested parties, such as parents, 'in the loop'. In addition, I had a conversation with the parent where I acknowledged that I had taken her requests on board by explaining the connection between enjoyment and performance. On reflection, these two steps were vital contributors to the parental involvement being a strength of the intervention. This allowed for me to lay the foundations of forming a trusting relationship with the parent. I believe this trust played a large part in the parent being invested and engaged in the consulting process. As a result, her actions throughout were helpful and aligned with the aim of the intervention. Based on this experience, in future I will take this approach of being open with parents from the beginning, when working with young athletes.

Another continual reflection was the role Emily's mum played in the delivery of the intervention. Her enthusiasm to be involved was refreshing and I felt confident that she would support Emily in tasks away from sessions. However, I also felt there was the risk that the parent may take the lead on the tasks away from the sessions. The conversation in relation to expectations conducted with the parent prior to the intervention helped with this (e.g., outlining that Emily is the focus of all tasks). To manage this during the intervention delivery, I designed most tasks where both Emily and her mum had a different role to play. For example, in one task Emily's mum was given the role of asking the questions and throwing the ball, while Emily was asked to catch the ball and answer the questions. Within the final game day plan, Emily's mum had her own focus of ensuring Emily had everything ready to feel prepared to complete the plan. I believe that giving the parent a specific role within the intervention enabled her to feel involved and share her enthusiasm without taking over on the task.

Finally, out of necessity the consultancy began virtually via an online platform. Although I was comfortable with online consulting, it would not have been my first choice due to the age of the client. I was aware from experience and literature (Hanley, 2009; Price et al., 2021; Suler, 2004) that online consultancy makes it challenging to use important non-verbal cues, which I thought may be even more challenging due to the age of the client. However, my main concern was how I would bring the fun, interactive elements of the consultancy alive over a video call. Face-to-face I feel that my personality and enthusiasm can drive this element; however, this would be more challenging virtually. As a result, I chose to be more creative in my practice and activities. I had to think outside of the box and develop tasks that would be fun and engaging despite their virtual nature. To account for this, I added an extra step to the planning of each session where I considered how the task would work online, would I enjoy doing the task and do I think client would enjoy the task? Overall, I believe that working online did not hinder the effectiveness of the consultancy. Due to the accessibility and creativity of the sessions I may even argue that the consultancy process was more effective online than it would have been face-to-face.

Conclusion

This chapter provides an insight into how a psychological intervention may be designed and delivered to a 9-year-old athlete via online consultancy. Moreover, the chapter demonstrates that consultancy online does not need to be a barrier to sport psychology effectiveness. If navigated appropriately and with thought, it can be beneficial for both the client and the practitioner. Finally, this case demonstrates how a parent can be successfully involved in the consulting process and can be an important ally in delivering interventions.

REFLECTIVE QUESTIONS

- What are your thoughts on a 9-year-old athlete seeking sport psychology support for performance enhancement?
- How might you make online consultancy with a youth athlete as effective as face-to-face consultancy?
- What are your thoughts and feelings towards parents playing a role within the consultancy process?
- What challenges do you envisage encountering when involving parents within consultancy and how might you manage these?
- With the response to the above question in mind, if you were to plan an intervention for a youth athlete, how may you work with and through the parent to develop and deliver this?

References

Andersen, M. B. (2005). *Sport Psychology in Practice*. Champaign, IL: Human Kinetics.

Andersen, M. B., Van Raalte, J. L., & Brewer, B. W. (2001). Sport psychology service delivery: Staying ethical while keeping loose. *Professional Psychology: Research and Practice*, *32*, 12.

Anderson, A. G., Mahoney, C., Miles, A., & Robinson, P. (2002). Evaluating the effectiveness of applied sport psychology practice: Making the case for a case study approach. *The Sport Psychologist*, *16*, 432–453.

Bailey, R., Hillman, C., Arent, S., & Petitpas, A. (2013). Physical activity: An underestimated investment in human capital? *Journal of Physical Activity & Health*, *9*, 1053–1055.

Bambling, M., King, R., Reid, W., & Wegner, K. (2008). Online counselling: The experience of counsellors providing synchronous single-session counselling to young people. *Counselling and Psychotherapy Research*, *8*, 110–116.

Bergin, J.J. (2004). Small-group counseling. In A. Vernon (Ed.) *Counseling Children and Adolescents* (pp. 355–390). Denver, CO: Love Publishing Company.

British Psychological Society. (2017). *Practice Guidelines* (3rd ed.). https://www.bps.org.uk/news-and-policy/practice-guidelines

Collins, R., Evans-Jones, K., & O'Connor, H. L. (2013). Reflections on three neophyte sport and exercise psychologists' developing philosophies for practice. *The Sport Psychologist*, *27*, 399–409.

Gilbert, J. N., & Orlick, T. (1996). Evaluation of a life skills program with grade two children. *Elementary School Guidance & Counselling*, *31*, 139–151.

Gould, D., & Maynard, I. (2009). Psychological preparation for the Olympic Games. *Journal of Sports Sciences*, *27*, 1393–1408.

Gould, D., Feltz, D., & Weiss, M. (1985). Motives for participating in competitive youth swimming. *International Journal of Sport Psychology*, *16*, 126–140.

Gould, D., Feltz, D., Horn, T., & Weiss, M. (1982). Reasons for attrition in competitive youth swimming. *Journal of Sport Behaviour*, *5*, 155–165.

Gould, D., Lauer, L., Rolo, C., Jannes, C., & Pennisi, N. (2006). Understanding the role parents play in tennis success: A national survey of junior tennis coaches. *British Journal of Sports Medicine*, *40*, 632–636.

Hanley, T. (2009). The working alliance in online therapy with young people: Preliminary findings. *British Journal of Guidance & Counselling*, *37*, 257–269.

Harris, B., & Birnbaum, R. (2015). Ethical and legal implications on the use of technology in counselling. *Clinical Social Work Journal*, *43*, 133–141.

Henriksen, K., Storm, L. K., Stambulova, N., Pyrdol, N., & Larsen, C. H. (2019). Successful and less successful interventions with youth and senior athletes: Insights from expert sport psychology practitioners. *Journal of Clinical Sport Psychology*, *13*, 72–94.

Johnstone, L., & Dallos, R. (2013). Introduction to formulation. In L. Johnstone , & R. Dallos (Eds.) *Formulation in Psychology and Psychotherapy* (pp. 21–37). New York, USA: Routledge.

Knight, C. J., Harwood, C., & Gould, D. (2018). *Sport Psychology for Young Athletes*. Abingdon, Oxon: Routledge.

Lindsay, P., Breckon, J. D., Thomas, O., & Maynard, I. W. (2007). In pursuit of congruence: A personal reflection on methods and philosophy in applied practice. *The Sport Psychologist*, *21*, 335–352.

Ludlam, K. E., Bawden, M., Butt, J., Lindsay, P., & Maynard, I. W. (2017). Perceptions of engaging with a super-strengths approach in elite sport. *Journal of Applied Sport Psychology*, *29*, 251–269.

Ludlam, K. E., Butt, J., Bawden, M., Lindsay, P., & Maynard, I. W. (2016). A strengths-based consultancy approach in elite sport: Exploring super-strengths. *Journal of Applied Sport Psychology*, *28*, 216–233.

Orlick, T., & Zitzelsberger, L. (1996). Enhancing Children's sport experiences. In F. L. Smoll & R. E. Smith (Eds.), *Children and Youth in Sport: A Biopsychosocial Perspective* (pp. 330–337). Dubuque, IA: Brown & Benchmark Publishers.

Partington, J., & Orlick, T. (1987). The sport psychology consultant evaluation form. *The Sport Psychologist*, *1*, 309–317.

Perry, J. (2019). *Performing under Pressure: Psychological Strategies for Sporting Success*. London: Routledge.

Peterson, J. (2004). The individual counseling process. In A. Vernon (Ed.) *Counseling children and adolescents* (pp. 355–390). Denver, CO: Love Publishing Company.

Poczwardowski, A., Sherman, C. P., & Henschen, K. P. (1998). A sport psychology service delivery heuristic: Building on theory and practice. *The sport psychologist*, *12*, 191–207.

Price, D., Wagstaff, C. R., & Thelwell, R. C. (2021). Opportunities and considerations of new media and technology in sport psychology service delivery. *Journal of Sport Psychology in Action*, *13*(1), 1–12.

Rogers, C. R. (1961). *On Becoming a Person*. London: Constable.

Sharp, L. A., & Hodge, K. (2011). Sport psychology consulting effectiveness: The sport psychology consultant's perspective. *Journal of Applied Sport Psychology, 23*, 360–376.

Snyder, C. (2014). The path to excellence: A view on the athletic development of U.S. Olympians who competed from 2000–2012. Initial Report of the Talent Identification and Development Questionnaire to U.S. Olympians (S. Riewald, Ed.), USOC Sport Performance and Coaching Education Divisions.

Suler, J. (2004). The online disinhibition effect. *Cyberpsychology & Behaviour, 7*, 321–326.

Van Raalte, J. L. (2003). Provision of sport psychology services at an international competition: The XVI Maccabiah Games. *The Sport Psychologist, 17*, 461–470.

Vealey, R. S. (2007). Mental skills training in sport. In G. Tennenbaum & R. C. Ecklund (Eds.), *Handbook of Sport Psychology* (Vol. 3, pp. 287–309). Hoboken: Wiley.

Visek, A. J., Harris, B. S., & Blom, L. C. (2009). Doing sport psychology: A youth sport consulting model for practitioners. *Sport Psychologist, 23*, 271–291.

Weiss, M. R. (1991). Psychological skill development in children and adolescents. *The Sport Psychologist, 5*, 335–354.

Winter, S., & Collins, D. (2015). Where is the evidence in our sport psychology practice? A United Kingdom perspective on the underpinnings of action. *Professional Psychology: Research and Practice, 46*, 175–182.

4

'MAYBE YOUR COACH DOESN'T LIKE YOU ... ' – A CASE STUDY AND REFLECTIONS USING REBT METHODS

Betsy Tuffrey

Introduction

The Author

When I embarked upon my journey within the field of Sport Psychology, the profession was somewhat in its infancy. There weren't many books of this nature; there wasn't the variety or flexibility of training routes to professional qualifications; and there were limited applied roles available. The roles that did exist were poorly advertised (perhaps this is still the case) and organisations didn't seem to know what they wanted from a Sport Psychologist. I intend for the following chapter to provide quality and insight into applied practice – to add value to trainee and early-career practitioners.

Based in the South of England, I have completed my education and training in the UK. I began a distance-learning degree (BSc) in 2006 and went on to complete a distance-learning Masters (MSc) – followed by Stage 2 Qualification in Sport and Exercise Psychology (also known as QSEP) with the British Psychological Society. I have Chartered Status as a Sport and Exercise Psychologist with HCPC registration. Heavily influenced by those who have taught and mentored me, I lean on a predominantly Cognitive-Behavioural (CB) approach. This chapter will guide you through a case study example of Rational Emotive Behaviour Therapy (REBT) – and I aim to provide you with knowledge of my personal experience, with a specific lens on REBT in applied Sport Psychology practice.

DOI: 10.4324/9781003263890-6

The Use of REBT

Why REBT?

The purpose of this chapter is not to explain at length what REBT is and how it works in detail. If you'd like to know more about the background, theory, and practical guidance for this therapy, there are some insightful books you can refer to.[1,2]

My first experience of REBT came when I was completing my Master's. More specifically, through Dr. Martin Turner.[3] Martin (who would deny this through modesty) was and still is one of my biggest influences and inspirations. When I began to explore REBT, I quickly realised how much sense this therapy seemed to make to me. Prior to completing the Primary Practicum REBT course,[4] I began using aspects of REBT methods interwoven into a more generalised cognitive behavioural approach to consultancy. Really, this didn't extend much further beyond the ABC model (we will explore this later). I looked into completing the Primary Practicum course and have now also completed the Advanced course via the Albert Ellis Institute. Both the Primary and Advanced courses can be a little hard to come by – there are many courses online which are not accredited by the Albert Ellis Institute so be aware of this if searching for training opportunities. There is currently only one centre in the UK which is accredited by the Institute, and the courses can be irregular. The Albert Ellis Institute based in New York now offers remote training, which allows for an improved access to REBT for candidates worldwide. Both the Primary and Advanced courses involve 3–4 days of intense training; the Primary course explains the therapy and allows you an opportunity to begin to practice therapy methods; the Advanced course extends upon this knowledge with further academic understanding and a higher standard of peer counselling expected. Both courses recruit across a myriad of therapy backgrounds, with peers joining from various professions and are therefore not sport-specific.

Throughout my journey with REBT, the more I learnt, the more I realised how it seemed to suit my understanding of psychology, and my personality – authentic, with the capacity to be somewhat blunt when required! I think these personal tendencies, and the philosophy of REBT (see Digiuseppe et al., 2022), work particularly well in the world of sport – where athletes working on performance barriers can demand tangibility when it comes to overwhelming and disorientating psychological challenges. What appealed to me when learning about REBT was what

---

[1] 'New Directions in Rational Emotive Behaviour Therapy' by Windy Dryden is an insightful book if you wish to learn more about REBT.

[2] 'Rational Emotive Behaviour Therapy in Sport & Exercise' Edited by Martin Turner & Richard Bennett is a great resource to learn more about applying REBT in sport and exercise contexts.

[3] Dr Martin Turner is leading the way in introducing REBT into sport and exercise psychology. His website: www.thesmarterthinkingproject.com is a fantastic, contemporary resource.

[4] Check out: https://store.albertellis.org/ for more information on REBT courses.

seemed to be a no-nonsense approach. In applied settings, the psychologist may have limited time and opportunity to work with a client, so using methods which are quick to get to the point makes sense to me. REBT also educates and is useful in encouraging clients to hold themselves to account when it comes to their thoughts, language, and behaviours. Such an approach – I think – has longevity. Once a client understands their own self-talk and language, they are more likely to develop an awareness of these things in the absence of the psychologist. The impact of REBT can therefore far outlast the duration of each, or any session.

I feel in many ways that REBT training has afforded me the opportunity to ask frank and direct questions; to get to the crux of a thought or behaviour relatively quickly compared to more commonly practised methods – it is no-nonsense! In doing this, I've often felt I am ridding my practice of some of the flaws that sports performers may associate with therapy or therapists. In my experience, there are many elite athletes that seem to have grown tired and wary of generic questions – for example the somewhat stereotypical tilt of the head and posing of the question: *'how are you feeling?'*. Of course, that question often allows an individual to express and explore, but we may do well to consider the client's existing perceptions of consultancy – for some, perhaps a soft questioning style such as this brings about negative connotations for the athlete regarding the therapeutic process and its potential for success. Yes, misconceptions of the psychologist most certainly still exist in sport (Pain & Harwood, 2004). REBT allows the client to feel collaboration and direction – with a degree of practical help achieved largely through using direct and specific questioning that drives to the root of an issue. This therapy allows not only the client, but also the practitioner, to keep on topic, with the therapist gaining permission from the client to interrupt or steer them back on track during consultancy. In my view, REBT also helps the practitioner to focus on the most pertinent aspects of concerns rather than trying to address innumerable points of potential interest. This further helps to keep things specific – allowing the client to stay focused on what matters most in their work with the therapist; but it also helps the practitioner to keep to a framework and to not deviate when they may otherwise be tempted to. It helps *me* to curb the endless quest of problem-solving each and every issue in a superficial, short-term, and relatively meaningless way. REBT gets to the point, and quickly (much like myself, some might say!). REBT largely focuses on single instances – one example; one irrational belief (iB); and therefore, one alternative message. Not that REBT is simplistic or rushed. On the contrary, it's complex but efficient. Simple, not easy.[5]

When Does REBT Work?

I have found REBT methods effective with both established and new client relationships – however that's not to say it's a 'one size fits all' method. Having

---

[5] See: http://www.rebtnetwork.org/library/personalreflections.html for further reflections from the REBT community.

well-defined, methodical boundaries can create quick yet strong rapport – but the challenges and directness which may at times be required by the practitioner can be challenging for the client to accept. Considerations about the level of rapport with a client may be relevant for the 'mic-dropping' moments of consultancy, but rapport is not an essential ingredient for successful REBT work. Using direct challenge to pose difficult questions can really open the door for the client to go through self-exploration and change. So, this 'mic-dropping' moment might come from asking: *'So **what** if your coach doesn't like you – why does that matter?';* to which the client might respond: *'I suppose it doesn't matter that much, I just don't like it'.* This type of questioning can certainly take courage from the practitioner – in my experience it can feel risky and against the instinct to support the client when you throw a strong comment (or grenade) aboard! In my experience, REBT works well if at least some rapport has been developed, to pave the way for challenging conversations. On reflection, I would not describe the relationship with the client in the following case study to have been particularly strong – if indeed present at all. That said, the selection of REBT was based on a need for direct clarity to progress consultancy – so again, rapport whether present or not is not the only factor to consider when deciding to use REBT methods.

When Doesn't REBT Work?

In many client-practitioner relationships, as the practitioner we often convince ourselves that the needs of the client should prevail. However, sometimes the needs of the client may not be the needs the client directly expresses to you. It is therefore important to discuss goals and expectations before you fire into the tough stuff. There may be times – particularly in an employed setting (such as a club or academy) where, as the practitioner you are available to clients 'on-tap', and they are not 'shelling out' on your hourly rate. In such instances, you may see a client who wants a 'half-hearted' conversation; a client who might want regular contact, a check-in, or to briefly discuss the meaning of life! This might be because they are not ready to delve deeply into their belief system, or it could be because they enjoy and benefit from a more general discussion or reflection. Specifically, I think REBT fails to work when clients have little or no willingness to be deeply honest and express true feelings or views. REBT methods keep a very specific focus, and do not always work well with a meandering loose-fitting conversation. When we force the use of REBT regardless of these considerations, we set REBT up to fail.

Do I always know from the outset that I will use REBT? No. It's important to consider the factors surrounding your client – their motivations and desires, and whether REBT methods are likely to help with their goals.

'Deep Diving' into the Sea of Negativity

I am not one for buzz phrases … so the title of this section challenges my inner, irrational fury! This section is about being prepared to sit comfortably with a negative outcome AND getting your client on board with this. REBT retains a negative 'end result' if you like. The goal is to replace an Unhealthy Negative Emotion (UNE) like anxiety – with a Healthy Negative Emotion (HNE) let's say, healthy nervousness. Let's take an example – a footballer is struggling with a UNE such as extreme anger whenever they are taken off the pitch in a competitive fixture. As a result of this extreme anger, they are wanting to (or are) throwing things around the changing room (this is called an action tendency – what we may do or wish to do in response to a situation). Neither the emotional experience nor the action tendency is helping the athlete in any way here. It's unrealistic and romantic for a client (or a practitioner) to suggest we will turn this around by means of miracle to a positive emotion such as – let's say, joy. That sounds ridiculous, doesn't it? Why? Because the situation is not desirable and that is okay. Does anyone really want or expect a player to skip off the field of play, delighted to be substituted? Of course not. Negative emotions are fine, however, the connotations associated with a UNE are not desirable or helpful for the individual and their performance and/or life goals. REBT guides a client to acceptance that an alternative negative emotion – an HNE such as frustration, where the action tendency might be to cross your arms on the bench and for 5 minutes feel a little hard done by is okay, and actually a pretty good goal for the situation.

The Case Study

The Client

The client was a 15-year-old footballer. I was contacted initially by their parents, who stated the reason for seeking assistance related to their child's lack of enjoyment in playing football, and their child's experience of pre-match anxiety. Specifically, the parents stated they wanted to ensure their child continued to play and train at their current club.

Initial Contact and Background

Due to location and the constraints of the Coronavirus pandemic, when the client's parents contacted me to enrol in consultancy, we agreed to conduct sessions remotely. The first two sessions included the client and one parent, to protect the gender. During these sessions, the client didn't disclose much, whereas the parents spoke at length about their own ideas and interpretations of their child's thoughts and behaviours. I suggested that it may be more fruitful if the client and I were to have a conversation without the presence of either parent. This of course would only go ahead with the parent's permission – and with any and all sessions recorded for safeguarding purposes. Therefore, subsequent sessions took place with the client absent of parental input. Throughout consultancy up to this point, I was trying to obtain a picture of the issue; how it was presented; what impact this was having on the client; and what the client's goals were. In the past I have found it can be challenging to get to the crux of the goal of consultancy with an under-18 client who may have been coerced or even forced to partake in consultancy. When I began working alone with the client, I felt I was losing my way. The responses from the client were vague, and at times contradictory to prior disclosures. I felt uncomfortable that three sessions in, I had little direction; all the while worrying about what the client was gaining apart from losing an hour of his time answering repeated and reworded questions in a vain attempt to progress the work.

I decided to propose REBT to the client – to assist in regaining some direction and structure in our sessions together. Refraining from divulging the entire theoretical back-catalogue of REBT since its formation, I gave an outline of what this therapy meant, and what the next session would look like – the client was happy to proceed. Before even beginning any 'nitty gritty' work, REBT allowed me even at this stage to 'have a plan'. What helped me to decide to change tack was a timely reassessment of how the sessions felt and the lack of progression we had made thus far. It's important to remain humble about how effective you may be as a Psychologist, whilst maintaining a balance of self-esteem regarding your abilities as a practitioner.

Know Your ABCs

Many therapies rely on obtaining a great deal of context from clients, be it their history; family circumstances; or past experiences. In contrast, REBT doesn't spend much time on this. Context is important, but what you're looking for with REBT is a specific problem AND a specific example of the problem (extrapolating outwards may happen later as an avenue for further discussion). As this type of therapy has specificity at heart, there may be times during a session that the client needs reigning in or refocusing – and so it's important to get permission for this prior to the start of consultancy. Failure to get permission can negatively impact the therapeutic alliance; for example, you may upset your client if you interrupt them or seemingly change the direction of conversation – appearing rude or disinterested. Importantly, this isn't about cutting off or diminishing the importance of any disclosed information from the client, but more about filtering. For example, you might say: *'Let's come back to that – for now let's really focus on this point'*. A crucial factor for REBT is to establish a goal early on with the client. It is important that neither the client nor the practitioner loses sight of the goal – in my practice I use the goal as a header for any notes or diagrams I record.

Together with obtaining a goal, imperative to REBT work is the 'ABC' framework. The ABC model is as simple as it sounds, and although the information that gets dropped into the framework may be less simple to decipher, the model is so widely applicable it's not only a great session intervention, but an excellent educational tool for use far beyond the session itself (Figure 4.1).

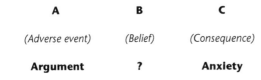

A	B	C
(Adverse event)	*(Belief)*	*(Consequence)*
Argument	**?**	**Anxiety**

FIGURE 4.1 ABC framework example

A simple way to illustrate the model to clients is to offer them the following diagram; I don't initially give the diagram in its entirety – I start with writing A and C and running through the A-to-C 'trap' before moving on. 'A' is the adverse event (sometimes called the activating event) – it's 'the thing'. 'C' is the consequence, 'what happens when "*the thing*" happens'. Us humans all too often fall into the trap of A-to-C thinking. We perceive (and often outwardly declare) that A has caused C. Breaking news – we are all guilty of this. Perhaps it's human nature; perhaps it's our language – either way, we so frequently attribute the consequence C to A without much thought. For example: *'That argument made me feel anxious'*, or *'They made me really angry'*. Such is the habitual automation of this connection, even the most well-versed practitioners may also fall into this trap! I have too been caught saying: *'So, what do you think is causing C?'*. Don't be scared to correct yourself in this way – this demonstrates humility as well as highlighting the human error we often all fall victim to when A-to-C thinking. Using parody and humour can also be effective here – try gaining agreement from the client that A is **causing** C. You will then "bamboozle" them as you highlight the new connection you are about to make (cue introduction of 'B'!).

What this model allows us to do is show the client theoretically and visually that there is a connecting factor to consider at 'B' – that a **belief** about A is resulting in C. I often pose to the client at this stage that if A did cause C, why is it that different people respond differently to the same adversity? Why is it that some athletes feel crippled by fear and anxiety pre-match; yet others feel nervous yet exhilarated at the prospect? If it were the 'rule' that A causes C, then we would respond in the same way; yet something different is going on for each of us. When initially discussing B, a key question could be: *'What are you telling yourself about this argument (A) that is resulting in you feeling anxious (C)?'*. There is extensive literature on REBT which will go into more detail about this, but here I'm merely showing that the acknowledgement of a B-to-C connection is key in this therapy.

So, let's take the example of a Cup Final resulting in performance anxiety for a football player. As explained above, I can be a little annoying at this stage for the client, as I encourage them to agree that the cup final (A) is **causing** anxiety (C). Before I shoot them down in flames and take the glory of highlighting the actual B-to-C connection, I usually ask the client to imagine a particularly nervous player who would be very anxious in this situation. Then, I ask the client to imagine the most positive of role models – perhaps an idol. I would ask whether this role model would be debilitatingly anxious at this event. They typically say no (I know what you're thinking – I'm full of tricks) and so this provokes some thought and discussion around why different people might produce a different C. The illustration that A surely cannot **cause** C (otherwise every player would be equally as anxious at a Cup Final) further reinforces that the A-to-C connection is flawed. Once the client understands that A-to-C thinking is problematic, we can start to discuss B. By illustrating that B is our belief we can start to discuss how B may be causing C for them as an individual. We might suppose in this example that B could be something like: *'I'm not good enough'*; if a player is thinking or saying this then it makes sense that they might feel anxious about this upcoming event.

I find this simple diagram a great way to annotate and share combined workings as you go through the client's ABCs with them. There are some useful tools out there which provide help sheets and structured pages to complete during an REBT intervention (Dryden, 2021) – these are excellent for sharing the progress of the intervention and key relationships between points A, B, and C during consultancy. In my experience, this sharing of work can be very helpful in both educating and building a collaborative relationship with your client; moving away from secretive note taking which can result in a sense of unease and judgement for the client. My new favourite toy is an electronic notepad, which allows live screensharing – perfection for this kind of intervention particularly when delivering remotely.

Sessions

Session 1 of REBT

I began session one by recapping with the client what we had already gleaned from our previous contact, to check understanding and clarify any grey areas or dis-agreements. The client and I began discussing pre-game anxiety (a topic which had come up frequently during consultation) and this slotted in nicely to the beginnings of an ABC discussion.

After I had used examples to check the client's understanding of the ABC model, we moved on swiftly to identify the client's own ABC model. We discussed what the client wanted to achieve from consultancy (the goal) which was to enjoy par-ticipation in football again. It is vital to discuss the goal for consultancy early on. This goal provides a tangible and relatable link throughout REBT consultancy; whether to illustrate how thoughts or emotions are not helping the client to achieve the goal; or revisiting the goal to enhance motivation with homework exercises. We iden-tified A as 'Competitive Fixture' and we identified C as 'Anxiety'. To satisfy REBT's encouragement towards a specific example, we discussed a recent game where anxiety felt at its strongest, or most debilitating for the client.

So, we had established A and C. The client identified the activating event or adversity (A) as the competitive game; and saw that the emotional consequence to this was anxiety (C). The client at this stage was of the mind that the competitive game is causing anxiety (A is causing C). In line with REBT, this A-C assumption is not accurate, and causes a skewed perception of reality. By running through some ex-amples of why A-to-C thinking is problematic, the client came to understand that A-to-C thinking is not true or logical. That said, the client was reluctant to ultimately agree that it is not the game that is causing the anxiety. In my experience with REBT, clients can be a little cautious or unconvinced; remember, we haven't really addressed anything detailed yet, so it would be unreasonable to expect the client to 'see the light' entirely at this stage and give up on what they may have been telling themselves for potentially a long time. We moved on to discuss what might be coming up for the client at B. When discussing B, ultimately your goal as a practitioner here is to drill down to uncover an iB. When conducting an REBT session, and when discussing B, there are a few things to look out for. Signs of iB's may come in the form of[*]:

- Awfulizing – Describing things as terrible; catastrophic; the worst thing ever, etc.
- Low frustration tolerance (LFT) – Describing an inability to cope or deal with something i.e.: *'I cannot tolerate it when I am disrespected'*.
- Demandingness – Rigidly specifying that something *must* be i.e.: *'I must be respected at all times'*.

[*] *This list is not exhaustive. Refer to REBT literature for more detail in this area.*

Clients may find it challenging to access or express what is going on at B. I started by asking the client: *'What was so anxiety provoking about that match?'*. Below is an illustration of the inference chaining process, which assists in identifying the iB. Note that I do not challenge the irrationality at this stage, as I might assume the adversity of making mistakes is true, rather than appeasing the client.

- *What was so anxiety provoking about that match?*
- Well, I'm going to make a mistake and that will be depressing
- *Depressing?*
- Yes – couldn't bear making a mistake
- *So, let's say you make a mistake, what is so bad about that?*
- I know I'll make a mistake, and my teammates are going to be annoyed or angry with me
- *And how bad would that be?*
- Terrible! Like, terrible!
- *So, if we scored that on a scale of 1–10 how terrible?*
- 10
- *Ok. So, what is so terrible about making a mistake*
- I feel a pressure to not make a mistake
- *Ok. So, when you do make a mistake, what does that mean to you?*
- People will think I'm bad
- *So what?*
- Maybe I am bad
- [silence]
- And they'll think I'm bad at everything, or rubbish, or a failure

Questioning in this way often guides the client and the therapist to the crux of the iB, which we agreed was: *'Making mistakes in a game is terrible. I cannot stand it when people think I'm bad — it means I am a failure'.* Once you've ascertained an iB, it's useful to get the client to recognise how this is resulting in anxiety, and indeed how this anxiety is not helping them in achieving their goal.

Session 2 of REBT – 'Negative Nora'

Recapping the prior session, the client and I reinforce the agreement that the iB statement isn't helpful. Before trying to figure out an alternative rational belief (rB), we talked about what an ideal C might look like. This is where Negative Nora comes in. Often, clients want to experience something positive — something good. They may also feel like that's the answer you're looking for them to produce. This is a bugbear of mine; in that there is often a misconceived idea that positive thinking is 'King' in psychology, and in life. I've rarely thought this was particularly helpful; and perhaps that comes from my own experiences — sometimes things are rubbish and that is okay as it is (we don't need to force an ingenuine positive spin on something). After all, it's not negative experiences per se that distress or disturb us, but our perception of these events. Considering this, it's important for a client to recognise that to progress rationally with their goal, C is still going to be negative in nature. Bear with me on this … What we are trying to get to is an HNE which is not debilitative to performance or goals. So, the client and I agreed that 'healthy nerves' would be a good, achievable, alternative to anxiety at C. It's important to link again to the goal — how healthy nerves allow the client to achieve the goal of enjoying football — more so than a UNE such as anxiety, would allow.

During the second session, I sensed that the client was starting to think a little more independently. This was a significant shift. Initially in consultation, much information seemed to be from the parent(s) — either directly, or by the client agreeing with the parents. When the client and I first met, I felt the client was looking to me for the answers and was reluctant to be open and honest. In my view, this recent shift was attributed to the client being better able to see the progression of the model in these REBT sessions — being able to see the work we were doing and trusting the work, and indeed me — a little more. Once the alternative HNE of healthy nerves at C had been identified, the next step was to start to think about rational alternatives at B which would allow healthy nerves to prevail — this is about identifying an rB alternative. We agreed on three statements for the client to practice; for example, one of these was: *'If I make a mistake, that is bad, but it's not awful'*.

I asked the client to reflect on the session and they reported feeling 'good' and understanding themselves better. With the goal of enjoyment of football at the fore, I tasked the client with homework. This was with the aim of initiating and practising new thoughts and behaviours which would assist in the adoption of the rB. It had come up during consultation that as a result of feeling anxious, the client would often refrain from attending training, or turn up late to avoid any inter-actions with teammates and coaches. To encourage new helpful behaviours, one aspect of homework was to arrive at training early and approach a teammate or coach for a short conversation.

Session 3 of REBT

During the recap of session two, I felt as though the client wasn't 'buying into' the new self-statements, or indeed the rB at all. The client had found it 'too difficult' to follow through with the homework task. This felt to me rather like a regression; however, I quickly realised that all was not lost – but I needed to reinforce some of the aspects of the prior session. This is quite understandable; what REBT is asking for is for clients to abandon their iBs (which they have held for some time and truly believe) in exchange for a brand-new rational alternative. Whilst we as practitioners can demonstrate the benefits of this in terms of the client achieving their goals and experiencing less distress, it is not an easy task for the client to undertake.

When I asked again whether the rational alternative was indeed to feel healthy nerves at C (HNE), the client was struggling with whether they wanted to feel the HNE as an alternative, or whether they even wanted to play football at all. This was impacting on the motivation to change and engage in the therapy. I asked the client why they play football, and what life would be like for them if they didn't play. Unexpectedly, this thought came with some relief and happiness, which seemed to help the client to see the truth of their experience – to entertain the idea of not playing. This is where this case study took on new meaning.

We began to think about what life without football looks like for the client. I started with: *'How would you feel if you only ever trained and didn't play competitively?'* and *'Why don't you give up altogether?'*. As is often the case with under-18 clients, the weight of the parental viewpoint is a factor, probably for both client and practitioner (after all, as a practitioner you have been somewhat employed by the parent – with their specific goal in mind). It seemed to me that although the idea of not doing the sport anymore brought about a sense of relief, it also appeared too distressing to entertain – with comments such as: *'How would my parents react?'*. The client was in a state of toying back and forth between the realisation that they didn't want to play football anymore, and the idea that if they could just feel less anxious the problem would go away (the problem being they didn't want to play). This was really the meaty end of the consultancy. When asked: *'What you would rather do if there were no repercussions?'*, the client struggled to answer and appeared conflicted. The idea that they may be able to change the anxiety (UNE) to healthy nervousness (HNE) meant perhaps they could carry on playing – thus pleasing their parents and ridding themself of this issue. But truly, they only wanted to explore this route because it was simpler not to let their parents down. The real golden moment perhaps was the disclosure from the client that training or informal bouts of play rather than competitive play was **their** goal. In my mind, this satisfied the health and activity concerns of the parents, and crucially satisfied the goal of the client to enjoy football.

The poignancy of REBT is sometimes about where you leave the session – not 'overworking the dough' so-to-speak, refraining from diluting good work with more content or over-explored, over-elaborate conversations about the same point. When a client leaves a session with new insight (an epiphany-like sensation), that alone can be a big deal which may need some time and space to sink in. Considering this, I was cautious not to explore this 'mic-dropping' realisation too much – instead allowing the client to mull over the poignancy of what they had arrived at themselves. Often there are 'big moments' that come from a realisation that emotions and beliefs are connected; that beliefs can be challenged, or that there is an alternative way of viewing the world. An athlete might receive these insights with amazement and hope, or with guilt and anger. It's not easy to realise that some of your emotional suffering could be self-perpetuated.

This session prompted the client to speak with his parents, who subsequently emailed me. In terms of ascertaining whether the intervention had been helpful to the client, this is where it got messy. The parents wanted their child to continue playing and training; but the client had realised they didn't want this to happen. The parents therefore had no interest in their child continuing work with me as they did not see this as helpful to their own goal. It would be easy for me as a relatively early career practitioner at this stage, to surmise that I had not conducted a successful round of REBT sessions as the outcome was not desirable to the parents who had initially engaged in my services (with adult clients, perhaps there is a more open-minded route to self-understanding). However, the client arguably achieved a truth and realisation which consultation helped them to arrive at.

Consultancy came to an end with a summary email to the client's parents, including potential avenues for discussion with their child. I suggested it may prove beneficial to discuss what the client felt about the sessions, and what thoughts were prevalent for the client regarding future participation in the sport. This type of discussion may provide a semi-structured platform for the client to share previously unshared thoughts and feelings, and indeed for parents to be responsible for their contribution to such a conversation in a more intentional way than every day, perhaps informal conversation. Irrespective of how this discussion may pan out, the outcome of consultancy in my view was positive. The aims of consultancy in many ways are to access the most real and true of emotions and thoughts to achieve true insight and change, desirable to the client.

Practitioner Reflections

Maybe Your Coach Doesn't Like You

In the current case study, instinctively perhaps I wanted to discourage the client away from negative thoughts – perhaps wanting to reassure that everything is fine, and that maybe the client didn't really feel like they wanted to give up, or that they probably don't feel as anxious as they think they do. I resisted this temptation, as in REBT it is inelegant to alter perceptions in this way; instead, I assumed that the experience was true. Rather than question the validity of the perception, I questioned what the client was telling themselves (B) about the adversity (A). This is about empowering the client to believe that even if A is true, they still have the capability and the responsibility to deal with the emotions that arise, and to move forward constructively. In REBT practice, dissuade the client from buying into the notion that their actions and emotions are caused entirely by external events. I help them to venture into the uncomfortable territory of emotional responsibility, sometimes even gently and empathetically pushing them into this territory, to face the world as it, not as it 'should' be. For example: *'I'm not agreeing that the coach thinks you are rubbish, I don't know either way, but let's assume they do for a moment'*. In this case study, some of this conversation centred around mistakes. I would entertain the idea of mistakes happening (as they do!) instead of going down the road of correcting said mistakes. That's not what's important here – what was important in this case study was to understand what mistakes mean to the client, and how assuming mistakes will happen may help the client to accept this adversity. In other situations, I might agree with the client's adverse thoughts: *'Fine – let's say the coach thinks you're rubbish and therefore the world will end!'*. Sometimes there's a balance to be had with po-faced seriousness, and sometimes using jest and sarcasm can be beneficial, with sarcasm forming a paradoxical argument against an iB (Turner, 2019). By agreeing with iBs and presenting them sarcastically, I allow the client to dispute and critique their own utterances and not treat them as precious and sacred beliefs. The client can see that there is an argument against their narrative for a situation. Helping a client to develop critical thinking skills allows in some ways for a continuation of the work by the athlete, in the absence of a practitioner.

Let's normalise that you want to please your client. You may want to take all their troubles away or miraculously transform them into wonderful rainbows of relief. This is not your job. Not only is this hard to get your head around, but it's also something you will need to remind yourself of time and time again. Sometimes a client will walk into consultancy with you, with concerns that the manager won't play them because the manager doesn't like them. And you know what – the manager might not like them.

Irrational Language

In elite sport, we hear and see a lot of strong messages being relayed to and between staff and players, and the general public. This could include irrational, extreme language, or the communication of a results-driven ethic with very small margins for error. For example, a game may be *'must win'* or an athlete may say: *'I'm devastated to lose'* or, *'This means everything to me'*. It's important to view these strong messages within the context of the environmental demands of elite sport, because in some cases strong language might be accurate and appropriate, it may be a conditional must (i.e., a must-win to progress in a cup competition – factual) and may not reflect deeply held iBs (Latinjak & Hatzigeorgiadis, 2020).

As REBT practitioners, we don't just walk around spotting 'musts' so that we can dispute them! I would be sure to educate any client on conditional musts, which may be accurate and not irrational, to firm up their understanding when they stand to hear the 'musts' in their own language. Some clients are argumentative when it comes to challenging this aspect of REBT, and so it's helpful to point out these exceptions to make it a sensible debate rather than petty disputation over the finer details of discourse.

Entertaining an Unplanned Resolution

In the current case study, REBT allowed myself and my client to explore what may have been the 'unthinkable' i.e., giving up or retiring. Asking a client whether they would consider leaving their sport can often provoke a defensive reaction, and often leads the client to realise all they love about their activity, and that of course they don't want to give up. However, occasionally – as was the case here – clarity may be gained from a realisation that exiting the sport is both an attractive and fulfilling prospect. Sometimes, the outcome of consultation isn't perhaps what you wanted or expected, and not what the athlete (or parent) thought would happen. But if you help the athlete to reach a realisation that may set them free of their problem, perhaps that doesn't always look like a neat resolution and continuation of performance. We, as practitioners, can become fixated from the very start of our careers, on making things 'better' for an athlete. But who gets to decide what is 'better'?

Final Thought

Throughout this chapter I have tried to retain my personality and style throughout. This leads me to a crucial piece of advice: recognise how important your own individuality is as a practitioner. Most practitioners have extensive knowledge and skills – but we are all simply a vehicle of delivery. How you disseminate your practice is what makes your practice. I urge you to remain true to your own style, values, and beliefs when considering your practice. This chapter has reinforced to me the connection I feel with REBT. I hope this chapter inspires you not necessarily to delve into REBT practice (although that might be the case) but to find your passion in practice. Then, you'll be able to focus on working with purpose and in turn, you will become the best vehicle of delivery of your own knowledge.

REFLECTIVE QUESTIONS

1. What might you consider before using REBT methods with a client?
2. How might you identify an irrational belief?
3. How could taking yourself through an example of inference chaining support your practice?
4. What might be some challenges for you personally, of using REBT?

GLOSSARY

REBT – Rational Emotive Behaviour Therapy
ABC – Adversity/Adverse event; Belief; Consequence
HNE – Healthy Negative Emotion (e.g., concern)
UNE – Unhealthy Negative Emotion (e.g., anxiety)
iB – Irrational Belief
rB – Rational Belief
Awfulizing – Describing things as terrible; catastrophic; the worst thing ever.
Low Frustration Tolerance (LFT) – Describing an inability to cope or deal with something i.e.: *'I cannot tolerate it when I am disrespected'.*
Demandingness – Rigidly specifying that something *must* be i.e.: *'I must be respected at all times'.*

References

Digiuseppe, R., Doyle, K., Dryden, W., & Backx, W. (2022). *Albert Ellis and the Philosophy of REBT*. Oxford Clinical Psychology. Retrieved 18 June 2022, from https://www.oxfordclinicalpsych.com/view/10.1093/med:psych/9780199743049.001.0001/med-9780199743049-chapter-1.

Dryden, W. (2021). *Reason to Change: A Rational Emotive Behaviour Therapy Workbook*. Routledge : New York (2nd ed.).

Latinjak, A., & Hatzigeorgiadis, A. (2020). *Self-talk in Sport*. Routledge.

Pain, M., & Harwood, C. (2004). Knowledge and perceptions of sport psychology within English soccer. *Journal of Sports Sciences*, *22*(9), 813–826. 10.1080/0264041041000171 6670.

Turner, M. (2019). REBT in Sport. *Advances in REBT*, 307–335. 10.1007/978-3-319-93118-0_14.

5

OUTSIDE THE ARENA: WORKING AS A SPORT PSYCHOLOGIST WITH NON-SPORTING HIGH-PERFORMANCE CLIENTS

Harley de Vos

Introduction

If you are like me, when you hear the term 'sport psychology' you probably think about sport, athletes, and coaches. And if like me, you embark on a journey to become a sport psychologist, you probably aspire to work in sport and to work with athletes and/or coaches. While working in sport can be immensely rewarding, there are a range of other settings outside of sport where the skills and expertise you gather in pursuing a career as a sport psychologist are highly sought after, and these settings can be equally rewarding to work in. Although I am a sport psychologist and work with athletes, I have also had the opportunity to work with several non-athlete high-performance clients. By non-athlete high-performance clients, what I mean is clients who are not athletes but whose vocation makes them a high performer or means they work in a high-performance setting. Think of professionals working in high-stress settings including surgeons, doctors, military personnel, pilots, firefighters, law enforcement officers, performing artists, CEOs, and business owners or leaders – these are people that I consider to be high performers, and in my experience, they respond well to sport psychology principles and approaches. To illustrate my point, although there are dozens and dozens of professional sporting teams and organisations across various sports in the United States of America, it is the U.S. Army that is the largest employer of sport psychologists in America (Weir, 2018).

In this work with non-athlete high-performance clients, I see myself as a *performance psychologist* as opposed to a sport psychologist. I must stress at this point that although I have some experience, I am by no means an expert in performance psychology. If you are interested in learning more about performance psychology or how to apply sport psychology knowledge and principles with non-athlete

DOI: 10.4324/9781003263890-7

high-performance clients, I would strongly encourage you to read widely across the relevant literature and engage in high-quality supervision.[1]

In this chapter, I am going to outline my approach to working with non-athlete high-performance clients. Using two case studies, I hope to showcase what I have learned thus far in my career and how I apply my skills working with non-athlete high-performance clients. The case studies will focus on my work with a military client and a training doctor. To protect the anonymity of the clients in these case studies, details have been altered or omitted.

What Is Performance Psychology?

There has long been conjecture in the field of sport psychology relating to how we define what we do and the scope of practice that we have. My Master's degree was in sport and exercise psychology, and my endorsement is as a sport and exercise psychologist. Because I do not work in exercise settings (in my opinion, exercise psychology is more closely tied to health psychology than sport psychology), I often drop the exercise part from my title. In many ways, sport psychology really is a subset of performance psychology and therefore, 'sport and performance psychologist' would be much more accurate I feel in terms of the work that I and many practitioners in the field do.

Hays (2006; 2012) defined performance psychology as helping people learn how to perform better and consistently in endeavours where excellence counts. Building upon this definition, Division 47 (Exercise and Sport Psychology) of the American Psychological Association proposed the following definition of performance psychology (Portenga et al., 2016, p. 6):

> 'Performance psychology is the study and application of psychological principles of human performance to help people consistently perform in the upper range of their capabilities and more thoroughly enjoy the performance process. Performance psychologists are uniquely trained and specialised to engage in a broad range of activities, including the identification, development, and execution of the mental and emotional knowledge, skills, and abilities required for excellence in performance domains; the understanding, diagnosing, and preventing of the psychological, cognitive, emotional, behavioural, and psychophysiological inhibitors of consistent, excellent performance; and the improvement of performance environments to facilitate more efficient development, consistent execution, and positive experiences in performers'.

The definitions provided by Hays (2006) and APA accurately depict the breadth of practice that performance psychology entails. These definitions also align closely

---

[1] One book I would recommend to anyone interested in performance psychology is 'Performance Psychology in Action' by Dr Kate Hays.

with my own personal experiences and approach to working in performance psychology, as I hope to demonstrate through my two case studies. When I am working with a non-athlete high performer, I am collaborating with them to help them achieve and maintain their optimal performance level. To help these clients, I will use psychological techniques and strategies that focus on performance enhancement, performance restoration, and/or managing wellbeing and mental health.

My Personal Therapeutic Approach

My therapeutic approach to sport (and performance!) psychology is influenced by my own experiences, the training that I have received, my beliefs and understanding about sport and optimising performance, and my personality characteristics. My training has led me to believe that performance and mental health cannot be separated, just like the physical and the mental ultimately cannot be separated. Consequently, I feel comfortable and competent helping an athlete or performer with a mental health concern that may or may not be related to their sport or performance domain. Equally, I also feel comfortable and competent helping an athlete or performer work on the mental aspects of their performance and helping them to optimise their performance.

As a practitioner, I believe strongly in the importance of the therapeutic relationship. My approach to working with clients is heavily influenced by the Rogerian therapist qualities of authenticity, genuineness, empathy, warmth, compassion, acceptance, and unconditional positive regard (see person-centred therapy or Rogerian therapy). Although, truth be told, I'm not sure I always display unconditional positive regard as much as Carl Rogers would want a therapist to!

As a psychologist, I believe in using evidence-based interventions. Above all else, we are scientists, and what we do should be based on good science. My therapeutic approach is based on acceptance and commitment therapy (ACT). I find ACT works well with athletes and high performers – the principles of mindfulness/present moment awareness, defusion, and values align closely with this population. There has been a great increase over the past few years in journal articles, books, and conferences/professional development focused on ACT in sport. My personal belief is that any sport psychology practitioners who are interested in ACT should first learn about ACT and how to use it in therapy before learning about how to apply it in sport.[2]

My scope of practice as a sport psychologist in working with non-athlete high-performance clients has been developed through my qualifications, professional development, supervision, continual reflective practice, and work opportunities.

---

[2] I would recommend reading the likes of Steve Hayes, Kelly Wilson, or Russ Harris, who have all published various books including textbooks, therapist manuals, and self-help books such as 'ACT Made Simple' (Harris, 2019), 'Get Out of Your Head and Into Your Life' (Hayes, 2005) and 'A Liberated Mind' (Hayes, 2019).

An important consideration for all psychologists relates to competence and not practicing outside your area of competence. An old supervisor of mine once told me that when it comes to matters regarding competence as a psychologist, sometimes it is up to us as the psychologist to upskill ourselves and gain competence to meet the needs of our client(s). This advice I have taken with me when working in a range of different settings (including sport/performance and general psychology) and when working with a range of different client groups. To be able to apply your skills and knowledge in sport psychology to other performance settings, first you must focus on being a good psychologist. Second, you need to ensure that you use evidence-based interventions in the work that you do. Third, always be willing to learn and improve as a psychologist – just like the sporting and non-sporting clients that we work with! And finally, be open-minded, adaptable, and enthusiastic to work on opportunities that may arise outside of sport. In the two case studies below, I demonstrate my process for developing competence as a psychologist when working with non-athlete high-performance clients.

Case Study One: Military Personnel

Prior to commencing work with Condor Performance, the sport and performance psychology consultancy that I am currently working with, I had little knowledge about military psychology or working with military personnel. It was not an area in which I had considered working. With the opportunity, however, to work with several military clients, it has become an area of interest for me. This interest stems from the regard in which I hold them and the work that they do. While I absolutely love working with athletes, if they don't perform well, the sun will rise again and life will go on. With military personnel, the stakes are very real. It is because of the potential consequences that I consider military personnel, especially those in high-performance areas such as Special Forces or Navy SEALS (in Australia we don't have SEALS but we do have similar personnel in our Navy), to be elite with what they do. Helping them to improve, to transfer my knowledge and expertise in sport psychology to their domain, and to learn constantly from them (which also helps better me as a practitioner) is something that makes me immensely proud. I consider learning from my clients to be an important part of reflective practice. I like to remain curious, inquisitive, and seek to understand what it is like to undertake and perform in their chosen endeavour. In the case of working with military personnel, I always seek to understand what their role and environment they work in requires of them, as well as learn through a process of ongoing introspection and interpretations of my client interactions, which strategies and techniques from sport psychology apply effectively to working in the military.

Joe is a 33-year-old male officer in the Australian Defence Force with operational experience as an infantry platoon commander in the Middle East as well as multiple deployments as an intelligence officer. He is interested in pursuing a career in the Special Forces and sought performance psychology services to help him set a solid foundation of mental resilience and to support him to achieve his career goal of becoming an officer and leader in the Special Forces. Joe also has a background as an endurance athlete, competing in marathon and ultramarathon events, and holds various military athletic records. In our first session together, I explored with Joe his current role, background experience, and reasoning for wanting to join the Special Forces. The latter is a goal he has had since before he joined the military. I also explored his family life, interests, and hobbies outside of his career. We discussed his career goals and what he wanted from our work together, which was to develop mental toughness to help him prepare for the selection process.

One activity I like to perform with all new clients after our first session is a self-reflective performance appraisal of that client's performance when they are at their best and when they are not performing well. I ask the client to complete this task as a written homework task after the initial session. I prefer the clients to write down this reflection, as I feel taking time to reflect and describe their experiences is more effective when written compared to when delivered verbally. This task, like all homework tasks, readings and handouts, and interventions I provide for my clients, is always optional. Part of suggesting this task as homework to my clients is to assess their engagement in our work, although I don't judge those clients who do not complete this exercise. In the case of non-athlete high-performance clients such as Joe, I tend to modify this activity slightly and focus on their strengths and weaknesses. My goal in asking clients to complete this task is to gain a greater understanding of what my client is good at, what they do well, and what their best performance looks like so that I can work with them to help them access that more consistently. As a sport and performance psychologist, it is important to remember that we cannot make our clients jump higher, run faster, or do anything better than what they are physically capable of. What we do well, however, is help them to get their head 'out of the way' so that their body can do what it is physically capable of doing.

In undertaking the strengths and weaknesses appraisal with Joe, he outlined that his strengths included strategic thinking, physical strength and endurance (he has a background in distance running), planning, and his experience. He identified that his weaknesses or areas for improvement included a history of injury, emotional regulation, managing stress when under fatigue, and performance anxiety when under assessment. Joe's history of injury and self-confessed "getting carried away" when exercising and undertaking physical challenge was immediately something I identified as a key area for intervention. I made this assessment based on his self-reflections, my therapeutic approach, and my beliefs about high performance. Understanding recovery, especially related to sleep and relaxation (as well as physical recovery techniques routinely used by athletes), is something I constantly strive to learn more about. Helping clients to sleep better, relax more, and focus on recovery in addition to training hard (for non-athlete clients this often presents as being 'productive') is an important area for intervention that sport psychologists are well placed to educate and assist clients with (see Halson, 2013). Joe did reveal that he struggles to switch off and insomnia can be an issue for him.

In our next session, Joe reported that he had spoken with an officer in the Regiment (Special Forces) who reinforced to Joe the importance of being clear with his intrinsic motivators for wanting to join the Regiment. In other words, know *why* he wants to join the Regiment.[3] Clearly knowing Joe's reasons for wanting to join the Special Forces is important for two main reasons – being able to clearly articulate his reasons to the selection officers and leveraging his why, to help him keep going when the selection process gets challenging, and his mind may start protesting and encourage him to stop.[4]

Following this information from Joe, I decided to introduce him to values and help him to explore and clarify his own values. When a client wants to work on motivation with me, I will approach it from a values perspective. This is beneficial to help clients understand what matters most to them, what their priorities are in life, and what gives them the most meaning. By understanding this information, clients can then take action based on their values, and low motivation should be less of a problem as a result. Joe reported that he found understanding his own values as well as aligning his values with those highly sought in the Regiment to be really helpful. In his own words, "the most valuable thing that I gained [in working with me] was the coaching that started my comprehension of the connection among goals, motivation, and values. I found significant benefit for developing a strong mental foundation by better understanding my values and connecting my daily activities and challenges to these values." This feedback from Joe was valuable to help my own professional development. I always encourage my clients to provide feedback regarding the skills I teach and my therapeutic style, although this is more informal and ad hoc rather than a structured process.[5]

An important part of my work with all my military clients, especially Joe, is my own professional development and learning. I am a big believer that as a psychologist we constantly need to strive to learn and expand our knowledge and skills. One of the requirements to earn and retain registration as a psychologist in Australia is to maintain continued professional development each year. I am unaware whether this is a registration/licencing requirement for psychologists in other parts of the world, but regardless I would strongly encourage all sport psychology practitioners to ensure they are continuing to learn and upskill. Completing your post-graduate studies in sport psychology is just the beginning of your knowledge development! Professional development can include attending conferences and workshops, reading books, supervision and mentoring, and other educational activities.

---

[3] To learn more about the importance of discovering and understanding your purpose or why, I suggest reading Simon Sinek such as 'Find Your Why'.

[4] For anyone wanting to learn more about the selection process and what it takes to join the Australian Special Forces, I highly recommend you check out the documentary 'Search for Warriors' (a two-part documentary available on YouTube).

[5] There are some great resources available regarding client session evaluations such as the Session Rating Scale (Johnson et al., 2000), and certainly incorporating this level of formal evaluation from clients is something that can improve practice.

In addition to my required professional development, I have made a habit of constantly seeking to learn more about my clients' performance domain, be that a sport I don't know much about or in Joe's case, what is required to be a Special Forces operative. I will often ask my clients if they can recommend any books/podcasts/documentaries, etc., related to their sport or performance domain that I can engage with to increase my knowledge. This process of working collaboratively with my clients relates to my philosophy that the therapeutic relationship is the most important component in therapy and aligns well with my interpersonal and client-centred approach. I also find it can aid a therapeutic relationship based on equality (I am never the expert!), reducing the potential for a power imbalance to emerge. The collaborative process demonstrates to my clients that I am invested in them and their journey, and I am keen to expand my knowledge base to best meet their needs and challenges.[6]

Alongside working with Joe on his values, we also discussed Stoic philosophy[7] and how he may implement elements of Stoicism into his preparation. Joe was well-read on Stoic philosophy, and our discussion focused more on reminding him of his knowledge about this and how he could implement it, rather than teaching him the principles per se. We spoke at length about the physical training he was doing to prepare and incorporating mental skills (such as committed action) during his physical training sessions. Recovery and the importance of sleep (for both recovery and optimising performance) were also important components of our discussions.

In our next session, Joe reported feeling anxious regarding his body and injury history. In particular, he was concerned about his hamstring and the impact that it might have on his ability to perform the weighted pack run (a key fitness test in the Special Forces selection process). When I work with a client with health/injury-related anxiety, as Joe was experiencing, I find that normalising the client's emotional experience can be helpful for reducing the anxiety and emotional distress they are experiencing. Regardless of the trigger for anxiety, I also like to explain the basic neurobiology (using evolutionary psychology) of where anxiety comes from in our brain, and how from an evolutionary perspective, anxiety is a key survival mechanism. As with normalising the emotional experience, I find that teaching clients about *why* they are experiencing anxiety also helps to reduce their emotional distress.

To help Joe manage his injury anxiety and deal with the challenges of preparing for selection, I chose to use self-compassion. As a sport psychologist, I am a big advocate for self-compassion as a crucial mental skill for helping optimise and achieve peak performance. In fact, for all clients that I have worked with and will

---

[6] For those interested in working with military personnel 'On Killing' and 'On Combat' by Dave Grossman, 'Can't Hurt Me' by David Goggins, and 'The Resilience Shield' by Ben Pronk, Dan Pronk, & Tim Curtis are great books. I would also recommend autobiographies of any Special Forces soldiers and 'Open' by Andre Agassi. I am a firm believer that you can learn something from everybody, and autobiographies often provide great pearls of wisdom and insights that you can apply personally and professionally.

[7] Author Ryan Holiday has written extensively on stoicism if you want to learn more.

work with in the future, I would argue that self-compassion is one of the most important skills that I teach my clients. My understanding of self-compassion and its effectiveness is based more on my own experience as a psychologist, rather than any formal training I have received.

My approach to teaching self-compassion is to combine mindfulness, being kind to yourself, and giving yourself permission to make mistakes/learning that mistakes are an important part of being human. Awareness of thoughts (developed through mindfulness) and self-talk is useful for teaching a client to be kind to themselves. I will often ask clients when they are noticing that they are being self-critical whether they would say what they are telling themselves to a friend or a teammate. Almost always, the answer is no. Giving yourself permission to make mistakes is also an important part of developing self-compassion. My approach is to ask my clients if professionals in their sport or performance area make mistakes, and always the answer is yes. I find this can be helpful to let clients understand that making mistakes is okay. Mistakes provide us with opportunities to learn, grow, and improve. If an athlete or performer is not making mistakes, I would argue that they are probably not improving. Joe reported that he found learning about self-compassion to be helpful and was keen to implement self-compassion to see how it could benefit him. In a military context, self-compassion is a vital component for high performance because the difficult challenges military personnel face, such as high-risk dangerous missions in hostile terrain, are hard enough without pitting yourself against your own critical and judgmental inner narratives.

An important sidenote on self-compassion: whether a client you are working with competes in a combat sport such as boxing or martial arts, or any other sport that has the potential to involve a high level of physical pain (e.g., endurance sports), or defines themselves as a "tough" competitor, or like Joe who is in the military, self-compassion will help them. Self-compassion is not the antithesis of toughness and competitiveness. It is an essential component.

In our next session, Joe prepared a detailed plan regarding the new few weeks of his preparations for the selection process, and we discussed this at length. A focus on short-term goals was part of our discussion. We also discussed planning mentally for the challenges ahead. My preference as a sport psychologist is to help clients to incorporate the skills and learnings that I offer them into their daily programme so that when they are working on physical or technical skills, they can integrate mental skills into their practice and preparation. With a military client such as Joe, helping them integrate mental skills into their preparation may involve their physical training (equipping the mind and body to do difficult things), study and tactical nous, and exploring ways to incorporate mental skills into their day-to-day work role (such as leadership, strategic thinking, and problem solving). The mind and the body work best together, and my approach is one of integration.

The next key theme for discussion between Joe and I was about developing and refining critical thinking skills when under pressure and experiencing fatigue. Now the levels of pressure and fatigue that we are talking about in the military and in Special Forces selection are unlike anything most high-performing clients will ever encounter. Total sleep deprivation over several days, yet still needing to perform operationally at a high level. Decisions that must be made quickly and decisively with literal life and death consequences. I must admit that I wasn't sure how exactly I could help Joe with his critical thinking skills, and I told him as much. As a sport psychologist, there will be times when a client asks a question or presents with an issue that you do not know what to do with, and being honest helps to strengthen the therapeutic relationship and gain you credibility. As a practitioner, it is totally acceptable to tell a client that you don't know and then go away to read up and learn about that topic so that you can help them.

In discussing critical thinking skills with Joe, I learned that he had operational experience on deployment where he had been able to develop critical thinking skills under pressure and fatigue. Leaning on his own experience, I reinforced to Joe what he had learned about what had and had not worked regarding his critical thinking skills. As sport psychologists, sometimes our job is not to teach clients new skills or pass on new knowledge, but to explore with the client their own experiences and how they can leverage off that to help them.

By now I had been working with Joe for several months, and the selection process for entry to the Special Forces was getting closer. At this time, Joe was dealing with some personal stressors that were having a detrimental impact on his ability to prepare as well as he would have liked. He was also having more physical issues with his body, this time a serious calf injury. In what turned out to be our final session together, Joe and I spent the session discussing whether he should proceed with his application and the selection process. Being a sounding board to clients is an integral part of what we do as sport psychologists, and it is important that as a practitioner we never underestimate the value in offering a compassionate ear, listening, reflecting back to the client what we are hearing (or are not hearing), and being able to offer our perspective on their situation.

As a sport psychologist, learning to support your clients when they come up short in their quest for 'success' is an important part of the profession. Whether it is chasing gold medals, championships, rankings, team selection, or any other outcome that our clients are often working towards, inevitably there will be occasions when they do not achieve their goals. And so, this proved to be the case with Joe. Due to an unfortunate combination of injury and personal circumstances, Joe decided to withdraw his application for the Special Forces. Does this mean that our work together was a failure? Absolutely not. It is my personal belief that anyone working as a sport psychologist who purely does so because they want to help athletes 'win' is in the profession for the wrong reasons. Sure, winning is nice and in professional and elite sport ultimately outcomes are important. But defining oneself solely based on these outcomes is foolhardy and will set you up for a long career of dejection.

I know that Joe valued the work that we did together. I know that I learned just as much, if not more, than he did through our journey together. I know the skills that I taught Joe will help him with all aspects of his life, not just his career and desire to join the Special Forces. I also believe that Joe and I will do further work together in the future when he is ready and in a position to attempt entry once again into the Special Forces. I look forward to the opportunity to help Joe further, and I know that I am a better practitioner as a result of the time I have already spent working with him. Now I would say that you can't ask for a better result than that.

Case Study Two: Training Doctor

Through my work as a sport and performance psychologist with Condor Performance, I have had the opportunity to work with a number of medical professionals including doctors, surgeons, and medical students. I really enjoy the opportunity to work with medical professionals – I find them to be great clients. There are several factors that in general make them great clients: they are highly intelligent so there is a wonderful opportunity for some insightful and interesting discussions, they are highly motivated and driven, they are willing to learn and improve, and helping medical professionals to improve their own performance helps them to help their patients more effectively. Altruism at its finest!

The client in this case study is Adam, who at the time he engaged in work with me was a mature-aged, fourth-year medical student. He initially sought performance psychology services because he was about to sit for major exams and wanted assistance to remain focused throughout the exams (which were three hours each in duration) and manage performance anxiety related to the exams. Adam was also keen for help dealing with the competitiveness and politics of his cohort and university studies including the stigma associated with poor exam performance. Dealing with the politics of studying medicine, university, and placements turned out to be a theme that we could deal with regularly throughout our work together.

In our first session, I was able to provide Adam with the assistance he was looking for to help him with his exams. He had a long interest in Eastern philosophy and engaged in regular mindfulness practice that he had maintained for several years. Adam's understanding and practice of mindfulness was something I was able to use to help him with his exam preparation and focus during his exams. It is my belief that optimal performance cannot occur unless someone can remain focused in the present moment, and therefore mindfulness – whether taught through deep breathing work, body scans, awareness of thoughts, or a combination of all these techniques – is a crucial skill to teach all athletes and performers.

Just as I did in my work with Joe (and indeed use with almost all my clients), I focused on a strengths approach with Adam. To help him prepare for his exams, I encouraged Adam to think about the experiences that he had and the knowledge that he had gained up until this point in his life, and how he can leverage off his own strengths and expertise to help himself with his exams. I like to remind my clients that when they have an upcoming major performance (such as a match, tournament, or even exam), they already possess all the necessary skills and attributes to perform well. They're not being asked to do anything that they don't already know how to do. The key is in the moment when it matters, being able to produce what they are capable of. I find that this can instil belief and reduce performance anxiety in clients and helps them to shift their focus from what could go wrong (outcome focused) to what they can do and what they need to do to perform well (process focused).

Adam reported that he found our first session beneficial, and he was able to perform well in his exams. Following this session, Adam decided that he did not want to continue working with me as he had passed his exams. When I start working with a new client, I always approach that initial session from the perspective that I am going to work with that client for an extended period of time. As I often tell my clients, if you were working with a technical coach on modifying your technique, you wouldn't see that coach once and expect your technique to change instantly. It requires ongoing work. The same is true of sport psychology. In saying this, I also believe in the importance of providing your client with value in the first session. This value may simply be listening to them, it may be reminding them of their strengths, or teaching a skill such as deep breathing. In private practice general/clinical psychology, for instance, the median number of sessions clients attend is one. Sport and performance psychology is not all that different. No matter how good you are as a practitioner, how strong you perceive your rapport was, or how eager the client appears to work with you, there will always be clients who you only see for one session. If you take nothing else of note from this chapter, I want you to know that not every client you work with will want to or will work with you. And that is totally okay. A "one-session wonder" is not a reflection of your prowess as a practitioner.

Fortunately for me (and for you the reader), Adam saw enough value in the work that we did in that initial session that he decided to return. This time, it was not for an additional session. In fact, Adam and I ended up working together for 12 months. Much of the work that we did together was centred around problem solving and discussing various scenarios that had arisen at work and university for Adam. In this way, I was very much a sounding board for him, providing guidance as required. This role is similar to how I have often worked with coaches, which is less focused on teaching specific techniques and more on providing guidance to help the coach be more effective. The conversations that I had with Adam focused on topics such as conflict management and resolution with colleagues and supervisors, patient interactions, and building rapport with patients.

As I mentioned earlier, one of the reasons Adam had initially sought performance psychology services was to help him deal with the 'politics' of studying medicine. This topic would prove to be one that we would discuss continuously throughout our work together. Ultimately, I could not change nor help Adam to change the culture of medicine. But through our work, I was able to help him to shift his focus to his values, his reasons for wanting to study medicine and pursue a career as a doctor, and to what he could *influence*. For Adam, that included focusing on his strengths, studying hard, his diligence, interactions with patients, colleagues, and supervisors, and on constantly learning from his experiences.

Due to the intense nature and constant scrutiny of studying medicine and the required assessments, we spent further sessions discussing how to handle the various assessment tasks Adam had to complete. These included role plays, exams, and placement observations. Strategies to help optimise his study time became a feature of our work together, such as taking short and frequent study breaks (e.g., a 5-minute break for every 45 minutes of study), focusing on one topic per day/at a time, study environment, and maximising his best time of the day for optimal productivity. For instance, if Adam is a morning person, then allocating time in his morning for study (as much as can be possible depending on his work and university schedule) when he is going to be at his most alert and productive is going to help him to study more effectively.

Conclusion

Irrespective of whether you work in sport, military, performing arts, or any other number of domains with high work stress and performance demands, what is going to help you to thrive as a psychologist is yourself. We must have a sound philosophy that underpins the work that we do. Spend time developing your philosophy and understanding your reasoning for doing the work you do (or want to do) – in other words, understand your *purpose*. It is one of, if not the best, professional investments you can make. When working with a client, seek to understand your client and their performance demands first before offering any guidance. We have two ears and one mouth, and we should use these accordingly.

Invest time in building relationships. If you work with individual clients, this may be the therapeutic relationship. In organisations, even if your work is with individuals, spend time getting to know the key staff. From coaches and support staff to management down to the property stewards and club stalwarts, take time to build relationships. Understand the ecosystem that you are working in, or that your clients are working in. Without strong relationships, it becomes very difficult for us to do our job effectively.

It is also my belief that as sport psychology professionals we must be willing to engage in ongoing learning and development. As psychologists, we have professional development requirements, and we absolutely must adhere to them. But beyond professional development, I hope I have demonstrated in these case studies how working as a sport psychologist requires us to always be learning. Whether this is directly from our clients, research we undertake, reading, listening to podcasts and audiobooks, watching documentaries and other TV shows, observing the daily training environment or workplace, or engaging in activities and experiences, we must constantly be seeking to learn. It is only through learning that we can grow as professionals.

These two case studies across two different performance areas have illustrated how sport psychology principles and interventions can be applied and adapted to non-athlete high-performance clients. The skills and expertise that sport psychologists possess are incredibly useful to help anyone wanting to improve their own performance and can be employed effectively across a whole array of industries and performance domains. I hope that this chapter has highlighted potential opportunities that exist as a sport psychologist, beyond working in sport. If you are willing to learn, to be adaptable, and are open to opportunities that may arise to use your skills and expertise in different performance settings, working with non-athlete high-performance clients can be incredibly rewarding as a sport psychology professional.

REFLECTIVE QUESTIONS

- Why did you want to become a sport psychologist?
- What is your practical philosophy as a sport psychologist? How might your philosophy inform your practice inside and outside of sport settings?
- Are there performance areas outside of sport (e.g., military, medicine, and aviation) that you would be interested in working within? Why?
- What ethical and practical considerations would you need to consider if you were going to work with non-athlete high-performance clients?
- What professional development opportunities would you need to undertake to prepare you if you were going to work with non-athlete high-performance clients?

References

Agassi, A. (2010). *Open*. HarperCollins.

Goggins, D. (2018). *Can't Hurt Me: Master Your Mind and Defy the Odds*. Lioncrest Publishing.

Grossman, D. (1995). *On Killing: The Psychological Cost of Learning to Kill in War and Society*. Boston: Little, Brown.

Grossman, D., & Christensen, L. W. (2008). *On Combat: The Psychology and Physiology of Deadly Conflict in War and in Peace*. Millstadt, IL: Warrior Science Pub.

Halson, S. L. (2013). Recovery techniques for athletes. *Sports Science Exchange, 26*(120), 1–6.

Harris, R. (2019). *ACT Made Simple: An Easy-To-Read Primer on Acceptance and Commitment Therapy* (2nd ed.). New Harbinger Publications.

Hayes, S. C. (2005). *Get Out of Your Mind and Into Your Life*. New Harbinger Publications.

Hayes, S. C. (2019). A Liberated Mind: *The Essential Guide to ACT*. London, UK: Random House.

Hays, K. F. (2006). Being fit: The ethics of practice diversification in performance psychology. *Professional Psychology: Research and Practice, 37*, 223–232.

Hays, K. F. (2012). The psychology of performance in sport and other domains. In S. M. Murphy (Ed.), *The Oxford Handbook of Sport and Performance Psychology* (pp. 24–45). New York, NY: Oxford University Press. DOI: 10.1093/oxfordhb/9780199731763.013.0002

Hays, K. F. (Ed.). (2009). *Performance Psychology in Action: A Casebook for Working With Athletes, Performing Artists, Business Leaders, and Professionals in High-Risk Occupations*. American Psychological Association. 10.1037/11876-000

Holiday, R., & Hanselman, S. (2016). *The Daily Stoic: 366 Meditations on Wisdom, Perseverance, and the Art of Living.* New York: Penguin.

Johnson, L. D., Miller, S. D., & Duncan, B. L. (2000). *The Session Rating Scale 3.0.* Chicago: Author.

Kerr, J. (2013). *Legacy: What the All Blacks Can Teach Us About The Business of Life.* London, U.K: Constable.

Portenga, S. T., Aoyagi, M. W., & Cohen, A. B. (2016). A working definition of sport and performance psychology. *Journal of Sport Psychology in Action.* DOI: 10.1080/21520704.2016.1227413

Pronk, D., Pronk, B., & Curtis, T. (2021). *The Resilience Shield.* Australia: Bolinda Publishing

Rogers, C. (1951). *Client-Centred Therapy.* Boston, MA: Houghton Mifflin.

Rogers, C. (1966) The necessary and sufficient conditions of therapeutic change. In B. Ard (Ed.), *Counseling and Psychotherapy: Classic Theories on Issues.* Palo Alto, CA: Science and Behavior Books.

Sinek, S. (2017). *Find Your Why: A Practical Guide to Discovering Purpose for You or Your Team.* New York: Penguin.

Weir, K. (2018). A growing demand for sport psychologists. *Monitor on Psychology, 49* (10), retrieved from https://www.apa.org/monitor/2018/11/cover-sports-psychologists

YouTube video - 'Search for Warriors' (two-part documentary), retrieved from https://www.youtube.com/watch?v=-zqaehQN9sw

6

EVERYONE IS FIGURING IT OUT ALONG THE WAY: DIVING HEADFIRST INTO THE WORLD OF ESPORTS

Bernadette Ramaker and Ismael Pedraza-Ramirez

In this chapter, we will introduce the work of applied sport psychologists in esports, a novel field of performance. Esports is a new and fast-evolving domain thus there are no clear guidelines or structures in place for sport psychologists. However, we inform our applied work based on scientific knowledge from traditional sports and recent work in esports. Thus, it is important to stay informed of the current initial steps in increasing the understanding of the role of sport psychology in esports (Leis & Lautenbach, 2020; Pedraza-Ramirez et al., 2020) and the development of high-performance systems (Nagorsky & Wiemeyer, 2020; Watson, Abbott & Pedraza-Ramirez, 2021). As we will primarily focus on our applied experiences, we will shed light on the initial challenges that sport psychologists can experience when transitioning from traditional sports into the field of esports while working online with players and coaches. We will describe how sport psychologists can find the balance in creating a strong and sustainable team culture without losing sight of the will to win or the individual player's needs. Additionally, in this chapter, we will answer important questions that we have encountered during this transition, such as, how does a practitioner assess the urgency of the team's needs? How does one build a sustainable team culture from scratch in a remote environment? How can one facilitate the creation of meaningful relationships from both a sport psychologist's perspective and between players and coaches? And how does one know that they are doing the 'right' thing? This chapter provides practitioners with real examples of how a sport psychologist can transition from their work in traditional sports into esports by addressing the challenges of adapting and fitting into an existing organisational culture and assessing the needs of this environment.

DOI: 10.4324/9781003263890-8

The Sport Psychologist's Transition from Traditional Sports to Esports

Our academic and practical training was in traditional sports, and we gained experience in the safety of sports environments that were familiar to us. As applied practitioners, like many trainees, we started in our sport, speed skating (Bernadette) and football (Ismael). This is where we gathered the initial experience, put in the hours, and made the mistakes you want to make as a rookie practitioner. While pursuing our sport psychology training and further accreditation we started venturing out of our familiar sports. Our networks opened the door to the esports world at different times but allowed us to move away from the comfort of speed skating and football towards an exciting and completely different performance domain. Ismael collaborated on the creation of a website called The Mental Craft[1] which aimed to share knowledge on the integration of these two fields and to offer sport psychology services to players, teams, and organisations. It was via this website that Ismael first gained experience with a professional esports team. In the case of Bernadette, an internship with a professional esports team allowed her to step into this completely different field of work. Even though transitioning into esports was challenging, they quickly realised that the performance demands in esports are similar to traditional sports.

Most importantly some differences required us to adapt our approach. Firstly, we needed to understand the language the players used. Second, it was important to have curiosity about the esports' nuances and the unique characteristics of each environment (i.e., Team A and Team B). Observing daily practice, reviews, and conversations, researching competition characteristics, game concepts, and meaning of the used language, and asking many questions were ways we used to familiarise ourselves efficiently and effectively with our new environment.[2]

The Current Environment

The esports organisation we for as performance coaches has multiple active teams in esports titles such as League of Legends, Rainbow 6 Siege, Rocket League, and Call of Duty. The title of a performance coach is common in esports and is often preferred over the title sport psychologist. Thus, we use performance coach and sport psychologist interchangeably throughout this chapter, depending on the situation and context. In our position as performance coaches, our focus is on overall player physical and mental well-being and overall performance enhancement. This role is different from the traditional sport psychologist role by including more performance aspects rather than focusing solely on mental aspects of performance. However, each

---

[1]   http://thementalcraft.com/
[2]   Listen to ZEPP FM podcast, episode 012, Sport psychology in eSports with Ismael Pedraza to understand the transition and early experiences of integrating sport psychology into esports.

performance coach in esports differs depending on their background and their position's assigned role or focus (Watson et al., 2021).

Throughout this chapter, the focus will be on the first author's (Bernadette) work as the performance coach of Team A of this organisation. Team A competes at the highest level of the European league and simultaneously in the national competition. It consists of five players, the head coach, the strategic coach, and the performance coach. Most of the time, the players work remotely. This means both scrims (i.e., training) and competitions are played from their homes. However, there is the exception for in-person competitions, so-called Local Area Network (LAN) events, where every team member travels to the event and competes from the same venue. Usually, these LAN events are bigger national and international competitions such as the world championship.

It is important to highlight that the work with Team A was based on an already established performance framework carried out by the second author (Ismael) on-site with Team B. This performance framework was developed aiming to establish a high-performance culture and optimise performance from a multidisciplinary and holistic perspective (i.e., sport science, performance psychology). Although the scope of this chapter does not allow for a focus on the specifics of the performance framework or the process of Team B, we will shed light on the development and implementation of the same high-performance framework within the online environment of Team A.

Developing the High-Performance Framework

In the organisation, the performance coaches worked towards creating a framework that combines performance elements from traditional sports (e.g., the inclusion of physical exercise routines, pre-performance routines, and psychological skills training) with the esports context.[3] The framework aimed to provide a sustainable guideline to achieve ultimate success across all the organisation's teams, targeting all parties involved: players, coaches, management, and staff. The goals were to (1) develop talent at a personal and professional level, (2) educate on how to perform consistently, and (3) create an overarching framework that can be implemented for all the teams. The framework's foundation was sport science and performance psychology while implementing a structured approach. The framework's structured approach combines physical and mental aspects of performance from three areas: psychology, exercise, and nutrition. The performance coach oversaw the implementation of all three areas; however, depending on the performance coach's education and background the inclusion of other experts may be the most optimal approach for the team(s).

The established performance framework was initially implemented in person with Team B. We then used learnings from this experience to inform the

---

[3]   For an example of a professional esports coaching staff structure and processes watch Rogue | #1 Coaching Team of 2021 LEC Spring.

implementation of the high-performance framework within a remote environment (i.e., Team A), which was particularly challenging. The performance coaches followed a standard three-phase procedure (see Keegan, 2015) to implement interventions. In the first phase, assessments (e.g., individual and team intakes) were completed with players, coaches, and others involved (e.g., general manager and team manager) to assess the current situation of the groups, their needs, skills, and abilities. The next phase was (psycho)education and the interventions for the target groups based on the initial assessments. The last phase functioned as an evaluation phase and a new starting point for the next cycle.

Firstly, it was necessary to make the team aware of the performance coaches' overall vision for the high-performance framework across both the organisation and the teams. This awareness was raised through a team meeting led by the performance coach at the start of the competitive season. In this meeting, the season's expectations, vision, and tone were explored. Secondly, strong working relationships were developed between the performance coach and players, the coaching staff, and among players themselves. I (Bernadette) chose to build relationships by conducting individual player and coach intakes to gather the most important and meaningful information about everyone in their professional roles and their backgrounds. This approach allowed me to understand their personalities and better anticipate how players might respond to each other.

Given that the organisation has expectations to compete at the highest level with all teams, providing adequate resources to players and coaches for performance was necessary while creating a sustainable competitive environment. It is important to highlight that in this environment not only the teams and coaches play a role in performance, but everyone who works for the organisation is involved and impacts the performance culture. Thus, it is integral to the performance approach to address everyone's involvement and impact to ensure that all parties are working efficiently towards the main goal of creating a sustainable culture for performance.

The First Steps in Esports

As the performance coach of an esports team, I am convinced that it is beneficial to have a certain understanding of the game. Therefore, I made it my mission to develop as much knowledge about the game before I started my work with the team. Nowadays, that seems simple enough with the limitless resources available. As I knew nothing about esports before my involvement with Teams A and B, I started from square one. I used different resources to gather as much information as possible, such as watching videos on YouTube that explained the games in detail;[4] reading descriptions on blogs; explanations of different maps, layouts, and call-outs; extending my knowledge of avatars

---

[4] Watch a complete Beginner's Guide to League of Legends.

(e.g., champions, heroes, operators); getting familiar with the competitive structures nationally and internationally; and watching old matches to understand what a game day looks like to prepare for what the players might need on match days. My first learning experience of my first esports game (i.e., Team B) was more challenging at times due to the lack of contextual knowledge. However, the second time around I used my previous experience of familiarising myself with esports, so I could speed up my learning process of the second esports game (i.e., Team A).

Thus, the second time studying a new esports game did not feel like I was thrown in at the deep end of the pool without any swimming lessons quite as much. When the work with the team started, attending scrims showed the obvious gaps in my knowledge. However, this allowed me to fill those gaps by specifically searching for the concepts I wasn't sure about yet, such as my understanding of the avatars (e.g., champions, heroes, operators) and why players choose specific avatars. This enabled me to understand players' roles and tasks more deeply. Additionally, the players and the coaches were always more than willing to explain concepts and were excited to help me build my knowledge. Asking for a client's help in the pursuit of gathering information requires a type of courage. First, to admit to yourself and others that you don't understand yet. Second, to ask for help and be willing to be the student. Third, to be humble enough but confident in your pursuit of understanding. This way of learning fits my professional values well, as I base my work on involvement, openness, and honesty.

Working as an Embedded Performance Coach

As a performance coach, it is a challenge in itself to become part of an esports organisation and accept the position of embedded performance coach in a different country than your own. Moving to a different country as a full-time or part-time position is an industry characteristic. Therefore, this adds another dimension to your work and life as you need to be decisive, move fast and grab the chances when they present themselves. When an opportunity arises, the only way to respond is by going all in. For example, jobs as a performance coach in esports do exist, and in some cases, a position can be created when there is a need for a team or in an organisation. When that need is recognised and the opportunity arises, it is then up to the person to commit and go in for that position. This represents the volatility and uncertainty of esports that everyone in the industry will be confronted with at some point in their career.

The nature of the work as a performance coach stays the same as in traditional sports, aiming to improve and maintain overall physical and mental well-being and performance enhancement of players and coaches. Naturally, working as a performance coach comes with challenges. The most prevalent challenges are determined by the performance coach's working position. There are four ways a performance coach can be integrated into an organisation or team: embedded onsite, embedded remotely, part-time onsite, and part-time remotely. A performance coach who is embedded onsite is integrated into the organisational system and is physically present in the same location as the team. A performance coach who is embedded remotely is also integrated into the organisational system but is not physically present and works online with the team. A performance coach who is part-time onsite delivers meetings with the team or individual players in person semi-regularly. Finally, a performance coach who is part-time and working remotely works with the team (e.g., providing team workshops and meetings) online on a part-time basis.

In the current organisational environment that I am involved in as the performance coach, I am embedded remotely in the overall organisational structure. As the embedded remote performance coach, attending most practice and scrim days and strategy sessions online, I can function as a bridge between management and the team (i.e., players and coaches). Having this position blurs the lines regarding who the client *actually* is. The organisation, the players, the team, the coaches, or a combination of all of those. This challenge also occurs for sport psychologists working within traditional sports. An embedded performance coach will experience that their position is much more nuanced and complex than having a black-and-white answer as to who their client is. In my experience, it was, therefore, important to find clarity in my responsibilities and tasks and agree upon what to report to management regarding the overall state and performance of the team and individual players while respecting the confidentiality of the players and coaches. As the performance coach that is part of the system, I realised that I also carried responsibilities in the bigger picture of the organisation. This makes my role different from when simply working with individual clients.

The role and tasks of the performance coach include facilitating all performance processes that range from big to small. For example, when the performance coach works on-site, they take care of the seemingly trivial things including taking away unnecessary stressors such as keeping players' phones when they enter the competition stage. When the performance coach works remotely, they check that players are wearing their jerseys on game days, have their recording software running, that they have eaten enough during the day, and integrate individualised approaches to cope with emotions and pressure more successfully. These and other external and internal stressors have been previously identified in elite esports while addressing coping strategies that can be used by practitioners (see Smith, Birch, & Bright, 2019).

As an embedded performance coach working remotely, you can see much more of the environment by regularly attending the online scrims, strategy sessions, and team meetings (see Swettenham & Whitehead, 2022). An insider perspective is sometimes beneficial because you can observe group discussions, players' reactions to feedback, and how the coach structures reviews. This allows you to directly observe situations rather than receive second-hand information which carries natural bias to understand the day-to-day and contextualised behaviour and thoughts of players and coaches. Thus, it allows for more in-depth conversations by challenging a player's train of thought through critical questions that force them to see situations from a different perspective than their own. However, there is also a flip side to this embedded position. Since you observe so much, you must be wary of your bias. For me, my philosophy revolves around maintaining strong relationships with my clients and understanding my clients' stories and experiences. Keeping a more objective perspective can be challenging when you have observed or been involved in situations first-hand. Thus, self-awareness as a performance coach is critical to working effectively. However, when stepping into esports you don't only step into a different type of performance domain but also a different type of communication. This meant I had to learn and understand the daily language that is spoken in the team, including words players and coaches choose and how they express themselves. During the first weeks with the team, I felt like the players were speaking a different language to me that I simply didn't understand, and sometimes I still need a 'translation' from someone to fully grasp the context and meaning of a conversation.

Furthermore, it is crucial to be able to adapt your way of working to the context of the players and the team. Team sessions or exercises need to be adapted to fit their context and how they experience their profession with the why of each session needing to be crystal clear. Based on my experiences with the team, the best practice is to keep team sessions brief, ideally around 30 to 45 minutes. This is because players lose focus and mentally check out when sessions take longer, especially when they are more theory focused. Therefore, team sessions are ideally set up to be interactive either in conversation or activity in which they can work together to keep their attention in the meeting itself. Furthermore, my experience is that online work with teams takes more time than in-person work, so this needs to be accounted for during preparation.

Working as part of the system and being fully integrated into the team culture comes with another challenge: you are usually the only expert in this area in the organisation. There is a lack of qualified colleagues who could give you valuable feedback on your work as a performance coach. There will always be some type of uncertainty and doubt on whether you are doing the 'right' thing, especially in esports, which is still developing and is not as established in its processes as traditional sport cultures. Within our support staff structure, however, where there are multiple active performance coaches in one organisation, a peer system can be implemented by integrating a peer intervision model. This means having someone to discuss ideas and exercises, having a second pair of eyes for observations, and on occasions the delivery of team meetings or sessions together. Not all performance coaches have the chance to work together with other performance coaches in the same organisation. Therefore, it can be immensely helpful to seek out other professionals to widen your network, have fruitful discussions, learn from each other, and ultimately develop the professional field of esports further together.

Consequently, regardless of whether the performance coach is on-site or remote, an embedded performance coach must find the balance between creating and maintaining strong relationships and being fully involved but still capable of keeping an objective eye and approaching challenges with a more distant per-spective. Therefore, an embedded performance coach has a different position than a performance coach who is not a part of the daily organisational structure but comes in to deliver their services only, such as individual meetings with players or team workshops.

Establishing the Team's Needs

I conduct my work with Team A remotely which means that all team activities, meetings, and work happen online via screens. The online nature of the work comes with challenges for the performance coach and the players, as they are expected to be fully engaged and interactive by keeping their full attention on the meeting (and not on Twitter). The roles and responsibilities of each coaching staff member must be clear from the start of the work to streamline working processes. This role clarity can be achieved by the performance coach communicating their view on their work and ensuring this is aligned with the rest of the coaching staff. The players and coaches will always be the game experts and gameplay experts. The performance coach is the expert on overall player well-being and overall performance enhancement. The expertise of the game and the expertise of well-being and overall performance en-hancement are often treated as separate concepts by the coaching staff. The assess-ment of the team's needs was completed via a team intake with players and coaches. This allowed players to express their thoughts on the team's strengths and weak-nesses and what they deemed important for good team performance. The intake process also involved having conversations with coaches, and discovering their vision of the game, and conducting individual intakes with all players to understand their backgrounds as people and their paths as players. This step is crucial in es-tablishing relationships and rapport with staff and players.

Relationships with others are created and based on making sure they feel seen, valued, and cared for. Creating relationships in a remote setting needs some creativity. In a regular physical setting, the creation of relationships will develop over time in formal and informal moments. Each moment can be seen as an opportunity to strengthen the interpersonal bond, for example at the dinner table, walking together to the office, or getting food together. However, in the remote setting, these moments need to be created. Therefore, the process of creating and nurturing relationships is mostly dependent on formal moments, such as team meetings, individual meetings, and moments before and after scrims. Not only do professional working relationships need to be created, but also the relationships between teammates need to be nurtured. Building and maintaining relationships is a continuous process that should be addressed proactively. This doesn't stop after the first weeks of the season; we actively keep building the environment of the team over time.

One of the first team meetings was specifically created and undertaken to create a better understanding of each other and create a team bond on a deeper personal level than just the in-game level. A day before the team session, I asked all players and coaches to find two pictures, a meaningful and a funny one. It was crucial for this activity that players made a deliberate choice for their pictures. During the activity, the players should be able to share with their teammates why this picture is meaningful to them and why they find it important that their teammates know about that specific story. The second picture should describe them as a person or player, but it should be a funny picture (e.g., a meme). Players should be able to explain what the picture tells about them and why they choose it.

The activity itself was set up so that the pictures were shared with the performance coach before the start of the meeting so that she could create a shared document that all players could access during the meeting. During the activity, the players were asked to guess whose picture was whose and explain why they thought so. This provided an element of surprise. In such team sessions, players can share personal stories that they usually don't get the space or time for. Additionally, it allows for humour by creating an opportunity to laugh about the funny pictures. In the debriefing of the activity, it is important to reflect on why such activities are important and raise awareness for players and coaches that creating relationships takes effort and time. It is also up to them to keep working on those interpersonal relationships besides the formal team sessions.

For this session, I actively encouraged all coaches to participate in the activity so that they were also involved in sharing personal stories. The coaches' participation adds a human element to their roles. This is important in creating relationships with the players as it shows players that the coaches have an identity beyond coaching. The session facilitated the players to get to know each other very well by sharing stories and creating space to ask each other questions. However, the success rate of this session depends on the attitude of players and coaches going into the session.

A few aspects concerned me before the session, namely whether players would have prepared their pictures and their stories in time, to what extent they would choose pictures that were meaningful to them, and how to ensure that it wasn't just a 'fun' session but also carried meaning. Looking back on this session, I was content with how the session turned out. Everyone took this activity seriously by choosing pictures that showed something important to them. This took the activity to the next level, making it even more valuable. I was impressed by the questions the players asked each other, which allowed players to gather more detailed information about each other. Each picture had its own unique story; however, two stories made a particular impact on all team members: one which explored an individual's physical health journey, and another which expressed the importance of family. This activity facilitated the team learning about each other's lives. A valuable variation on this activity could be encouraging people to find meaningful pictures from various life periods (e.g., youth, teenage years, adult life) to allow the team to talk more about their development over time. Players and coaches also reflected on this session as a valuable way of learning more about each other personally. The stories inspired them and helped them discover elements they had in common.

Roster Changes

In esports changing the lineup of players and transferring to a different team is called a roster change. Roster changes are part of the competitive process. In the competitive structure of Team A multiple transfer windows per year exist, usually before the start of the competitive season. Roster changes can influence the process and plan implemented in the team and can affect group dynamics, performance, and cohesion. The main challenge of a roster change is the effective integration of the new member inside and outside of the game.

Players and coaching staff who stay on the team can experience the changes and their effects differently. Unlike traditional sports where coaches and players could be in one team for many years, in esports players and coaches change relatively frequently, sometimes negatively affecting the developmental process of the players and the team. Roster changes in esports seem to have a higher impact than in traditional sports due to the frequency of changes and the total number of players on one team. Depending on the game, an esports team usually consists of three to five players. Thus, when one or two players are replaced, this amounts to already 20 or even 40 percent of the team. Some players have negative experiences with roster changes as they need to keep explaining existing strategies to their new teammates and they do not only lose a teammate but also a friend. However, roster changes can also positively impact the team in terms of group cohesion, performance, and leadership.

The role of the performance coach in the process of roster changes depends on agreed tasks, roles, and duties. For example, the performance coach could play a role in the selection process by facilitating and providing more information about the candidates through in-depth conversations to understand each candidate inside and outside the game. Facilitating the understanding of one's personality, background, and one's motivation, drive, and experiences so far could be valuable to consider in the decision-making process of who could be a good fit for the team. After the selection process, the performance coach could be involved in integrating new team members by introducing them to the existing culture and facilitating space for the old members to cope with the changes. A roster change creates a new team, however, the performance structures such as regular team meetings, individual player sessions, and the corresponding expectations surrounding performance coaching are maintained. Despite this, having new energy in the team means that shifts in team values, goals and identity may occur. By looking at the phases of team development (Tuckman, 1965; Tuckman & Jensen, 1977) in which groups go through forming, storming, norming, performing, and adjourning, the team naturally starts again from the forming phase which brings the challenges of defining new team dynamics, tasks, and roles.

Bootcamps

The online nature of the team influences the way we work together. In a remote environment, it is possible that players and/or coaches have never met each other in real life and only know each other from playing together online. Since the professional community is relatively small, pro players often find each other when they are playing online during their practice before or after training with the team. Some of the players may have seen each other at LAN events either as teammates or opponents. Therefore, there are limited physical encounters that naturally affect the relationships that exist between the players. These mostly online interactions will never be quite the same as when they spent time together in a physical setting for a longer duration, like playing from a common office or gaming house, or even a bootcamp (i.e., training camp). Thus, the impact of a physical bootcamp for a team that usually practices remotely can be significant because a bootcamp creates an environment where outside distractions and stressors are absent. Players and staff are in a temporary, focused, performance bubble. Therefore, the increased focus and limited distractions in a bootcamp environment allow the performance processes to be sped up. To illustrate, players improve their individual and team gameplay faster, in-game strategies can be adapted more easily by showing others your in-game perspective, and team cohesion is created more quickly. Similar to traditional sports, bootcamps are implemented in esports as a training camp for esports players at the start of the season or before big competitions. The duration, location, and how the bootcamp is organised depend on the team's needs and organisational resources.

The bootcamp that was set up by our organisation for Team A was a seven-day bootcamp before the start of a competitive season. The purpose of the bootcamp was to nurture the team bond among players and staff, create a team culture and working environment, and improve gameplay in a focused setting. An overall goal for the full duration of the bootcamp and daily focus points for scrims allow the team to improve gameplay step by step. The bond and relationships between all key stakeholders need to be developed. Everyone invests time in getting to know each other both in-game and on a more personal level. The team culture is created from the first moment the team comes together. Common team culture is characterised by establishing a team identity, common team values, setting up routines and talking about goals, and expectations, and reinforcing productive behaviours (e.g., San-Fu & Bor-Shiuan, 2005; Cruickshank & Collins, 2012). Effective communication is a big component of a healthy and productive working environment.

An onsite bootcamp changes the way the team works and the working style of the performance coach. The shift from remote to onsite is important to consider when creating effective team sessions. Being onsite requires you to adapt and allows you to use different interventions, exercises, or activities that simply work better when the group is physically in one place. For example, exercises requiring players to use the physical space and exercises involving items like balls and ropes are possible in an onsite setting. In remote sessions it can be challenging to get players in individual and team meetings to turn on their cameras, so we have a better understanding of everyone's engagement and understanding of the topic. The onsite sessions are easier in this respect as everyone is physically present.

Therefore, one of the advantages of onsite bootcamps is that conversations are easier when you can see full body language and not just a cropped version of only the head and the shoulders. Thus, this all-together onsite period offers a fantastic opportunity to create a stronger rapport with everyone in person.

Players experience great benefits from the bootcamps as it allows them to spend time with their teammates and coaching staff, especially after practice, which is rare in remote conditions. Therefore, bootcamps are usually intense for those who are involved. Naturally, bootcamps require different energy from everyone involved when you are together in person versus when you are together online. The relationships are built quicker and become more solid when players get to spend time together. It is important to find a balance between spending time together and being aware of their own needs to recharge on their own. This also applies to the practitioner, being physically present at a bootcamp requires you to be 'switched on' all the time. Thus, it is key to implement your own recovery strategies to perform well in your job while keeping your mental and physical state in check. For example, making an active effort to get enough hours of sleep, committing to an exercise and meditation routine to keep my energy and concentration levels up, and incorporating some alone time to charge my social battery again have been useful strategies for me.

Learning Experiences and Recommendations for Future Practitioners

We would like to conclude this chapter by sharing some lessons we took from working in esports. Firstly, getting started as an applied practitioner in esports is the first challenge one will encounter when one is interested in becoming full-time in esports. How can you get your foot in the door? Esports is similar to other sport fields in which networking plays a significant role and influences your opportunities. Establishing and educating yourself, making sure you develop your expertise well to professionalise the esports scene further. Practitioners can access evidence-based work to better understand esports performance and its nuances, and implement strategies in their practice (e.g., Swettenham & Whitehead, 2022; Watson et al., 2022). Furthermore, entering the fascinating world of esports is mostly achieved by engaging in internships and creating relationships with those who have already established themselves in the esports field, regardless of their professional position. In some cases, it might be possible to create an intern position together with the organisation even when they did not publish an official vacancy for such a position. It requires courage, creativity, and being bold enough to approach those to ask for something.

Second, new esports practitioners must understand that challenge is the norm and that they will be confronted with challenges daily. Challenges occur in every environment, especially in professional competitive scenes, and esports is no exception. The nature of the encountered challenges can vary significantly. On a performance level, performance coaches may support players to cope with their emotions. At the same time, players might also need help outside of the game with structuring their day more effectively by setting up daily routines including physical exercise and sleep schedules. As a practitioner, it is challenging to be part of the system and work effectively by providing a safe space for players and coaches.

Lastly, to increase effective team sessions, we ensure to consider during the preparation a three C's criteria which stands for a Clear, Concise, and Context based sessions. The purpose of meetings needs to be addressed and *Clear*. Why is this meeting important? When some might doubt the relevancy of meetings, the buy-in from players (or coaches) is missing, which is crucial for improvement. The sessions need to be *Concise* and to the point. Some will lose focus and mentally 'check out' when meetings take too long. In those situations, players will simply not pay attention to their full capacity, and as a practitioner, you are confronted with half efforts. The last criterion is to ensure that meetings are translated to fit the esports *Context* and the context in which the team is currently functioning. When that translation is missing, the message will either get lost or will not be as impactful as intended. This potentially could create friction where some might argue that they are not optimally using their time.

Conclusion

Everyone involved in the professional esports scene desires to win, perform, and compete at the highest competitive level. As this desire is already there, the performance coach can just nurture this desire more for those on the team. The bigger challenge for the performance coach is balancing the expectations to compete at the highest level and ensuring the team's and individual players' needs are met to be able to perform to their full potential sustainably. The performance coach can assess the urgency of the team's needs by establishing in-depth conversations with stakeholders from the start of the work with the team. To ensure the focus is on the right aspects the performance coach can align the team intake with the individual player intakes.

Additionally, the relationships and rapport with players and coaches should be established early on and continuously reinforced over time to ensure the sustainability of the team culture itself. A sustainable high-performance team culture includes everyone who is part of the organisation, and a remote environment is not any different in this aspect. Therefore, the performance coach should address everyone's involvement. A sustainable team culture in a remote environment is created by a common team identity, team values, and routines, including the team's goals, expectations, and preferred methods of communication. It is crucial for everyone to have the same understanding of what an ideal team working environment looks like to ensure the durability and sustainability of the culture. Implemented methods to get everyone on the same page are having structured team meetings, and individual sessions but also identifying more informal moments that aid the overall environment and the interpersonal relationships. The creation of meaningful relationships is at the core of the work of a performance coach in esports. One can go different routes in creating meaningful relationships, however, the main and most crucial factors are time and effort. Relationships are created by spending time together, online and in person, having a genuine curiosity and interest in others, and making sure everyone feels valued and cared for. Every moment can be seen and used as an opportunity to strengthen interpersonal bonds further. Once those relationships in the team are created, they need to be maintained and actively nurtured over time. Working as a performance coach and being the hired qualified expert comes with the challenge of prioritising the right things for the team. Since esports is still in the developmental stages, the performance coach needs to adapt, be flexible, and creative by implementing and translating concepts from traditional sports. We recommend creating a system where multiple performance coaches work together and serve as an internal support system. However, this professional support network can also be created outside of the organisation by widening your contacts to discuss anonymised cases and work-related questions with qualified colleagues who might also be active inside (or outside) of esports to ultimately continue the professionalisation of esports.[5]

REFLECTIVE QUESTIONS

After reading this chapter, your interest may be sparked to dive headfirst into esports. We want to challenge you to reflect and prepare yourself by answering the following questions.

- What are the overlapping and distinct characteristics of esports and the field you are working in now and how can you use those?
- How can you start to create your professional support network whom you can contact in case of challenging work-related questions, exchange ideas, or ask for advice?
- How can you ensure to implement your style, philosophy, expertise, and way of working in a newly developing field like esports?

GLOSSARY

Call of Duty – 4v4 game, first-person shooter game. Aim of the game is objective based. Depending on the game type this could for example be to eliminate all enemy players or to secure a site of enemy players.

---

[5] Watch the keynote talk of the Esports Research Network Conference 2021 for more information on the lessons learned while building well-being in high-performance teams.

Call out – Directions that players use to indicate locations in the game.

Champion – Avatar played in the game with unique characteristics, strengths, and weaknesses for the esports League of Legends.

Hero – Avatar played in the game with unique characteristics, strengths, and weaknesses for the esports Dota2.

LAN – A LAN event is an in-person esports tournament. LAN stands for Local Area Network, referring to the fact that everyone participating is playing on the same local network. Team members travel and compete from the same venue.

League of Legends – 5v5 game, multi-player battle arena game. Aim of the game is to destroy the base structure of the enemy team. Players play avatars called Champions.

Meme – Ideas, behaviours, images, or styles that are shared via the internet, often via social media platforms.

Operator – Avatar played in the game with unique characteristics, strengths, and weaknesses for the esports Rainbow Six Siege.

Performance Coach – Performance coach is the person in the position who is focusing on multiple areas of performance more than only mental aspects. However, still often interchangeably used to describe the position of sport psychologist.

Rainbow Six Siege – 5v5 game, first-person shooter game. Aim of the game is to either complete the objective (protect or defuse the bomb) or eliminate all enemy players. Players play avatars called Operators.

Rocket League – 3v3 game, sport-based videogame. Aim of the game is to score as many goals as possible. Players play the game with rocket-powered cars.

Roster Change – Roster change is the process of swapping the lineup of players of a team.

Roster – Roster is the lineup of a team.

Scrims – Scrims are the team training. The training is played out versus an opponent (enemy team). The enemy team could be from the same competition structure and region, or of similar skill and competitive level.

References

Cruickshank, A., & Collins, D. (2012). Culture change in elite sport performance teams: Examining and advancing effectiveness in the new era. *Journal of Applied Sport Psychology*, *24*(3), 338–355. Doi: 10.1080/10413200.2011.650819

Keegan, R. (2015). *Being a Sport Psychologist*. Palgrave Macmillan.

Leis, O., & Lautenbach, F. (2020). Psychological and physiological stress in non-competitive and competitive esports settings: A systematic review. *Psychology of Sport and Exercise*, *51*, 101738.

Nagorsky, E., & Wiemeyer, J. (2020). The structure of performance and training in esports. *PloS one*, *15*(8), e0237584.

Pedraza-Ramirez, I., Musculus, L., Raab, M., & Laborde, S. (2020). Setting the scientific stage for esports psychology: A systematic review. *International Review of Sport and Exercise Psychology*, *13*(1), 319–352.

San-Fu, K., & Bor-Shiuan, C. (2005). Assessing sport team culture: Assessing qualitative and quantitative approaches. *International Journal of Sport Psychology*, *36*, 22–38.

Smith, M. J., Birch, P. D., & Bright, D. (2019). Identifying stressors and coping strategies of elite esports competitors. *International Journal of Gaming and Computer-Mediated Simulations (IJGCMS)*, *11*(2), 22–39.

Swettenham, L., & Whitehead, A. (2022). Working in Esports: Developing team cohesion. *Case Studies in Sport and Exercise Psychology*, *6*(1), 36–44.

Tuckman, B. W. (1965). Developmental sequence in small groups. *Psychological Bulletin*, *63*, 384–389.

Tuckman, B. W., & Jensen, M. C. (1977). Stages of small group development - Revisited. *Group and Organizations Studies*, *2*(4), 419–427.

Watson, M., Smith, D., Fenton, J., Pedraza-Ramirez, I., Laborde, S., & Cronin, C. (2022). Introducing esports coaching to sport coaching (not as sport coaching). *Sports Coaching Review*.

Watson, M., Abbott, C., & Pedraza-Ramirez, I. (2021). A parallel approach to performance and sport psychology work in esports teams. *International Journal of Esports*, *1*(1). Retrieved from https://www.ijesports.org/article/52/html

7

COACHING PERFORMANCE EXCELLENCE: A PERFORMANCE PSYCHOLOGIST IN THE ROLE OF SPORTS COACH

Guy Matzkin

Introduction

In this chapter, I highlight the importance of applied psychological preparation on the field rather than in the clinic (i.e., one-to-one away from the sporting environment) as the factor underpinning the Israeli archery team's success story. I occupied the role of both head coach and performance psychologist, which I recognise is quite a rare position to be in. Therefore, this chapter highlights an approach to applied psychological work that performance psychologists can implement while working with coaches as well as the athletes on the field.

Before we dive into how and why the combination of a sport psychologist and a coach is, in my opinion, a good one, I feel that a little background to this story is warranted. I started archery as a teen in a country where it is not a big sport. At around 200 active competitors on a good year, archery is one of the smallest and least funded sports in Israel. As you would expect, the conditions to succeed are poor, with lack of funding, facilities, and good coaching a common cause for early retirement. Apart from brief and sporadic international successes in the mid 90s and early 10s (the latter ones were my own glory days), Israeli archers have not appeared on any international podium of significance. At the twilight of my career as an archer, I finished my performance psychology studies in Edinburgh in 2018 and headed home, keen to use my newfound knowledge to promote Israeli archery. This is where this story starts. The story ends with Olympic success, a world record, two European records, and many medals at the international circuit. Let's begin.

DOI: 10.4324/9781003263890-9

The Beginning: Reforming an Organisation so That Talent Can Grow (Zero Psychology Involved!)

Upon returning to Israel in 2018, I met with the newly elected president of the Israeli Archery Association to discuss how we can improve the level of archery in Israel. I suggested importing ideas from the British archery scene and pointed out areas that needed to be improved for archers in Israel to achieve their potential. I was assigned to the professional committee of the Association, and together we worked on a ten-year development programme that highlighted these required changes.[1] While these changes were organisational in essence, they were critical, nonetheless, to our later success. As I feel that this aspect in the work of applied performance psychology (i.e., organisational optimisation considerations) can sometimes be overlooked, it is the first point I will make in this chapter. A properly designed organisation is fundamental for success and proper talent development, and in our case, the complete lack of a performance orientated and enabling organisation was perhaps the most important contributor to the poor performance on the international circuit over the years. I want to highlight the three main issues that were addressed in this reformation and how, as this might help you in future work.

Lack of a Development Pathway & Role Models

Over the last couple of years immediately prior to 2018, there were no national or club structures that promoted professional development for youth or senior archers (e.g., youth or senior national/club squads, a position of national coach, development sessions, etc.). Therefore, there were no achievements at the international level, and due to the lack of a clear development pathway and prospects to succeed in archery, there was a >99% dropout rates of young archers. As I perceived this to be the biggest issue, it was the first one to be addressed, and a clear pathway was created. This pathway consisted of three simple stages that promote better skills, performance levels, and knowledge while increasing athlete retention.[2]

1. Feathers and arrows programme (FA) – a system equivalent to belts in combat sports.
2. Youth Development Squad (YDS) – for archers aiming at international representation.
3. National Youth Squad (NYS) – for archers ready to compete at the highest levels of our sport.

---

[1] This plan is available in English on the Israeli Archery Association website at https://www.archery.org.il/documents

[2] The programme is available for those interested in the full guidelines.

Establishing these programmes served primarily one purpose; to make it clear for a young archer joining the sport exactly what are the steps they need to follow from day one until they compete internationally. As unprecedented success on the international stage, and especially of young archers, started piling up, it became clearer that this pathway was successful, which in turn boosted youth retention, improved the overall performance levels, and increased the team from 5 members to 16 members at the end of 2021 and 26 at the end of 2022. As the team grew, a Youth Captain position was created which highlighted an archer who worked hard, striving for excellence, to model these ideals to young archers while also serving as a link between the coaching staff and the archers on the team. Some impressive results followed including various European and World records.

Running the Squad as a Coach and Performance Psychologist

So, there I was running a newly created team, with only one internationally experienced archer. As I am a performance psychologist and the mental part is the most important factor for elite archery success (Kim et al., 2015), planning training sessions to promote their growth as competitors and mental skills was the top priority. I had a clear approach for promoting excellence and performance which was based on my experiences as an athlete and my studies in Edinburgh. The best tool I had for the job was the use of psychological characteristics for developing excellence (PCDEs; MacNamara et al., 2010a, 2010b). My attraction to the idea of PCDEs stems from my overall holistic approach to sports and my preference to applied on-the-field work rather than working in one-on-one settings.

While there are recommended texts on PCDEs (e.g., Chapter 6 in *Talent Development: A Practitioner Guide* [Collins and MacNamara, 2017]), I will try and do it justice with a short summary. In a nutshell, PCDEs are both trait characteristics and state-deployed skills that are demonstrated to be important for the realisation of talent and elite athletic success (Gould et al., 2002; Hill et al., 2019; MacNamara et al., 2010a, 2010b). These traits and skills vary between studies, but in general, they include commitment, goal setting, quality practice, imagery, realistic performance evaluation, coping under pressure, competitiveness, the importance of working on weaknesses, self-belief, focus and distraction control, self-awareness, planning and self-organisation, actively seeking social support, and resilience. As Collins and MacNamara (2017) state:

> "PCDEs allow young performers to optimise development opportunities (e.g., first time appearances at a new level of competition, significant wins, and losses), adapt to setbacks (e.g., injury, slumps in performance), and effectively negotiate key transitions (e.g., selection, demands for increased practice) encountered along the pathway to excellence"
>
> *(Collins and MacNamara, 2017 p. 69).*

Developing these mental skills together with traditional skills (e.g., technique, physical conditioning) is what I like to think of as mental 'injury prevention'. Helping young athletes develop strong mental skills from an early stage and in their chosen activity, and especially in a mental sport like archery, is where I thought I could have the most impact when working with the newly formed Israel archery team.

The first step to use PCDEs successfully with athletes is to define the PCDE behaviours in the context that is required. This step is open for interpretation based on the beliefs and the philosophy of the coach according to the behaviours they are looking for. The important thing to consider is that these behaviours must be positive (i.e., not the lack of something), behavioural (i.e., something that can be promoted), and visual (i.e., something that can be seen). For example, if one takes "planning and self-organisation" and breaks it down to such behaviours, here is a possible list of behaviours you may expect in an archery setting.

1. Showing up for practice with stretchy bands for warm up.
2. Allocating sufficient time at the end of practice for specific physical strength exercises.
3. Planning the equipment and kit needed for international competition.

Each one of these behaviours is a different example of what 'planning and self-organisation' might look like in an archery context and what I, as a coach, expect archers who plan and self-organise to exhibit. While different coaches will define behaviours differently for each PCDE, it is also important to note that you should also promote different behaviours depending on the level of the athlete. For example, showing up for practice with a stretchy band will be advocated for beginner archers who are new, unaware of good practice habits, and might not have any skills in preparation for activities – especially if they are young. Therefore, such an easy behaviour is the perfect first step to promote and develop the 'planning and self-organisation' PCDE. Something considerably more complex such as planning the equipment and kit needed for the international competition will come later in the development pathway.

This concept can be easily employed to identify key behaviours to be promoted, with the characteristics I mostly focused on in my work with the team being goal setting, imagery, quality practice, realistic performance evaluation, focus and distraction control, commitment, and coping with pressure. The reason I chose these specifically can be attributed to weaknesses I identified with the archers' performance capabilities and necessary improvements for future success in major events and 'good practice' procedures I felt were lacking (e.g., quality practice, imagery, goal setting). But how can you actively promote said PCDEs as a coach? Or, more realistically for sport psychologists working with coaches to improve athletes? Collins and MacNamara (2017) suggest two important concepts to do exactly that: coach systems and coach behaviours. These concepts suggest that the way a coach acts (coach behaviours) and the system in which they work (coach systems) are critical for the promotion of a PCDE. They also suggest that it is better to focus only on a couple of PCDEs at a time. Consider the following example for 'commitment'.

The commitment behaviour I aimed to promote was showing up to practice on time, setting up the bow, and warming up in time for practice.

Coach behaviours:

1. I show up to practice 30–45 minutes before it starts, and finish preparing everything well before session starts.
2. I remind the archers of the importance of showing up early to ensure pre-training preparation can be completed before the practice session begins. I congratulate archers who arrive early and reprimand archers who are late.[3]

Coach systems:

1. Make sure the field is open so that early archers are not stuck waiting outside the gate.
2. It is known that archers who are late will face consequences. Such fixed standards included five push-ups per one minute of being late and carrying out the targets while setting up the field. This was a 'system' that aimed to discourage unwanted PCDE behaviour (i.e., being late).

If all works well, between coach behaviours and systems, the required behaviour will be promoted until it is inherent to the archer's behaviour. It is worth noting that although I discuss 'coach behaviours' and 'coach systems', these concepts are also relevant for performance psychologists, whose behaviours can also influence athletes. Furthermore, as consultants to coaches and athletes, performance psychologists are well-positioned to influence clubs/teams/programmes in promoting PCDEs to the athletes.

Bringing Challenge to the Training Environment

The activity that had the most positive impact and was also in direct contrast to the way clubs were approaching training was how we incorporated archery-specific drills and games with the aim of promoting distraction control and coping with pressure. These activities introduce challenge into the training environment while maintaining a supportive environment to foster PCDE growth. In contrast, typical practice sessions for the archers on the team in their own clubs comprise technical work, with the occasional scoring session, all in a quiet and peaceful setting which

---

[3] It should be noted that research into how to apply PCDEs and examples of applied use are lacking. This is merely my approach into PCDE application, which is based on concepts of operant conditioning (i.e., rewards and punishments). While this might be an acceptable and a prevalent exercise in my country (Israel), you should acknowledge cultural considerations when planning your own PCDE work.

may in some ways limit their preparation for competition. Therefore, my aim with the team was to make practice, at times, more demanding than competition.

Let's take 'Lord of the Gold' for example. This game was born as a result of my improvising during practice, with it becoming one of the best challenges to prepare the team for competition. The rules are simple.

Each archer shoots one arrow with the aim of achieving a certain score based on their ability. If an archer achieves their desired score, they move into the next round of the challenge. If an archer scores less than their desired score, they are out of the challenge. The game continues until every archer is out of the challenge, apart from the winner who achieved their desired score each time. Throughout the challenge, I announce whether each archer continues into the next round or whether they are out. As archers are knocked out of the challenge, they attempt to distract their teammates to apply more pressure and test their focus.

While this game sounds simple, it worked considerably well for several reasons. First, it levelled the playing field and would allow an intermediate archer newly on the team to compete with the more experienced archers, as each archer was given a different standard to maintain. Second, as it is a quick game, we can hold many rounds of it in a short time. Third, the kids love it, and beating each other and being proclaimed as Lord of the Gold was something each one of them really wanted. This gave the drill meaning and winning and losing had importance for all of them. In my personal experience, one of the biggest challenges working with some athletes is that in practice sessions there is no significance if they fail or succeed in something. This puts them at a disadvantage in competitions because in competition, unlike practice, succeeding or failing has meaning. Therefore, the biggest advantage of Lord of the Gold and the reason it worked well is that it had meaning for all the archers on the team and added challenge to their training sessions.

Another example of when I introduced a challenge to prepare the team for competition was my use of 'oooooohhhhhh!' during practice. Occasionally, I would sneak up on an archer when they were scoring their performance – especially if they were doing well – and I'd say something like 'ooooooohhhhh! All your arrows are in the gold! So much PRESSURE! Will you be able to put the last one in?'. I find that this active challenge of an archer's task orientation with ego-orientated statements is considerably important to help them do well in competition. The rationale is that their self-talk during competition can present as something similar; therefore, I like to challenge them with such scenarios in the safe setting of practice. If they do not perform well as a result, we frame it positively to encourage growth (e.g., noting how much they improved at this over time and how it will help them in the future), and if they succeed, they are empowered to handle such occurrences in future competitions.

It is my firm belief that one of the reasons why the members of the team were significantly stronger mentally than their peers around the world is this kind of unorthodox approach to practice and, as a result, their resilience while competing. Practice must be formulated to help an athlete to succeed in competition, and therefore applied on-the-field work is crucial for psychologists. Sometimes coaches may miss this in the endless pursuit to make an athlete stronger and technically superior, and this is exactly where sport psychologists can and should intervene to work collaboratively with coaches. If you perceive that training sessions are not constructed to facilitate performance, you should take note of this and approach the coach to explore this. To encourage buy-in from the coach, in my experience, it is important to begin with only one or two suggested changes and involve the coach in the process by asking them for their views on your observations and suggestions.

The Olympics as the Ultimate Test

The mental preparation for the Games started back in 2018. Every aspect of the plan was designed to develop a mentally tough archer who was ready to compete at the highest level. Critical to this was my active role as a performance psychologist within training sessions and competitions.

This section will highlight some key considerations when working as a performance psychologist and preparing for an international competition. Although attending the Olympic Games is not something that all performance psychologists will experience, these reflections and considerations can be readily applied to the preparation for any major sporting event.

The Importance of Goals

Even with the challenges that can come from being overly focused on outcome goals, during the Olympics they served tremendous use for us. After qualifying for the Olympics last minute mere weeks before the Games, and it being the first time an Israeli archer was attending, it was easy to get sucked into celebrations set out to just 'give it a go'. Nevertheless, I was fortunate that the archer and myself had the same mindset of 'we are going to compete, not to participate'. Therefore, an afternoon of celebrations on the day was allowed, but the next day we were back to business. While discussing what we would consider a successful Olympics, it was apparent that the archer and myself were very aligned as to what we thought a successful Olympics would look like – winning two rounds at least. With inexperienced archers, I tended to take the lead more when setting outcome goals, as I find they either aim too low or too high. With experienced archers, it is more of a collaborative endeavour, where I encourage them to do the 'aiming' and only intervene if I think they are not being realistic enough with their goal setting. The goal of reaching one-eighth finals at least – even though a 100% outcome goal which normally I would never use for such an event – saved the Games for us. The archer's ranking round at the Olympics was lacklustre, and they only qualified 60 out of 64 archers. Now that they had to face the fifth ranked archer in the first round, all hopes seemed lost. This is where the goal of reaching one-eighth round steered us to the right place. I highlighted that even if he did well in the ranking round, he would still, realistically, only place at around 35th, which would guarantee a top ten archer in the second round. As he would have to compete against a top ten ranked archer at some point in the competition, the slow start merely meant that they would face a tough opponent in the first round rather than the second. This realisation returned motivation and perspective and the archer proceeded to win both these matches.

Cue Words

The use of cue words is common amongst members of the team, with this technique being critical to our success at the Olympic Games. The archer had a major loss of confidence in their shooting technique upon arriving in Tokyo, resulting in several of the worst practice sessions I've ever seen from them. In a nutshell, their automatic shooting sequence became highly conscious and non-automatic. I began to use cue words based on the concept in Mallett and Hanrahan's (1997) work, and we simplified the archer's shot routine into words: 'open', 'stabilise', 'centre', and 'powerful' to describe the draw, anchor, aiming, and release technical stages. While the goal setting step was more of a collaborative effort, I had more influence on the selection of cue words. The goal setting session took place prior to arriving in Tokyo when the archer was level minded and functioning well. But when we worked to simplify their shot routine into four cue words, they were feeling pressured and panicked. Therefore, I decided to introduce the use of cue words which focused on four important stages of their shot routine. Once we had discussed potential cue words to represent these aspects of their shot routine, the archer chose words that resonated with them. These words were chosen to reflect what great shooting looked like for them. These cue words filled their head while performing, and I kept repeating them out loud while they were performing at all stages. I cannot emphasise enough how effective that was in very challenging conditions.

Midnight Talks

During the Games, myself and the archer shared a room which allowed for midnight talks: what I would describe as some of the best 'sessions' I've had with an athlete throughout my career so far. Being in the role of a coach performance psychologist gave me inequivalent access and professional possibilities that coaches and sport psychologists by themselves don't often have. These sessions allowed the archer to share thoughts, worries, and plans and reflect, relax, and plan for their performance. Having these conversations gave me the opportunity to help reframe some inaccurate thought patterns they were having that affected their ability to perform at their best. They also helped to maintain the archer's motivation and confidence throughout the event when facing challenging situations. While this kind of one-to-one access to athletes is not always possible, I would encourage fellow practitioners to seek opportunities for less formal, more spontaneous conversations (e.g., water fountain chats, in hotel lounges, during table tennis games). In these more relaxed settings, I found the athletes were more comfortable to divulge more than they usually would in formal training or competition environments. These were moments where I felt I could have a significant impact.

Preparation is Everything

Before the Olympics we held two simulation events in Israel. We had a crowd of family and friends, live feed over social media, music, a commentator, a line judge, high-level opponents, journalists, and even 'rain' (which was a teenager holding a hose imitating a potential typhoon). It was a 'poor man's' version of the Olympics, but it was a major key for the success in Tokyo. During these simulations, the archer had the opportunity to prepare for different scenarios against different competitors. All the elements we introduced were designed to simulate the Olympic Games and to apply some pressure and distraction to help the archer better manage challenging moments when out in Tokyo.[4]

After the Olympics the archer reflected and attested to the effectiveness of the simulation, saying that even when they were presented to the (non-existing) crowd in Tokyo they felt like they had done this before and felt comfortable just by the merit of the simulations. I genuinely believe that a major setback in performance for the archers who performed less successfully in the Olympics stemmed from the difference between their training and preparation and the reality of the Olympic Games environment.

As our archer's preparation was dramatically more encompassing and challenging pre-Tokyo, their sense of familiarity and preparation supported their performance when competing in the Olympic environment. Reflecting on this intervention, if I were to use this approach in future, I would become more familiar with the competition venue to ensure that simulations could be as accurate as possible to increase the athlete's familiarity and comfort when attending the competition.

Integrating Sport Psychology Into Coaching

This case study has explored how I worked to integrate sport psychology within my coaching practice. Working in this way enabled me to create a psychologically informed training environment, something which performance psychologists and coaches can work collaboratively to create. However, I also recognise that being in the role of both coach and performance psychologist may have discouraged archers from sharing certain reflections and insights. To manage this, I encouraged all archers to have a personal performance psychologist that I was able to regularly coordinate with. As an example, the Olympian's performance psychologist and I coordinated well – especially throughout the Games – and he was able to highlight things I may have missed and provided me with critical reflections to improve our work. My takeaway from this is to work collaboratively with others, whether this is with coaches, performance psychologists, or support staff.

---

[4]   See Low et al., 2022 for further information on the role and creation of pressure in training.

Final Reflections

Below are some of my reflections from my work as both the Israeli archery team coach and performance psychologist.

1. Being on the ground is crucial: I don't think it was stressed enough while I was studying, but going to the field and watching the athlete in their sport is critical for the work of a sport psychologist. Working only in one-to-one private sessions is not enough, both for the impact you can make and the information you gather.
2. Educational sport psychology is key: making an athlete knowledgeable gives them a competitive edge. Knowing multiple psychological tools is of course beneficial for athletes, but so is teaching them concepts in sport psychology. Athletes who can identify arousal and how it can be beneficial for them, question their own worries with logic, and use a multitude of skills when appropriate are truly an effective way to make self-sufficient champions.

Conclusion

This chapter is a culmination of several years of hard work. By sharing my experience, I hope to have given you four main takeaways to consider when developing your practice moving forward. First, a good organisation and a clear development pathway are critical for success. If a development pathway is unclear, athletes may not develop to their full potential. It may be useful to reflect on your role in encouraging a clear development pathway for athletes. Second, athletes need to be supported to develop important mental skills over time (including in training as well as in competition settings) to optimise their performance at the height of their careers. Third, in my experience, sport psychologists can be most impactful when they are present at training sessions and competitive events, working closely with coaches to create training plans and promote the growth of psychological skills. Finally, since high-level competitive events require high-level preparation and skill execution for athletes, coaches, and support staff, it is worth reflecting on how you can contribute to the preparation for these events and beyond.

REFLECTIVE QUESTIONS

1. Do you go on the field, and have you met your client's coach face-to-face?
2. Is your client's training setting being conducive to elite-level performance? How can you – as a sport psychologist – help shape their training settings to help them perform well under pressure?
3. Is there a clear development pathway in front of your client? Can you help clarify the pathway for them or help their organisation to formulate a clearer one?

References

Collins, D., & MacNamara, A. (2017). *Talent Development: A Practitioner Guide*. New York: Routledge.

Gould, D., Dieffenbach, K., & Moffett, A. (2002). Psychological characteristics and their development in Olympic champions. *Journal of Applied Sport Psychology*, *14*(3), 172–204. 10.1080/10413200290103482

Hill, A., MacNamara, Á., & Collins, D. (2019). Development and initial validation of the psychological characteristics of developing excellence questionnaire version 2 (PCDEQ2). *European Journal of Sport Science*, *19*(4), 517–528. 10.1080/17461391.2018.1535627

Kim, H. B., Kim, S. H., & So, W. Y. (2015). The relative importance of performance factors in Korean archery. *The Journal of Strength & Conditioning Research*, *29*(5), 1211–1219.

Low, W. R., Freeman, P., Butt, J., Stoker, M., & Maynard, I. (2022). The role and creation of pressure in training: Perspectives of athletes and sport psychologists. *Journal of Applied Sport Psychology*, *0*, 1–21.

MacNamara, Á., Button, A., & Collins, D. (2010a). The role of psychological characteristics in facilitating the pathway to elite performance: Part 1: Identifying mental skills and behaviors. *The Sport Psychologist*, *24*(1), 52–73. 10.1123/tsp.24.1.52

MacNamara, Á., Button, A., & Collins, D. (2010b). The role of psychological characteristics in facilitating the pathway to elite performance: Part 2: Examining environmental and stage-related differences in skills and behaviors. *The Sport Psychologist*, *24*(1), 74–96. 10.1123/tsp.24.1.74

Mallett, C. J., & Hanrahan, S. J. (1997). Race modeling: An effective cognitive strategy for the 100 m sprinter? *The Sport Psychologist*, *11*(1), 72–85. 10.1123/tsp.11.1.72

CASE STUDIES: IN CONCLUSION

Erin: *In conclusion then when looking at the case studies, I think we've got a real variety but also a real depth of experiences that were shared across all the chapters. These case studies really give the readers a sense of some of the work they might look to do in the future or perhaps challenge them to think differently about their work.*

Tim: I think a great example of this is Beth's chapter (Chapter 3). What stood out for me in this chapter was the creativity Beth was able to apply in the way she worked with the young athlete, how she took educated risks when delivering her service to a person younger in age, and for me most importantly, how she was able to use the athlete's parent as a resource throughout that intervention process.

Erin: *The chapters encourage you to think outside of the box when approaching work with clients. One of the chapters that stood out for me in that way was Betsy's chapter (Chapter 4) which focuses on Rational Emotive Behaviour Therapy (REBT). Although I'm familiar with REBT, this chapter encouraged me to further reflect on my approach when using REBT with clients. I think Betsy's chapter really expresses the vibe of REBT and not only gives readers an idea of what it is, but also what does it actually look like when working with a client, and how does it feel to work in this way as a practitioner? I think it will really give readers a sense of whether REBT is an approach they'd like to explore.*

Tim: The variety across the chapters also showcases the breadth of challenges that practitioners often have to deal with. In Anna's case (Chapter 2) when identifying athletes' needs surrounding mental health support, she created a new role for herself and steered her career in a new direction. This is something other practitioners may wish to do – and in some cases, this may require further training – but Anna demonstrates how you can be the architect of your own future as a practitioner.

DOI: 10.4324/9781003263890-10

Similarly, Harley (Chapter 5) talks about how sometimes you may come across opportunities that encourage you to think outside of the box. So, looking at the world around us through the lens of a performer, rather than just as a sports performer. For me, this chapter captures how despite practitioner training perhaps focusing on sport, in particular, practitioners can successfully apply psychology to different performance contexts to broaden the scope of their careers.

Erin: *And these are just some of the things we've picked up on from the case study chapters. I'm sure some readers will share similar reflections, but they will have also taken away their own key learnings based on their own experiences, and I think that's what we really want for the readers, for them to be able to look at all these case studies and think, as a practitioner, as a person, what can I take away from this section of the book?*

REFLECTIONS: AN INTRODUCTION

Erin: *We really wanted this section of the book to be novel and something a bit different to the case studies. These reflections are an opportunity to give readers an insight into the experience of being a sport psychologist, rather than simply thinking about the process of doing sport psychology. Here we explore some of the realities of navigating the early stages of your career as a practitioner. This section – as with the whole book – is about being a bit less polished, a bit less clear-cut, and moving away from sugar coating a sport psychologist's experiences – and in so doing, reflecting the reality of working within the profession. The reflections within the book are very varied, honest, and open, so we're really hopeful that readers can learn from other practitioners' experiences of perhaps some high points in people's careers but also some of the more challenging moments.*

Tim: What's very clear in the reflections is that the authors have focused down onto something very specific and have given a detailed account of their experience in applied practice. So, I hope that readers will be able to draw on that detail to help them to understand some of the real-world challenges of the profession and how practitioners have dealt with them.

Erin: *The first chapter in this section – Chapter 8 – is a reflection by a practitioner who completed a PhD alongside undertaking her applied qualification. This author shares her experience of having one foot in research and one foot in applied practice and how these roles can complement each other and reduce the gap we often see between research and practice.*

Tim: The second chapter in this section – Chapter 9 – looks at the challenge of coming into sport psychology as your second career. The practitioner shares their experience of entering a new career path and training route later in life and reflects on the skills and experience they have brought from their previous career into their practice.

DOI: 10.4324/9781003263890-11

Erin: *Chapter 10 of the book presents another novel perspective from a sport & exercise psychologist who is a former elite athlete. This chapter focuses on the opportunities and challenges of transitioning from being an athlete to a practitioner psychologist in sporting environments. The author reflects on using her sporting knowledge to gain entry, how her experience of sport psychology as an athlete has shaped her practice, and some of the benefits and challenges of self-disclosing her own experience to clients to build rapport.*

Tim: Chapter 11 focuses on how a practitioner in the early stages of their development and training was able to develop an understanding of themselves which then impacted their philosophy of practice, encouraging readers to reflect on how their values and beliefs can shape their careers.

Erin: *Then we've got Chapter 12 which reflects on the importance of understanding how you want to approach your training and career. The author discusses carving out your own path during the training process and explores some of the important considerations practitioners may have to make throughout their careers. For example, deciding whether to accept or decline unpaid work. The following chapter – Chapter 13 – then introduces us to the world of exercise psychology which is a relatively untapped area of our profession. Here the author shares her experience of getting started as an exercise psychologist and reflects on key challenges she has faced including gaining entry into fitness settings and working effectively with key stakeholders such as personal trainers to maximise her impact.*

Tim: Chapter 14 gives us insight into the practitioner's experience of their first international tournament as a psychologist. The author reflects on the importance of clarifying their role within the tournament environment, understanding how to work effectively as part of a multi-disciplinary team, and then the value of self-care to ensure that they are looking after their mental health and can bring their best selves to work. Finally, Chapter 15 shares an open and honest discussion between two early career practitioners regarding some of the more challenging conversations they have had with others throughout their careers, and they reflect on how reminding themselves of their values helped them to navigate these difficult situations.

Erin: *There's such a range of fascinating, candid reflections to get stuck into. I think this section will really encourage readers to consider not just what we do as practitioners, but how we go about navigating our way through the profession, making important personal, professional, and ethical decisions.*

Tim: While on the surface some of these chapters may seem challenging to read because of their candid nature, each chapter is very much an honest reflection of the fuzziness that comes with applied practice, where we are not always 100% sure about our decisions and their impact. So, we ask readers to embrace the fuzziness and explore how these personal stories resonate.

8

PURSUING A DUAL CAREER WITHIN SPORT PSYCHOLOGY: REFLECTIONS ON COMBINING PRACTITIONER TRAINING WITH ACADEMIC TRAINING

Charlotte Hinchliffe

Introduction: An Overview of My Career Journey in Sport Psychology to-Date

Establishing a career in sport psychology was not, for me, a lifelong ambition or childhood dream. In fact, I never knew what I wanted to do as a career growing up. I just knew I wanted to do something I was passionate about and interested in. I chose to study psychology at Undergraduate level, having always been interested in understanding human behaviour, but not having had the opportunity to formally study this subject at school. I thoroughly enjoyed my Undergraduate degree and finished it wanting to continue doing something relevant to psychology, but again still did not really know what this might look like in terms of a career. I found the research side of psychology interesting, but I associated this with sitting behind a desk for a large part of the day, which was not what I wanted to do for a living. I therefore started to explore the applied side of psychology, looking at how I could use my knowledge and understanding of the subject in a more direct role working with people. After some research into the various applied fields, I decided that sport psychology was the one for me. I had always enjoyed playing sport myself (albeit at amateur level) and as I started reading around the area, became fascinated by accounts of how psychology could influence performance. It seemed like the perfect career to me – using my knowledge and understanding of psychology to work with people and help them to become the best they could be.

I embarked on my professional training having investigated the British Psychological Society's (BPS) training process and identified that I could complete it within three years (one year to complete Stage 1 – a Master's in sport and exercise psychology; and further two years to complete Stage 2 – the BPS qualification in sport and exercise psychology (QSEP)). I remember thinking at the time that three years felt like quite a long time to commit to, especially having

DOI: 10.4324/9781003263890-12

already completed a three-year Undergraduate degree; as the typical analogy went among my fellow psychology graduates looking to pursue an applied career in the field: you can graduate from a Medicine degree in less than the combined time of this. However, having identified that this was a career path I wanted to pursue, I committed myself to this process and spent a year living back home with my parents to enable me to save for my Master's degree.

After completing my one-year Master's, I felt I was still on track with my three-year plan and launched myself enthusiastically into my QSEP training with the aim of completing it full-time within two years. Despite QSEP being an independent training pathway, I managed to retain my links with the university where I had completed my Master's, through my supervisors who were both based there, and through various employment opportunities that I either applied for (part-time lecturing) or was offered through the network I had built at the university (research assistant work, applied practice work). These roles at the university enabled me to meet my professional training development needs (the four competency areas of ethics, consultancy, research, and communication), while also providing me with a source of income to help fund my training and living costs.

As I approached the second year of my QSEP, I was making good progress with developing my competencies across all four key roles. However, the research competency required me to produce my own independent research project (not just act as a research assistant for others' research projects). The research needed to be done to a high standard (i.e., beyond Master's level and acceptable for the peer review process), and therefore required a significant time investment. However, this was something I had neglected in my first year of my QSEP, as I focused myself on what felt like the more immediate priorities of up-skilling my consultancy and lecturing skills and delivering research outputs in my paid roles. Recognising this gap in my development requirements, I set to work planning a research proposal which I felt I could deliver to the level required within the remaining timeframe, accepting that this might mean I had to turn down paid research-assistant opportunities to focus on my own research.

At a similar time, however, a fully funded applied PhD opportunity became available at the university. The funding attached to the PhD would provide me with an income to focus on my own research activities, in addition to a budget to put towards my continuing personal development funds. However, it was the applied emphasis of the role that really caught my interest: a researcher-practitioner role in talent development, comprising ten hours a week of applied delivery across two talent development environments (who were funding the PhD), with the remaining time allocated for research activities. Firstly, this meant I would be working in an applied role, which meant my previous worries of being chained to a desk while employed in a full-time research role were waylaid. Secondly, I recognised the opportunity this role represented in integrating the fields of research and applied practice, to help bridge the so-called 'research-practice' gap[1] (i.e., the divide between what is being re-searched, written, and read; and what is being done in practice and helpful for practitioners to know more about; Hassmén, Keegan, & Piggott, 2016; Keegan et al., 2017).

The research-practice gap was something I had been frustrated by myself fre-quently during my training journey. For example, when consulting the literature to inform my applied work, I would either struggle to find anything that repre-sented the context I was working with, or if I did find something relevant was left feeling at a loss as to how to actually put into practice what I had read. The literature seemed to focus on *what* researchers had found when implementing an intervention, as opposed to *how* and *why* they had implemented the intervention. Indeed, the research-practice gap results in detrimental consequences for practice (which is not adequately evidence-based and, therefore, potentially ineffective), but also for research (which is not fulfilling its purpose of informing and improving practice; Hassmén, Keegan, & Piggott, 2016). This in turn creates challenges for training competent professionals (Keegan, 2016) and building confidence in the profession (Keegan et al., 2017). A key solution to this problem, is for practitioners to start writing about the processes and mechanisms that underpin applied practice (Hassmén, Keegan, & Piggott, 2016; Keegan et al., 2017). This PhD presented me with an opportunity to do just that, rather than continuing to be part of the problem by not sharing my applied experiences.

Having been so focused on completing my applied training and forging an applied career, taking on a full-time (three-year) PhD was not a light-hearted decision, as I knew this would delay the completion of the remainder of my professional training by splitting my focus across the two qualifications. Luckily, both the applied and research activities involved with my PhD complemented my training requirements well, and I was able to advance both qualifications simul-taneously, albeit at a slower pace. I completed my practitioner training two years after commencing my PhD (after five years of training in total – one on my Master's (Stage 1) and four on QSEP (Stage 2)), and my PhD four years after this (after six years in total). The final three years of my PhD were completed part-time, after my three-year funding came to an end and I had to look for an alternative income. During these last three years, I balanced part-time work as a Performance Psychologist with the English Institute of Sport (an organisation that contracts out support services to Paralympic and Olympic sports in the UK) alongside completing my PhD.

At the time of writing, I am still working in my role as an applied practitioner at the English Institute of Sport, which forms about 60 percent of my working week. The rest of my time involves a combination of other applied work with private clients; continued professional development activities; and dissemination activities

---

[1]   See Leggat et al. (2021) and Keegan et al. (2017) to learn more about the research-practice gap within sport and exercise psychology.

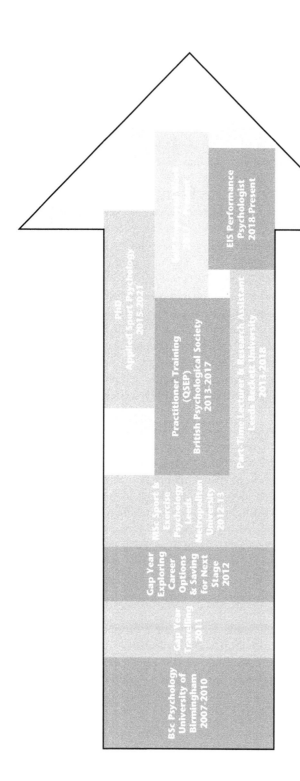

FIGURE 8.1 Timeline of my professional journey in sport psychology so far

(e.g., guest lectures at universities). I am not currently involved with any active research projects, having only recently completed my PhD and wanting to focus on publishing some papers from this first. However, continuing to contribute to the applied research field (and bridge the research-practice gap) is something I am keen to remain involved with going forwards. A timeline of my career journey outlined above is illustrated below in Figure 8.1.

Reflections on Combining Practitioner Training and Academic Training in Sport Psychology

Combining my practitioner and academic training was not something I originally set out to do. It has been an extremely challenging, but also rewarding experience, that has provided me with opportunities and experiences that would not necessarily have been available to me had I chosen to pursue only one of these pathways. Both pathways have their challenges and benefits, and there are similarities and differences that exist between these. Having experienced what it is like to be focused on just one area of training (both academic and practitioner), and what it is like to combine them, I have used these experiences to inform my reflections below on the benefits and challenges of each of these training pathways and domains of work, both independently and in combining them. Hopefully, this will provide a useful comparison for those currently considering which pathway to choose, or whether to combine these two pathways.

For me, the primary benefit of combining academic and practitioner training has been the complementary nature that each has on the other. At a practical level, this meant that my work towards one qualification helped me to advance the other qualification (and vice versa). For example, I was able to use the activities associated with my PhD to demonstrate my competence in the research area of my QSEP training; and as an applied PhD I was also able to dedicate one of my QSEP case studies to my PhD work. Equally, the skills I had learned to support my consultancy delivery in my practitioner training (e.g., rapport building, active listening, questioning, and observation skills) enhanced my ability to deliver in my academic role (e.g., agreeing a research focus with my funders, interviewing participants, observations in the field, delivery of interventions). This was particularly relevant given the applied focus of my PhD, which comprised developing, delivering, and evaluating an intervention with athletes, parents, and support staff in a talent development environment. I therefore needed the skillset of a practitioner to undertake this research effectively (i.e., have the competence to design, deliver, and evaluate an intervention); and the skillset of a researcher to produce a rigorous and trustworthy output (e.g., through use of recognisable research methods and writing to peer-review standard), which I could use to inform and shape my ongoing practice delivery (and potentially publish to enable others to learn from this too). The practice enabled the research, and the research improved the practice.

As well as the symbiotic nature of my skill development and outputs for each qualification, another key benefit for combining the two training pathways and domains of work was the opportunity to reap the benefits that each one offers, and to help offset some of the challenges associated with each pathway when pursued individually. For example, QSEP is an independent training route, which can feel isolating at times as there are no structured opportunities to spend time with other trainees. Working in the applied world can also be quite isolating, as practitioners typically either work in a self-employed manner or, if they work for an organisation, are often the only sport psychologist employed. This limits the opportunities for learning from and being supported by peers and colleagues with an understanding of the field in which we are working. Contrastingly, as a PhD student I was part of an institution where many other sport psychology academics and trainee academics were situated. This provided more readily available social support, which has been invaluable in my training journey (and beyond).

In addition to the isolation associated with undertaking an independent training route, I also found the unstructured nature of the QSEP challenging. I had to take responsibility for planning how to structure my training to meet the competencies required of the qualification. At the outset of my training journey, unaware of what I needed to know to be an effective practitioner, this was quite challenging, and I felt I often had to respond reactively to situations, learning after the event rather than a priori, which would have enabled a more proactive approach. While QSEP trainees are required to plan and identify their own development opportunities, PhD students at the institution I attended were offered regular research training workshops, which covered areas that had been identified as useful for postgraduate students to understand. This provided me with some much-welcomed stability and structure around the development of my research competency for QSEP, that I was lacking in the other competency areas.

One of the most fundamental benefits of combining a PhD with my practitioner training was the funding I received for the former. I was given a bursary to fund living costs, my supervision and course fees were paid for by my funders, and I was able to apply for additional funding for any supplementary development opportunities I identified would be useful that were not provided by the university's internal program. This contrasted with my experience of practitioner training, where I was required to self-fund qualification fees, supervision fees, and personal development activities, in addition to living costs. In the two years of my practitioner training before I commenced my PhD, managing these financial demands was challenging. I was unable to generate enough income from my applied work to provide me with a 'living wage'; therefore, I had to supplement this with other paid roles (reducing the time I had to focus on developing the required competencies) and financial assistance from family (something I was lucky to be able to access, but which others may not, potentially limiting this career path to those from more privileged socioeconomic backgrounds (Hu et al., 2020), creating a barrier to diversity and inclusion in the field). Taking on a PhD alongside my practitioner training therefore provided some financial stability to my time in training. While not all PhDs are funded, there are far more opportunities for this than for receiving funding for practitioner training (I am yet to come across anyone who has had their practitioner training funded). Indeed, the increased level of stability offered by research training over practitioner training is an extension of the increased level of stability in maintaining employment in the academic world compared to the high turnover rate of employees in the applied world (Mujika & Pyne, 2022).

While my academic training had some clear benefits for my applied training, this relationship was also reciprocated. The main challenge for me with my PhD was maintaining motivation and focus over such an extended time on one area and disciplining myself to dedicate the time to the activities I enjoyed less (sitting behind a desk and writing up my research). In the academic world there is a focus on depth rather than breadth of knowledge and taking the time to understand things to inform action, rather than doing these in parallel. For example, it took me the best part of my first year to establish a research question and gain ethical approval for my research, before being able to collect any data. It then took me nearly another year to analyse this data, meaning I was unable to start fully implementing my findings into my applied work until my third and final year in my role as a researcher-practitioner. Being able to engage with my practitioner training and applied work alongside my PhD helped provide the variety that I needed to keep motivated. In the applied field, I was working with lots of different people, across many different environments, supporting various areas of focus.

Of course, the varied and fast-paced demands of the applied world can be challenging for trainees who are still learning their profession, requiring practitioners to respond quickly/in the moment to situations as they unravel. While I enjoyed the variety this brought to my working days, I also felt pressure to quickly gain knowledge and understanding of a wide array of applied practice topics (feeling a bit like a 'jack of all trades, master of none'); and at times felt overwhelmed with how much knowledge there is to acquire (feeling firmly at the bottom of what has been termed 'The Dunning-Kruger Effect' (Kruger & Dunning, 1999)). Being part of the academic world, with its slower approach to responding, enabled me to safeguard time to explore existing research in depth to inform my practice and increase knowledge and understanding; and time to pause and reflect on the research and practice I was conducting. This time is something many practitioners are not afforded given the demands of working in a fast-paced, high-performance industry, and was something I valued in helping my development and confidence as a practitioner.

Most importantly, I believe that training in both these areas has made me a better practitioner and a better academic than I would have been had I chosen to focus on just one of these domains. Training as a practitioner has enabled me to identify and deliver research that is relevant and impactful to the field, a type of research described as 'translational research' (Collins, MacNamara, & Cruickshank, 2018). It has also enabled me to bring valuable context to teaching and dissemination activities, through using examples from my applied work to bring research and theory to life for the audience. Training as an academic has enabled me to keep up to date with the latest research to inform my practice and has developed my ability to critically appraise and reflect on myself and the services I provide and safeguarded the time to do this. These are examples of the research-practice gap being narrowed, and I believe it is important for our profession that more of this takes place, rather than people with different skillsets operating in their own domains and not bringing their work together.

Finally, a more obvious benefit of combining academic and practitioner training is that it increases the available career options to those associated with both these domains, rather than just one or the other. Given that most practitioners and academics have not undergone both areas of training, it may also support applications for employed roles by providing a competitive edge over other candidates. This may be increasingly important given the finite opportunities available to sport psychologists in comparison to the number of those who undertake training in this area, especially in the applied field. Indeed, having a PhD provides you with an area of expertise which can set you aside from other more generalist practitioners; and having practitioner training sets you aside from academics who do not have this additional contextual understanding and expertise from the applied world.

While these benefits are appealing, it is also important to be mindful of the challenges associated with combining these qualifications. I have already alluded to the investment required to complete both QSEP and a PhD. It is a full-time commitment to do one, therefore, taking on two qualifications simultaneously is a huge demand on the trainee. This inevitably places additional stress on trainees over and above that associated with completing one qualification (which, by all accounts, can be stressful enough in itself), and can create challenges around wellbeing and maintaining a healthy life-balance. With few people undertaking both qualifications, this can also feel quite an isolating experience, with others not always understanding the demands you may be experiencing.

With these demands in mind, it is impractical to contemplate completing the qualifications in the timeframe they would take to complete independently. Even with the complementary nature of the two, there are additional requirements that do not overlap within each qualification, which means further time needs to be factored in. For example, QSEP requires three submissions over the qualification plus a viva, and evidence of a variety of different examples of applied practice delivery (e.g., range of clients, contexts). This needs to be managed alongside the requirements of a PhD, which tends to include annual reviews and a focus on one research area/context, with one submission at the end plus a viva. All of this, inevitably, elongates the amount of time spent as a trainee. For me, this equated to both qualifications taking double the amount of time they would have taken on their own (i.e., four years for QSEP, and six years for my PhD). I know of others who have completed both in less time than this but, in all cases I am aware of, it still takes longer than the independent timeframes (at least four-five years in total).

Splitting your focus across two training areas can also detract from the pace of your development in each. While you develop competencies across the academic and applied fields, you are spreading yourself thinner than those who choose to focus on one of these areas and may therefore be able to advance their development quicker. I am not far enough into my career to know whether there will come a time when this disadvantage plateaus, but currently I feel less advanced in both areas than colleagues I know who have specialised in one.

Overall, there are several benefits and challenges associated with combining academic and practitioner training. These should be considered ahead of deciding whether to undertake both qualifications simultaneously. Having provided an overview of what it is like to undertake each of these professional qualifications, and what it is like to combine them, I will now share some of the lessons I have learned from my experiences, in the hope this will help others considering or already undertaking a similar path.

Lessons I Have Learned from My Experiences of Combining Practitioner and Academic Training in Sport Psychology

The most important thing I have learned from my career journey so far is the value in making sure you enjoy what you are doing. Neither of these training pathways are easy, with both providing many challenges at several different levels. You also need to dedicate a good number of years of your life to doing them. For these reasons, it is vital that you enjoy what you are doing. I have found there are parts of both roles I enjoy more than others, and some environments I enjoy working in more than others. Understanding what my preferences are, and then building my work to meet these preferences as much as possible has been important for maintaining my motivation to continue my training over such an extended period (more than nine years in total).

Secondary to harnessing intrinsic motivation, is building a good support network around you, both professionally and personally. Even if you love every single part of your training, it is still a highly demanding undertaking, and it can be lonely and isolating at times. Having support around me from people who understood what I was going through and/or were there for me when I needed them was crucial for me. I was lucky that my supervisory team was the same for both my QSEP and PhD, which meant that my supervisors understood the demands of both qualifications and were able to support me to meet the demands of each at the relevant times. This is not always the case for dual trainees though, and it is important to ensure expectations are managed and kept transparent across supervisors and other relevant stakeholders, so everyone is on the same page. I was also privileged to go through much of my training journey with a close colleague of mine, and to build connections with others going through the training journey too. Having peers who were going through the same or similar training and facing similar experiences reduced the potential isolation I could have experienced during my training and provided a valuable resource for peer reflection in addition to the formal supervision I had from my supervisors. I am also grateful to have such a supportive family, partner, and friends, who have supported me emotionally and (especially in the early days of my training) financially with my endeavours.

Thirdly, I think it is important to recognise the demands of each of these qualifications in advance, so that you go into it with open eyes and are not surprised or caught off guard by the realities. Before starting both of my training experiences I tried to speak to as many people as I could who were already working in these fields and/or had undergone these training pathways. The practitioner training in the UK was still in its infancy when I commenced my training, and the QSEP was the only option available for me, but there are now additional training pathways to consider in the UK, for example, Professional Doctorates offered by certain universities, or the BASES Sport and Exercise Psychology Accreditation Route (SEPAR) which provide similar yet differing routes into the profession. Investing time in understanding what your options are, speaking to those who have already experienced these, and identifying which is right for you is an important step to take before making any decisions. Within this, it is important to consider your end goal. Where do you want to be working at the end of your training and beyond? For example, if you want to only work in the applied world then there might not be as much value in a PhD as a Professional Doctorate or just focusing on QSEP/SEPAR. If you solely want to be an academic, then a PhD might be more important. Furthermore, if considering combining training areas, look for opportunities that enable you to optimise the complementary areas of both. For me, this comprised of undertaking an applied PhD which meant I was able to advance both of my qualifications simultaneously with more ease than what I imagine a non-applied PhD might have allowed for. As well as helping to streamline the process of completing two qualifications, this also provides an opportunity for more active researcher-practitioners working across the research and applied domains to help bridge the research-practice divide, which is crucial for developing our field going forwards.

Finally, look to develop and refine your own psychological skills and characteristics. The qualities that we help athletes to develop to perform at their best are transferable to other contexts (MacNamara & Collins, 2009), and are certainly relevant to coping with the demands of professional training. Commitment, planning and preparation, social support seeking, resilience, motivation, focus, maintaining a life-balance, and self-care (to name a few) will all be important in enabling you to navigate the demands of, and ultimately succeed in, your professional training.

Summary

In this chapter, I have provided an overview of my career journey in sport psychology so far, including my experiences of practitioner training, academic training, and combining the two, as well as lessons learned. Of course, these are just my personal experiences, and it is important to note that other people who have undergone the same training pathways will bring their own differing experiences. Ultimately, the important point to recognise is that whichever training pathway, or combinations of pathways, you choose to undertake, there will be benefits and challenges to all that need to be navigated. It is important to go in with a clear understanding of what is involved, and the personal resources to help you to meet these demands. It would be fantastic to see more people in our field qualified in both the academic and applied domains, to encourage a closing of the research-practice gap and ultimately to enable the field to continue to grow and develop in an impactful manner. To support this, it would be encouraging to see applied organisations joining forces with academic institutions to provide a more structured, stable route for those willing and interested in pursuing both careers. Importantly, this should include access to adequate funding and a realistic time-frame to complete both qualifications in (at least four- to five years full time).

REFLECTIVE QUESTIONS

- Where do your key interests lie/where do you see yourself in ten years' time – working in the applied world, the academic world, or a combination of both? Which qualification(s) will best meet these interests/assist you in achieving these career goals?
- Who is in your support network that you will be able to go to for support when you need it? Who else do you need in this network to meet your personal and professional support needs?
- Mapping out the demands of professional training and the personal resources you have to help you to cope with these demands, where are your strengths and where are your development needs?
- Regardless of whether you are planning to focus on practitioner training, academic training, or a combination of both, what could you do to help bridge the research-practice gap in our field going forwards?

References

Collins, D., MacNamara, Á., & Cruickshank, A. (2018). Research and practice in talent identification and development—Some thoughts on the state of play. *Journal of Applied Sport Psychology*, *0*, 1–12.

Hassmén, P., Keegan, R., & Piggott, D. (2016). Research and practice in applied sport and exercise psychology. In P. Hassmén, R. Keegan, & D. Piggott (Eds.). *Rethinking Sport and Exercise Psychology Research: Past, Present and Future*. London, UK: Palgrave Macmillan.

Hu, S., Hood, M., Creed, P. A., & Shen, X. (2020). The relationship between family socioeconomic status and career outcomes: A life history perspective. *Journal of Career Development*, *49*(3), 600–615.

Keegan, R. (2016). *Being a Sport Psychologist*. London, UK: Palgrave.

Keegan, R. J., Cotterill, S., Woolway, T., Appaneal, R., & Hutter, V. (2017). Strategies for bridging the research-practice 'gap' in sport and exercise psychology. *Journal of Sport Psychology, 26*(4), 75–80.

Kruger, J. M., & Dunning, D. (1999). Unskilled and unaware of it: How difficulties in recognizing one's own incompetence lead to inflated self-assessments. *Journal of Personality and Social Psychology, 77*, 1121–1134.

Leggat, F. J., Wadey, R., Day, M. C., Winter, S., & Sanders, P. (2021). Bridging the know-do gap using integrated knowledge translation and qualitative inquiry: A narrative review. *Qualitative Research in Sport, Exercise and Health*, 1–14.

MacNamara, Á., & Collins, D. (2009). More than the 'X' factor! A longitudinal investigation of the psychological characteristics of developing excellence in musical development. *Music Education Research, 11*(3), 377–392.

Mujika, I., & Pyne, D. B. (2022). Moving on in sport science. *International Journal of Sports Physiology and Performance*(Ahead of Print), 1–2.

9

LIVING THE 100-YEAR LIFE: REFLECTIONS ON THE (RE)TRAINING PROCESS FOR A SUBSEQUENT CAREER IN SPORT AND EXERCISE PSYCHOLOGY DURING MID-LIFE

Steven Vaughan

As we live longer, the lure of excitement associated with seeking new experiences may lead to embarking on alternative careers and changes in career pathways as one reaches mid-life. This chapter offers readers insight into some of the subjective experiences associated with embarking on a subsequent career. It describes how life experiences have led to reflecting about who I am, my philosophy and approach to practice. I believe that my approach to resolving these issues has been different as a mature trainee, than perhaps it would have been in my 20s. Finally, I reflect on how life experience has influenced the way I have managed changing dynamics, which enabled me to deal with tensions and challenges. This has led to developing an approach to practice which aligns with the practitioner I want to become.

Readers will gain insight into the experience of approaching a career in sport psychology from a viewpoint which differs from the more common progression directly from university to a first career. Those embarking on a subsequent career will be presented with some considerations that may be relevant for their own journey. Readers planning on working in sport psychology as their primary career may take some food for thought regarding lifespan implications to incorporate as they develop their professional and personal values for practice.

Practitioner Identity: What Is My Core Self?

Values and Motivators

Trainee Sport and Exercise Psychologists are taught about the importance of values in developing practice philosophy (Poczwardowski, Sherman, & Ravizza, 2004). If our values represent the guiding principles of life, it is interesting to

DOI: 10.4324/9781003263890-13

recognise how some may have changed over time. My values appear to have a split, where some are the same now as they were 30 years ago though others are different. My core values (using value cards; Miller et al., 2011) such as honesty, family and industry/hardworking have remained consistent throughout my life. However, when younger, values which appear to be extrinsically driven aligned to achievement, wealth and seeking to be accepted were important. For the sake of transparency this meant being successful, gaining material wealth and being popular, i.e., related to the impression I created. These values are noticeably different today where self-knowledge and self-acceptance are more important than being popular (though popularity is always nice!). Whilst I still strive for tangible success, this emanates from trying to be the best version of myself and being primarily motivated from an intrinsic core.

Considered in relation to Achievement Goal Theory (Nicholls, 1984, 1989) this shift shows a move from an ego focus towards task orientation. The younger self would judge success on results and performance relative to others, though mastery of the task for its own sake was not always on the agenda. Self-referencing to be the best version of me through effort, collaboration, and enjoyment is more the order of things today. It would be disingenuous to say that tangible results are not important, they provide benchmarks, material benefits, and social positioning. However, on a training course after describing what I did, I was asked to explain *why* I did it. This simple question led to something of an aah-hah moment in relation to being honest with myself about the way I worked and what was important. My focus was on achieving targets/outcomes (this is a *what*). I had chased paths of least resistance to get a result, and the next result, and the next, which in turn secured upward career progression. Being clear about the benefits, my work provided in securing services for others (my *why*[1]) enabled me to take a personally more enriching approach by doing things properly, even if this was sometimes corporately challenging. In respect of training to become a Chartered Sport and Exercise Psychologist I want to meet the measurable outcomes and personal growth challenges authentically and consistently with what is important to me; for example, completing placement opportunities in sporting contexts congruent with my interests rather than for the sake of accruing necessary practice hours.

Interestingly, studies have found that values can change over the course of a lifetime (Robinson, 2013; Vilar, 2020); achievement and excitement are more highly valued when younger, whereas social values and seeking greater benevolence are higher in older adults. At face value, seeking achievement through career change in mid-life puts me out of kilter with these findings. However, the reasons for making a career change were very much aligned with connection. Firstly, work was affecting the social connection with family and friends i.e., I wanted a

---

[1] There are many books to help understand your why. I think it is summed up quite nicely in a three-minute YouTube video 'Know your why' by Michael Jr (2017), https://www.youtube.com/watch?v=1ytFB8TrkTo.

better work/life balance. Secondly, not feeling connected directly to the provision of services, my previous leadership role fundamentally involved creating an environment to enable others to deliver hands-on services; basically, I went to meetings, dealt with emails, and wrote (well, mainly edited) corporate papers. What I craved was a role where I could develop a deeper connection with individuals that enabled them to derive personal benefit. I guess another way to describe that is wanting to stop directing the action and start delivering it. There is an additional reason, I accidentally fell in love with psychology and decided to link my life-long engagement in sport with it.

Recognising One's Authentic Self

Several years before making the decision to pursue sport and exercise psychology, there was a difficult period at work. The context is not relevant to this piece, but it led to significant reflection about me, my role, team, environment, etc. As well as identifying things that were important to me (links to my *why*), my learning and what I might have done differently, I tried to consider psychological factors at play. I recognised that apart from snippets gleaned during management development, I knew very little! This led to me undertaking an MSc in Applied Psychology alongside work, where among many other things this degree made me consciously consider humanism and provided a formal introduction to Carl Rogers.

Management training had focused on Maslow's (1943) hierarchy of needs and his concept of self-actualisation. By grossly paraphrasing Maslow's definition, fulfilment is achieved by doing everything one is capable of. What I wrongly believed was that expectations associated with getting to the top of the career tree would deliver me to this place, in effect I ticked off each level as I got older and achieved more success, such as gaining promotion. However, Rogers (1961) identifies differences between being authentic and inauthentic, where self-actualisation involves moving to 'being the process which one inwardly and actually is' (p. 175). In essence, self-actualisation is not a self-development process as our true self already exists, it involves recognising and acting consistently (authentically) with what one is. With the benefit of hindsight, I now recognise that it was external expectation and reward which had compromised my ability to be authentic in this sense. I am not sure that I consciously considered values in my 20s, as a reader of this chapter you may already be cognisant of yours and therefore affected less by outside influence. If you are not sure perhaps take some time to do this.

As I have described earlier, a change to some of my values (guiding principles) has occurred over time giving rise to acting more authentically. Though I must acknowledge this is easier given Maslow's (1943) physiological, safety, and belonging needs are met – I would not be writing this if selling the house had been a requirement of embarking upon a subsequent career! In describing self-determination theory, Ryan and Deci (2000) differentiate between intrinsic and extrinsic forms of motivation. Recognising how these factors affect our decisions is key. In this situation, as an older trainee I do not see any difference from my younger peers in terms of the intrinsic motivation to complete our training. What may be different are the extrinsic influences affecting my decision making. For example, one reason that we work is the need to earn, it may not be the main motivator but is important to enable us to live how we choose. As a mature trainee this situation is perhaps a little clearer as many of life's bigger fiscal decisions (e.g., buying a house) have already been taken. Though the underlying principle relating to how we consider the interaction between different factors to enable our decision making still applies. Interestingly, as I moved from student to trainee practitioner this interaction had a bigger impact on me than I expected.

How Experience Shapes What You Think You Want to Be

Stages of Professional Development

This reflection has so far considered how changes over time have led to me acting more authentically. Moving on to consider my development towards becoming a Sport and Exercise Psychologist, I have noticed that my life experiences appear to affect the typical stages of moving from trainee into practice. For counsellors and therapists six phases of development were identified by Rønnestad and Skovholt (2003, 2012) which have informed research investigating practice of applied Sport and Exercise Psychologists (for example see McEwan, Tod, & Eubank, 2019). These phases describe the journey from pre-trainee, through training, entry to practice and ultimately becoming a senior professional. However, as a mature trainee life experience has led to having a clearer picture of my self-concept and identity, which could be considered inconsistent with the development journey within this literature. Rønnestad and Skovholt describe 'building consistency and coherence in the personal/professional self' (p. 20) not occurring until the Experienced Professional phase. Any advantages associated with being able to integrate self-concept with a coherent professional self at an earlier stage are unknown, though this has led to other challenges in aligning my practice and theoretical orientation.

The personal attributes required for successful delivery of my previous operational leadership responsibilities were being empathetic, trustworthy, and authentic. These mirror some of the inherent requirements for being an effective Sport and Exercise Psychologist. However, for me becoming truly authentic was something that developed with age and experience. This does not mean my beliefs and practice were not authentic when younger, I probably did believe I was being authentic in my 20s too. It is with the benefit of hindsight that I can see how I may have been more influenced externally by what I thought people wanted me to be, rather than who/what I am; for example, if the tutors on my Sport Psychology MSc had all leaned towards existentialism, the younger me would probably have started to practice from this viewpoint. This was not the case as I thought I knew the type of practitioner I wanted to be, which has led to frustration and much reflection during my early experiences of practice.

Finding My Approach

The Advanced Student phase (Rønnestad & Skovholt, 2003, 2012) is typified by a desire for perfection whilst beginning to develop a sense of individualisation, which may give rise to possible conflict. Establishing theoretical orientation and approach to practice are key parts to developing this sense of individualisation. Keegan (2015) describes four mutually exclusive philosophies which are aligned to specific approaches to practice (Table 9.1). As I began career transition exploring theoretical orientations and philosophical approaches to practice, I assumed I would fit neatly into the construalist/client-centred box.

My leadership knowledge and approach were based on many years of diverse practical experience and had spent many hours participating in continuous professional development. Reflecting now, it is clear to see how this leant towards humanist principles, that is focusing on the individual and their agency. In work I rarely took a position akin to that of practitioner knows best, combining my inherent personal characteristics with professional training. Having not read about humanistic approaches in detail prior to my journey into psychology I began to discover a difference between thinking that you know what you are, and what that means. Having enthusiastically dived into exploring Rogerian principles and practice, I immediately became frustrated when it came to applied practice. This was because in the early months of working with athletes I found that in sport performance situations the client was often seeking a quick (e.g., mental skills type) solution. To make this seem worse, the client was looking to me to decide what that intervention would be. Whereas my desire was to deliver a Rogerian person-centred approach ensuring therapeutic conditions were in place and change was able to follow (Rogers, 1957). At the first step on the path to applied practice, I had found the Advance Student conflict (Rønnestad & Skovholt, 2003, 2012).

Being in a form of conflict led to repeating the same reflection whilst gripping tightly to the principle that it was necessary to get into one of Keegan's (2015) philosophical boxes. Wanting to be client-centred meant the construalist box was the one to open. However, Merry (2012) stated 'the person-centred relationship is not "instrumental" in that it does not constitute the "context" of therapy, nor is it preparation for techniques and strategies. The person-centred relationship *is* the therapy' (p. 42). This meant these early practical experiences appeared to count this

TABLE 9.1 A summary of potential theoretical orientations and approaches to practice (simplified from Keegan, 2015, Table 3.1, p. 53)

Philosophy of Science	*Approach to Practice*
Certaintism	Practitioner-led, aligns with cognitive behavioural approaches
Construalism	Client-led, aligns with humanistic approaches
Pragmatism	Eclectic, do what works
Fallibilism	Eclectic, very cautious gathers evidence to minimise risk

orientation out or accept a potentially different outlook for client work. This difficulty seemed to be enhanced when considered in conjunction with the mutual-exclusivity of cognitive-behavioural and person-centred approaches. For example, a cognitive approach which considers the cause of a runner's pre-event anxiety to be the irrationality of their belief leads to an intervention that challenges their beliefs. Whilst providing a benefit, i.e., enables them to perform next week, it seeks to 'alter and not understand what the client thinks' (Worsley, 2012, p. 170).

Something about seeing this statement written down in a discussion outside of trainee texts provided the catalyst to resolving this conflict. My perception from university teaching and Keegan's (2015) descriptions of eclectic practice seemed to imply a reductionist view of pragmatism, where practitioners randomly select approaches to fit the situation. Having strived to be a perfect client centred practitioner, I had avoided giving proper consideration of what pragmatism and fallibilism were as I had decided that they are places good practitioners do not populate. To resolve the conflict meant recognising that I use a combination of client and practitioner led approaches and that I aligned with the philosophy of pragmatism.

The question for me was, why did becoming comfortable with my preferred philosophy of practice consume so much of my emotional energy? Professional practice literature offered a potential avenue to explain. Individuation within professional development relates to experimenting to find fit between practitioner and the environment. Dynamic in nature, it reflects an ongoing process which ultimately leads to finding a balance of personal satisfaction and meaning (Tod, Hutter, & Eubank, 2017). In practitioner research, McEwan, Tod, and Eubank (2019) explain that 'Trainee Sport Psychologists adjusted themselves to the job of sport psychology, whereas Experienced Sport Psychologists adjusted the job to themselves' (p. 8). At the heart of this statement were the practitioner's life experiences which had occurred in parallel to their sport psychology development. For example, Tod et al. describe how life events help with specific elements of personal development, such as bereavement or divorce with improved empathy. During the early stage of development on the one hand I mapped to that of trainee, though my experience of life was more akin to that of an experienced practitioner. Considering my situation through this lens it appeared I was analysing in a way that may have been atypical for an early-stage trainee. Accepting my pragmatic core provided the release to enable me to freely (but safely) develop my approach to practice. The process of defining my version of pragmatism is ongoing. In short, this is about ensuring that practice is not randomly eclectic but based on principles which do not compromise building the relationship in a Rogerian person-centred way, where the client takes the lead. I have found the Performance Interview Guide (Aoyagi et al., 2017) to be helpful in formally supporting, and documenting, the early stages of client interaction which enables intervention to evolve from what the client wants. Importantly, this journey is not done alone, supervision, and peer support are key.

Support Structures

Through the training route there is a ready-made community of practice in place consisting of fellow trainees. The creation of sessions for trainees provides opportunity to discuss educational and practical experiences with peers. In sessions I attend, we usually find that everyone has encountered some challenge in their practice, thus generating avenues for further group and individual reflection. My fellow trainees have engaged in debate regarding explanations of my challenges and questions to them regarding their own experiences. These discussions are of great value, as well as facilitating opportunities to develop a peer network which will enable ongoing support for career-long learning. My advice to new trainees is to make the most of these opportunities. When I was younger, I did not always fully engage in peer learning, but over time I appreciated the benefits.

The key area of support has come through my excellent supervision, I am very lucky. The objective of supervision is to support trainees 'ensuring positive professional development, client welfare, and general ethical practice' are maintained (Lubker & Andersen, 2014, p. 161). My supervisors have facilitated plenty of opportunity to work through challenges and reduce the incongruence associated with this dilemma. Though through reflection about this process, I recognised how my position as a trainee was different in relation to the dynamics of this relationship. In my former career I held a position of authority and influence, in some respects could be deemed an expert at what I did, as well as providing oversight and guidance to teams. In this subsequent career situation, there has been a reversal in roles as I moved from mentor to mentee.

Tackling Changes in Relationship Dynamics

Academic Journey

By way of introduction to this final section, a brief overview of my educational journey associated with this subsequent career identifies points where I have experienced different relationship dynamics with my peers. Returning to university as a student has generally been a positive one, as a life-long learner being back in a classroom was enjoyable. Though I have not really considered whether the presence of a mature student creates any issues for those delivering the tuition. My training route involved an MSc Psychology conversion course before an MSc in Sport Psychology. There was a difference between the two courses in terms of how it felt to be an older learner. With several other mature students on the general psychology degree, unless discussing something social such as taste in music, differences from other students were not apparent. Though on occasion it felt that younger students thought our experience meant we had additional knowledge or skills creating expectations to lead, help or support them in set tasks. This was not the same for peers within sport psychology where the majority came from a sport science/psychology background therefore had more relevant specific knowledge than me. In addition, I felt like I stood out, interestingly other mature students have also described experiencing similar feelings of awkwardness in the sport psychology learning environment. In this situation it was important to re-cognise I was different but use my experience to build relationships within the group. As one may suggest to clients, I focused on what was within my control and set my own objectives.

Supervised Practice

The journey through supervised professional practice is individually driven within the frameworks prescribed by professional societies (in the UK these are the British Psychological Society and British Association of Sport and Exercise Sciences). As practitioners we interact with several groups including clients/employers, educa-tional providers, and peer groups. However, for me the key relationship is that with the supervisory team, it is constant throughout every element of the journey. Supervision provides opportunities for regular discussion, seeking advice/guid-ance, reflect on reflection, and so on. Of central importance to the efficacy of this relationship is ensuring, as we would with clients, that the right conditions are in place. This begins with making sure you have selected the right supervisor. I have supervision provided as part of my course though it was still important to choose the right one.[2] With the structure in place, it then takes time to develop the professional and working relationship.

The process of developing this relationship is not necessarily straight forward. Rønnestad and Skovholt (2012) reported that research in counselling had found supervision could be frustrating, examples included differences in professional philosophy or a realisation that a supervisor may not be significantly more knowledgeable than the trainee. This begs a question regarding how do trainee practitioners ensure a supervisory experience which will benefit them and reflect onto their interactions with clients? At the heart of these relationships is the power between the individuals involved, for example, supervisor -> trainee practitioner, and trainee practitioner -> client. Arrows indicate the traditional expert led direction of power transfer, where one party exerts influence over another within the relationship. However, my lens will be different from someone else's and how this dynamic works needs to be considered from the appropriate perspective. As discussed in previous sections, client led preferences mean I prefer bidirectional relationships rather than linear transfer from expert to novice. I think principles of the British Psychological Society's Power Threat Meaning Framework (Johnstone & Boyle, 2018) offers a nice structure to explore this further. I would recommend reading this as it combines narratives around the structure of Power, Threat, and Meaning to describe an individual's story.

---

[2] If information is required about the process of selecting a supervisor, Tomlinson and Alexander (2017) provide an informative short guide.

My story is: a clear and formal mentor/mentee relationship with a supervisor exists, previous experience meant I was aware of my preferences which helped me take control when making my choice; for example, I know that I am quite an informal but reactive type of person, so sought that type of relationship with my supervisor. I would be frustrated working with someone who restricted access to, say, a weekly email and monthly meeting – I am not saying this structure/formality is a bad way to work, but not for me. The meaning I attribute to our relationship and constructive nature of feedback given, mean that I feel I am guided rather than being told. This enables me to reflect and develop appropriate steps to move forward, ultimately solutions are co-produced as the relationship is not a unidirectional advice transfer. I feel comfortable and supported rather than in a position of weakness. Our underlying positions are different, my lead supervisor comes from a practitioner led background, which means on occasion that we both experience some form of challenge during the process. However, and I think this is key, I can draw on life experiences and previous mentoring activities to gain a sense of perspective which influence my responses. My former colleagues would testify this is more interactive than how my younger self responded in similar career development situations!

Qualification Requirements

Finally, there is one power dynamic not often discussed, meeting the qualification requirements within prescribed time limits. My course is three years in duration; year 1 was affected by the COVID pandemic. As the second year approached, whilst not in dire straits, I identified a need to increase my consultancy hours. Paid roles for trainees come up infrequently and competition is fierce as there is currently an oversupply of MSc level graduates in a small market – this could be the subject of a whole different reflection. A three-day per week role was advertised (note that the recruiter's process was excellent, providing a practical learning exercise for candidates as well as an interview). Whilst driving home, immediate reflections were that I was not sure this was the right job for me but could not put my finger on why. Ultimately, I was unsuccessful. However, with more structured reflection and supervisory discussion, I recognised this was perhaps fortuitous. My response to the perceived threat of not having enough practice hours had been to apply for the role. Reflection led me to recognise that I like the autonomy associated with practicing independently, was not ready to give up working with a portfolio of clients and most importantly not compromise the flexibility in work-life commitments I sought from changing career. My experience of life told me that other opportunities would come up, they did, and the immediate threat passed.

Now What (in Conclusion)

This reflection has considered three independent, but related experiences during the early part of professional training. It has focused on how the trainee, who is embarking on a subsequent career in mid-life, has identified life-span changes influencing them during this journey. Central to this is recognition in understanding the importance of their values and authentic true-self, and how it has affected them in establishing practitioner identity. Importantly, recognising that values and experiences that affect the individual across lifespan have changed. For the older trainee, this life-experience may lead to feeling different to their peers and change how they interpret and deal with challenges as their career develops. It is important to manage, often self-generated, anxiety when finding it difficult to marry self-concept with philosophy and practice. All trainees have access to significant supervisory and peer support, which they should unconditionally engage with, embrace, and use to become a better practitioner. If it feels odd to go from expert to learner, do not be afraid of this. Be consistent with your why, draw on previous experiences, engage in your journey, and enjoy it.

REFLECTIVE QUESTIONS

- Do you know your why, values, and how you want to position self?
- Are you being true to your authentic self? (Though recognise that this may change during your lifetime.)
- How are you engaging in training, supervision, and peer support activities? (This will support you when experimenting with approaches in a safe space, but always make sure it is the client's interest being served.)
- As a subsequent career trainee do you feel different? Are you drawing on relevant previous experience whilst establishing self within sport and exercise psychology?
- If you identify apparent conflicts, how are you going to reflect, and engage with supervisors and peers?

References

Aoyagi, M. W., Poczwardowski, A., Statler, T., Shapiro, J. L., & Cohen, A. B. (2017). The Performance Interview Guide: Recommendations for initial consultations in sport and performance psychology. *Professional Psychology: Research and Practice, 48*(5), 352–360. doi:10.1037/pro0000121

Johnstone, L. & Boyle, M. withCromby, J., Dillon, J., Harper, D., Kinderman, P., Longden, E., Pilgrim, D., & Read, J. (2018). *The Power Threat Meaning Framework: Towards the Identification of Patterns in Emotional Distress, Unusual Experiences and Troubled or Troubling Behaviour, as an Alternative to Functional Psychiatric Diagnosis.* British Psychological Society. www.bps.org.uk/PTM-Main

Keegan, R. (2015). *Being a Sport Psychologist.* Macmillan International Higher Education.

Lubker, J., & Andersen, M. B. (2014). Ethical issues in supervision: Client welfare, practitioner development, and professional gatekeeping. In E. Etzel & J. Watson II (Eds.), *Ethical Issues in Sport, Exercise, and Performance Psychology* (pp. 151–162). Fitness Information Technology.

Maslow, A. H. (1943). A theory of human motivation. *Psychological Review, 50*(4), 370–396. doi:10.1037.h0054346

McEwan, H. E., Tod, D., & Eubank, M. (2019). The rocky road to individuation: Sport psychologists' perspectives on professional development. *Psychology of Sport and Exercise, 45*, 101542. doi:10.1016/j.psychsport.2019.101542

Merry, T. (2012). Classical client-centred therapy. In P. Sanders (Ed.), *The Tribes of the Person-Centred Nation: An Introduction to the Schools of Therapy Related to the Person-Centred Approach* (2nd ed., pp. 21–45). PCCS Books.

Miller, W. R., C'de Baca, J., Matthews, D. B., & Wilbourne, P. (2011). *Personal Values Card Sort.* University of New Mexico.

Nicholls, J. G. (1984). Achievement motivation: Conceptions of ability, subjective experience, task choice, and performance. *Psychological Review, 91*, 328–346. doi:10.1037/0033-295X.91.3.328

Nicholls, J. G. (1989). *The Competitive Ethos and Democratic Education.* Harvard University Press.

Poczwardowski, A., Sherman, C. P., & Ravizza, K. (2004). Professional philosophy in the sport psychology service delivery: Building on theory and practice. *The Sport Psychologist, 18*, 445–463. doi:10.1123/tsp.18.4.445

Robinson, O. C. (2013). Values and adult age: Findings from two cohorts of the European Social Survey. *European Journal of Ageing, 10*(1), 11–23. doi:10.1007/s10433-012-0247-3

Rogers, C. R. (1957). The necessary and sufficient conditions of therapeutic personality change. *Journal of Consulting Psychology, 21*(2), 95–103. doi:10.1037/h0045357

Rogers, C. (1961). *On Becoming a Person.* Houghton Mifflin.

Rønnestad, M. H., & Skovholt, T. M. (2003). The journey of the counselor and therapist: Research findings and perspectives on professional development. *Journal of Career Development, 30*(1), 5–44. doi:10.1177/089484530303000102

Rønnestad, M. H., & Skovholt, T. M. (2012). *The Developing Practitioner: Growth and Stagnation of Therapists and Counselors.* Routledge.

Ryan, R. M., & Deci, E. L. (2000). Self-determination theory and the facilitation of intrinsic motivation, social development, and well-being. *American Psychologist, 55*(1), 68–78. doi:10.1037/0003-066X.55.1.68

Sanders, P. (Ed.). (2012). *The Tribes of the Person-Centred Nation: An Introduction to the Schools of Therapy Related to The Person-Centred Approach* (2nd ed.). PCCS Books.

Tod, D., Hutter, R. I., & Eubank, M. (2017). Professional development for sport psychology practice. *Current Opinion in Psychology, 16*, 134–137. doi:10.1016/2017.05.007

Tomlinson, V., & Alexander, B. (2017). Finding a supervisor. How can you create the right match? In A. Pope-Rhodius, S. Robinson, & S. Fitzpatrick (Eds.), *Excelling in Sport Psychology: Planning, Preparing and Executing Applied Work* (pp.24–33). Routledge.

Vilar, R., Liu, J. H.-f., & Gouveia, V. V. (2020). Age and gender differences in human values: A 20-nation study. *Psychology and Aging, 35*(3), 345–356. doi:10.1037/pag0000448

Worsley, R. (2012). Integrating with integrity. In P. Sanders (Ed.), *The Tribes of the Person-Centred Nation: An Introduction to the Schools of Therapy Related to the Person-Centred Approach* (2nd ed., pp. 161–186). PCCS Books.

10

AN INSIDE JOB: THE JOURNEY FROM ELITE ATHLETE TO SPORT PSYCHOLOGIST

Karla Drew

Introduction and Background

I am currently a lecturer in sport and exercise psychology at Staffordshire University in the UK. My educational background has followed the typical progression from BSc, MSc, to PhD which was completed at Liverpool John Moores University. For my professional training, I have undertaken the British Psychological Society's (BPS) qualification in sport and exercise psychology (QSEP) route which I successfully passed in 2020.

In terms of my sporting background, I have dedicated myself to track-and-field for over 15 years of my life. I have represented Great Britain in the Heptathlon and Pentathlon from 2010 to 2018. Throughout these years, I have had to negotiate numerous challenges which are common amongst many athletes such as moving away to university, experiencing a change in coach and training group, and trying to balance my various commitments inside and outside of sport, just to name a few. Taking part in competitive sport has allowed me to develop several skills and attributes (e.g., work ethic, commitment) that are applicable to other domains of my life (e.g., lecturing, education, applied practice).

The aim of this chapter is to reflect on some of the benefits and issues associated with carrying out applied sport psychology practice through the lens of an ex-international athlete.[1] Specifically, the chapter will share my journey from athlete to sport psychologist, reflecting on the impact of receiving sport psychology provision as an athlete on my development and practice to date. This chapter

---

[1] For further insight into sport psychology from an athlete's perspective, check out 'Learnings from Five Olympic Games' by former Great Britain Olympic Rower Frances Houghton MBE and 'Mind Games' by fellow former GB Olympic Rower Annie Vernon.

DOI: 10.4324/9781003263890-14

introduces the complexities of practitioner self-disclosure and highlights some key considerations of self-disclosing in applied sport psychology practice. Finally, this chapter concludes by offering some reflections regarding the benefits and pitfalls as a sport psychologist with a background as a competitive athlete.

The Other Side of the Fence: The Impact of Sport Psychology Support

In 2012, I began working with a sport psychologist following the recommendation of my coach. At the time, I was studying for a BSc in Psychology but despite being a committed athlete, I had little understanding of sport psychology and what it involved. In fact, I remember thinking that sport psychology was a bit 'fluffy' and all you needed was a positive mental attitude and you would be well on your way to success and glory. During my degree, I thought a career in clinical psychology awaited me – that was until I met Chris Marshall.

Chris was a sport psychologist at the English Institute of Sport (EIS). The EIS is lead supplier of sport science support to Olympic and Paralympic sports and the largest employer of sport psychologists in the UK. My coach introduced us and hoped Chris would be able to support me with a few performance-related issues I was experiencing. Over several months, I met with Chris regularly as we worked on developing some strategies for alleviating the identified problem. The work we did was not ground-breaking; we used simple techniques that were effective in helping me to overcome certain barriers to my performance. The sessions with Chris helped me to stay in control of my own performance, but they were *so* much more than that.

During our consultations, my interest in sport psychology was ignited. Chris must have seen this and took the time to educate me on various topics. Chris did not just equip me with the techniques to improve my performance, he educated me on the underlying principles and mechanisms involved in implementing these strategies. For example, Chris recommended I read a paper by Shiv and Fedorikhin (1999) which helped me to understand that if my process resources are constrained during competition (i.e., I am overthinking, focusing on unnecessary information) then I am likely to make decisions based on affective (e.g., emotional) rather than cognitive (e.g., logical) reactions which we felt was likely to hinder my performance. Chris would regularly explain relevant theories, models, and research to me to help me understand the rationale for our work together. Although this would not necessarily be a successful approach with all athletes, I enjoyed this a lot. I liked to understand why we were taking a certain approach to improve my performance and I think understanding the rationale increased my 'buy in' and acceptance of certain strategies. As I began to understand that sport psychology was more than having a *positive mental attitude*, Chris had not only ignited my interest in sport psychology but had helped me to find my passion and future career.

Being an athlete receiving psychological support has clearly shaped me today. It has shaped my sporting achievements, personal development, and professional development. Whilst writing this chapter I reflected on some of the benefits of being on *the other side of the fence* and receiving psychological provision, and particularly how this has impacted my practice today. Gaining genuine experience of assuming the role of both the client and the practitioner has given me insight into what this relationship might look like from both perspectives. Looking back as the client, I can appreciate the vulnerability of seeking help and understand the dynamics of the practitioner-client relationship as well as the therapeutic process.

Being on the other side of the fence has given me the opportunity to increase my own self-knowledge and consider how this may impact my own practice. Petitpas, Giges, and Danish (1999) highlighted the important of self-awareness in effective applied sport psychology practice. They emphasised the importance of self-knowledge and recommended that practitioners should reflect on their knowledge of themselves and the world to ensure that they are meeting their clients' needs rather than their own. Exploring myself with the support of a sport psychologist has helped me to understand myself better as an athlete, person, and practitioner.

Similarly, Tod (2007) has suggested that sport psychologists can learn important lessons from other psychology disciplines, such as clinical or counselling psychology. Certainly, within the clinical and counselling profession, personal therapy is strongly endorsed for personal and professional development (McEwan & Tod, 2015), but much less has been discussed in relation to sport. For example, it may be beneficial for trainee practitioners to engage with sport psychology services, or personal therapy for their own personal and professional development. Specifically, personal therapy may increase practitioners' self-awareness of how their own issues can impact client interactions. The use of personal therapy for personal development has been advocated to be included as a component of applied sport psychology training (Petitpas, Giges, & Danish, 1999) as it encourages an in-depth self-examination as well as increasing awareness of the therapeutic process (McEwan & Tod, 2015). Engaging with sport psychology provision helped to increase my own awareness and understanding of applied sport psychology and the therapeutic process.

CASE VIGNETTE: IT'S NOT ME, IT'S YOU

Whilst I believe working with a sport psychologist has helped to increase my self-awareness, it still requires constant reflection when working with clients. For example, whilst I was a trainee sport psychologist, I was working with a client, David*. David also competed in track-and-field, like me, but in terms of our approach to competition we were quite different. When I was competing, I loved to have structure in my approach to performance, I liked to know exactly what I would be focusing on for all my disciplines and would keep notes in my kitbag which I would take to each event to help maintain my focus. David on the other hand preferred a more flexible approach and his performances were fuelled by his strong competitive drive and focusing his energy into progressing towards his goals. David would be willing to make more 'risky' and confident decisions at the prospect of winning the big prize. After a thorough needs analysis and identifying some of the performance issues David was experiencing, I reflected that there were some similarities to one issue I had previously worked on with Chris. With David, there were times during his performances, usually at the pinnacle of the competition, where he needed to hone his attention in to focus on task-relevant information. In terms of my performance issue, sometimes when I was competing, particularly during one event of the heptathlon – the shot putt – I struggled to recover psychologically from a poor throw. This event at the time was one of my weakest out of the seven disciplines and if did not manage to get a good distance with my first throw, I would struggle to remain calm and focused for my remaining two throws, which as you can imagine would often result in a disappointing performance. Generally, I maintained a calm, logical, and structured approach to my competitions, but in my early days of competing, when things would go wrong, I often produced an internal, emotional response, where I would then struggle to maintain my attention on appropriate task related information. Chris and I worked together to develop, what we called a 'mental warm up'. Part of this warmup involved the use of a pre-performance routine for the shot put, which was used to help me maintain task-related attention.

Whilst working with David, I remember thinking that if the intervention worked for me, then it could work for David too. However, I think this is where the benefit of engaging in sport psychology support and education helped me to understand myself and what works for me, but importantly, how my view of the world can be vastly different to those of other athletes, including my clients. I shared with a mentor that I sometimes find myself considering an intervention for a client that I know would be likely to work for me, rather than them. Increasing my self-knowledge through sport psychology provision has made me more self-aware of my own behavioural preferences. It has helped me to reflect before I act, and I have found self-management strategies such as seeking advice from a mentor, to be crucial in my professional development.

Finally, being on the other side of the fence and receiving sport psychology support has also helped me to understand the type of psychologist I want to be. It helped me to recognise the practitioner qualities that I value as the client (e.g., authentic, approachable, respectful) and again, consider and reflect on the psychologist I want to become. Before even applying for a Master's degree, through my work with Chris, I already recognised the importance of the client–practitioner relationship; having complete trust in the practitioner to allow myself to be vulnerable and open in our conversations. Chris was not solely focused on 'fixing' my performance issues but instead took the time to support my development away from the athletics track. From the early days in my journey to becoming a sport psychologist, it has been important to value the client sat in front of me, that is the whole client, not just them as a sports performer. This is something that has developed from my own experiences of receiving psychological support and has informed my practice to date. In fact, there have been times during consultations where I have shared with clients my own experiences of receiving psychological support and the impact this had on my own performance and wellbeing. I have found that these types of disclosures can enhance the therapeutic alliance and help demystify the therapeutic process (Kaslow, Cooper, & Linsenberg, 1979).

Self-disclosure

As briefly mentioned, another topic discussed within counselling and clinical psychology settings, but less so in sport and exercise, is practitioner self-disclosure. Knox et al. (1997) broadly defined self-disclosure as, 'an interaction in which the [practitioner] reveals personal information about him/herself, and/or reveals reactions and responses to the client as they arise in the session' (p. 275). There are many different subtypes of disclosures, for example, disclosure of facts, feelings, strategy, and insight, are among a few (Knox & Hill, 2003), all of which can be used to serve a different purpose and can have a different impact on our practice.

At this juncture, it may be useful to share that I practice applied sport psychology from a humanistic perspective. Broadly and briefly summarised, humanistic practitioners focus on the interpersonal relationships to make sense of the moment-to-moment experiences of the client (Poczwardowski, Sherman, & Ravizza, 2004). Humanistic therapists subscribe to the underlying assumption that each individual (e.g., client) has their own unique interpretations of the world. In contrast to more traditional therapeutic approaches (e.g., psychodynamic), many humanistic psychologists allow for the use of open self-disclosures.

The use of self-disclosure in applied sport psychology consultancy is likely to be impacted by your philosophical orientation, especially if congruence between the practitioner's philosophy and methods has been achieved (Lindsay et al., 2007). Your philosophical orientation will impact your perception of practitioner self-disclosure and whether you deem it to be an appropriate technique to use during consultations. However, from a humanistic paradigm, practitioner self-disclosure can be used to demonstrate genuineness and authenticity, which can in turn prompt clients' openness, develop an empathic understanding and trust (Knox & Hill, 2003). Practitioner self-disclosure can be used to normalise clients' feelings and worries while equalising the power dynamic in the therapeutic relationship (Bradley, Tufton, & Hemmings, 2019). Furthermore, practitioner self-disclosure may also help the client to feel understood and build a connection with the practitioner, as well as being a useful tool to develop rapport (Way & Vosloo, 2016). Practitioner self-disclosure can also be a useful tool to help to create a psychologically safe environment in which the client feels comfortable to share their own experiences. As described by Jourard (1971), 'the most effective way to invite authentic disclosure from another is to take the risky lead and offer it oneself, first' (p. 184). I have also found self-disclosure to be useful when supporting clients to understand and apply certain psychological skills or interventions. For example, when working with a young athlete to develop a pre-performance routine, I have shown them my own competition routine to illustrate the process and provide a real-life example. This type of disclosure is known as disclosure of strategy (Knox & Hill, 2003). This disclosure helped the athlete grasp the concept of a pre-performance routine and what we would be looking to develop during the session. I personally have found when working with youth athletes, they can often find it beneficial to see an example to aid comprehension as quite often they are learning about sport psychology for the first time.

Whilst I have been lucky enough to have only positive experiences when using self-disclosure, I subscribe to the literature which generally states when it comes to practitioner self-disclosure *less-is-more* (Way & Vosloo, 2016). That is, if practitioner self-disclosure becomes too frequent it may impact ethical boundaries particularly when trying to maintain a professional relationship (Hill & Knox, 2002). As Dr Martin Turner explained (see MacIntyre, Campbell & Turner, 2014, p. 69), he felt that excessive disclosure on a train journey with the client had a detrimental impact on their professional relationship, 'I felt like he had seen the "real me" and now he was sitting with the "sport psych me". I realised that I couldn't work with him anymore' (While I generally see self-disclosure as a tool to develop rapport, and demonstrate an empathic understanding with the client, it is important to use with caution and avoid inadvertently shifting the focus from the client to yourself.

Although based on clinical provision, Knox and Hill (2003) provided useful suggestions for practitioners when considering self-disclosure, which I like to reflect on before and after self-disclosing. First, it is important to use appropriate content in practitioner self-disclosures. More common disclosures include content that is related to my professional background (e.g., education, professional training route, sporting background) which is generally perceived as being better received than overly personal disclosures (e.g., political, and religious views, sexual orientation; Knox & Hill, 2003). Disclosures that are excessively personal may frighten or burden the client and may also represent boundary issues in the therapeutic relationship. Another important consideration when making disclosures, is to only disclose about personal problems that have been resolved. It is likely that if I were to self-disclose about issues that were ongoing the focus of the consultation could shift from the client to the practitioner to address their own needs. Moreover, it would prove difficult to remain objective when discussing current personal issues and is likely to be unhelpful for the client.

Second, it is important to question your reasoning and purpose for self-disclosing. What are your motivations for self-disclosure? Simply put, self-disclosures should be used to serve the client and can be used to provide information, offer a different perspective, normalise, and validate client experiences, enhance connection and perceived similarity between practitioner and client (Hill &

Knox, 2002). You may decide against disclosing if it is likely to shift the focus from the client to the practitioner, disrupts or interrupts the client, does not serve the client, may burden, or confuse the client, and may blur professional practice boundaries. In contrast, practitioner self-disclosures that are intended to serve the client and enhance the provision of psychological support have been cited as having powerful effects such as promoting a positive working alliance (Ruddle & Dilks, 2015).

Finally, after self-disclosing it is important to return the focus back to the client. For example, I may choose to disclose information to normalise the client's feelings but ensure I finish the disclosure by returning the attention back to the client, perhaps with an open question (e.g., does that sound similar to how you are feeling?).

CASE VIGNETTE: A WELCOMED DISCLOSURE

The following case vignette details an example of where I chose to disclose information to the client during one of our consultations. Nicole* was a university student who took part in a team sport and was struggling to come to terms with a season-ending injury. Nicole had ruptured her anterior cruciate ligament (ACL) and had recently undergone ACL reconstruction surgery, from which recovery can often take as long as 12 months. Nicole was feeling disconnected from her teammates and coach, as she was undertaking her rehabilitation programme and training on her own or with her physiotherapist. Nicole's teammates were preparing for their most important competition of the season which exasperated her feelings of isolation. Nicole felt frustrated that no one understood how she was feeling because none of her teammates had ever experienced a significant injury like she had sustained. At this point, I perceived that there was an opportunity to normalise and validate how Nicole was feeling (e.g., frustrated, isolated) as well as developing our working alliance. I disclosed to Nicole that when I was an athlete, I also ruptured a ligament in my knee that meant I missed a year of sport and important competitions. I normalised her feelings by sharing that I had similar feelings at the time (e.g., frustrated by training hard during the off-season to then lose the chance to compete, feeling isolated from training partners and having to watch them train). Nicole looked genuinely happy and understood; a big smile beamed across her face 'Yes, exactly!'. Through this simple disclosure, I felt Nicole and I generated a deeper personal connection, she knew I understood what she was going through, which I perceived to positively impact the professional relationship.

Self-disclosing is a practitioner skill. You must be able to recognise and be self-aware of when disclosing might be constructive to practice, or when in fact it may be destructive. Self-disclosing must be in the interest of the client and your rationale for disclosing should be clear and purposeful. In this example, my intention was to share my own personal insight of experiencing a similar injury, normalising Nicole's feelings and experiences and increasing the relatedness between Nicole and myself.

My background competing in sport for over 15 years has meant that I have amassed a wide range of experiences (e.g., injury, underperforming, being a student-athlete, non-selection, retirement etc.), most of which many athletes have also experienced and can even serve as the basis of their help-seeking. This has meant the opportunity for self-disclosure can present itself quite often during my consultations. There are various practitioner skills (e.g., self-awareness, empathic understanding, reflection) that are likely to determine the use of self-disclosure (Cropley et al., 2007), as with much of applied sport psychology practice this can come down to our professional judgement. Before and after using self-disclosure, it is worth reflecting on the following three points:

1. Is the content of the disclosure appropriate? Ensure that the content is not too intimate or personal and does not reflect a current issue you are struggling with.
2. What are your motivations for self-disclosing? Make sure your disclosures serve your client and have a purpose.
3. After disclosing information to the client, be sure to return the focus back to them.

I have found practitioner self-disclosure to be a helpful therapeutic tool, particularly when drawing on my own sporting background. When used appropriately and effectively, self-disclosure can enhance the therapeutic relationship, facilitate client disclosure, and normalise the client's feelings.

Athlete-Sport Psychologist: Benefits and Pitfalls

Individuals who have experience of competitive sport, irrespective of their level of performance, will have acquired valuable skills and life lessons that will be applicable to other settings outside of sport (Bernes et al., 2009). For example, throughout my career as an athlete I have learnt several transferable skills that I can now apply to my work as a sport psychologist including dedication, performing under pressure, organisational skills, and self-motivation. I feel as though my background as an athlete has provided me with several benefits as an applied practitioner, but there are also pitfalls to consider.

First, as an athlete, I have gained practical experience of working with a sport psychologist. Specifically, receiving psychological support gave me insight into a few practicalities of delivering sport psychology provision, that I otherwise may not have been exposed to if I did not come from a sporting background. I was supported to develop knowledge of several psychological skills (e.g., imagery, relaxation, pre-performance routines), but more importantly how to apply this to *my* life, well before I had even considered undertaking a professional qualification in sport psychology. This means through supervision, I was supported to practice and master various psychological skills, as well as testing them under pressure in the performance environment. Ravizza argued that as a sport psychology practitioner 'You should never be taking a group through any activity, exercise, or technique that you really haven't gone through yourself' (Simons & Andersen, 1995, p. 463). I have first-hand experience as to what it might feel like as an athlete receiving psychological support and intervention, which I have also found to be a useful tool to develop rapport with the client. However, there are potential pitfalls to avoid if we hold multiple roles such as a former athlete and sport psychologist. For example, it is crucial that I do not let my own sporting experiences and perceptions lead to a loss of objectivity when working with a client. Furthermore, if we hold multiple roles, it is possible to blur the lines of our practitioner role, which can impact our professional and ethical practice. One such example comes from when I was still an athlete and also a sport psychologist in training. There were numerous times when I was at training and a coach would approach me and ask me if I wouldn't mind *having a chat* with one of their athletes who was experiencing *insert performance issue here*. There was never any mention of payment, and my services were framed and devalued as a *chat*. It was these instances, when working in situ it was difficult to shift the working relationship from *athlete* to *sport psychologist* and consequently change the nature of the already formed relationships. I have learnt that it is crucial to set expectations and boundaries from the outset, one free chat with an athlete is often followed by more requests, which can make broaching the conversation about payment more difficult the further you progress with the support. As described by Andersen, Van Raalte, and Brewer (2001), laying ground rules at the beginning of working with potential clients will help avoid awkward moments regarding payment.

That being said, I have found having insider knowledge to be beneficial particularly in understanding the performance environment and having contextual intelligence (Brown, Gould, & Foster, 2005). The professional practice literature suggests that a background in high performance sport can serve as a basis for building rapport and developing trust within the practitioner-client relationship. Athletes have indicated that they value sport psychology consultants who can 'walk the walk' and 'talk the talk' (Woolway & Harwood, 2020). That is, athletes preferred consultants who had experience of competing in the high-performance environment as well as having a good sport-specific knowledge and can talk the language of the sport. That's not to say that all sport psychologists need a background in sport or need to have experience of competing in the high-performance environment. In fact, the foundation to my philosophical approach to professional practice is to explore what the athlete is thinking and feeling and to understand what meaning they attribute to their situation, rather than my interpretation. However, having the sport-specific knowledge and experiences opens the door of mutual respect and understanding and provides the foundation for developing a greater connection and rapport with the client. I feel it is important to consider how we, as sport psychologists, can encourage that connection with our clients. Whether that is through shared experiences, or common interests, take the time to find that common ground.

Concluding Thoughts

This chapter looked to provide personal reflections of my journey from elite athlete to sport psychologist whilst outlining potential key considerations for future or current sport psychologists who either have a sporting background or do not. As reiterated through the chapter, my message is not that experience of competing within elite performance is necessary to do effective consultancy. Instead, I have shared my reflections regarding how my background has influenced my own applied practice, how the use of psychological support has helped to increase my self-awareness as an athlete, person, and sport psychologist. I have also shared how I have used practitioner self-disclosure as a means to facilitate a genuine working alliance, whilst also being mindful of potential pitfalls of ineffective disclosures. It is hoped that by sharing my thoughts, this chapter encourages practitioners to reflect on themselves and their experiences that they bring to the consultation room and how this might impact their practice.

REFLECTIVE QUESTIONS

- Do you have any experience of what it feels like to be *on the other side of the fence*? Can you appreciate what it might feel like to be sat in the position of the client, seeking help?
- Can you think of a time when you have been an insider or an outsider within your applied practice, and how this might have impacted your delivery?
- Consider opportunities to increase your self-awareness and how your own experiences, thoughts, and beliefs might impact your applied practice. For example, personal therapy, journaling, self-reflection, mentoring, and supervision.

References

Andersen, M. B., Van Raalte, J. L., & Brewer, B. W. (2001). Sport psychology service delivery: Staying ethical while keeping loose. *Professional Psychology: Research and Practice*, *32*(1), 12.

Bernes, K. B., McKnight, K. M., Gunn, T., Chorney, D., Orr, D. T., & Bardick, A. D. (2009). Life after sport: Athletic career transition and transferable skills. *Journal of Excellence*, *13*, 63–77.

Bradley, S., Tufton, L., & Hemmings, B. (2019). Self-disclosure within the sport psychologist athlete relationship. *Sport & Exercise Psychology Review, 15*(1), 3–12.

Brown, C. H., Gould, D., & Foster, S. (2005). A framework for developing contextual intelligence (CI). *The Sport Psychologist, 19*(1), 51–62. doi:10.1123/tsp.19.1.51

Cropley, B., Miles, A., Hanton, S., & Niven, A. (2007). Improving the delivery of applied sport psychology support through reflective practice. *The Sport Psychologist, 21*, 475–494. doi:10.1123/tsp.21.4.475

Hill, C. E., & Knox, S. (2002). Therapist self-disclosure. In J. C. Norcross (Ed.), *Psychotherapy Relationships That Work: Therapist Contributions and Responsiveness to Patients* (pp. 255–265). Oxford, UK: Oxford University Press.

Houghton, F. (2021) *Learnings from Five Olympic Games.*

Jourard, S. M. (1971). *Self-Disclosure: An Experimental Analysis of the Transparent Self.* New York, NY: Wiley.

Kaslow, F., Cooper, B., & Linsenberg, M. (1979). Family therapist authenticity as a key factor in outcome. *International Journal of Family Therapy, 1*(2), 184–199. doi:10.1007/BF00926717

Knox, S., Hess, S. A., Petersen, D. A., & Hill, C. E. (1997). A qualitative analysis of client perceptions of the effects of helpful therapist self-disclosure in long-term therapy. *Journal of Counseling Psychology, 44*, 274–283. doi:10.1037/0022-0167.44.3.274

Knox, S., & Hill, C. E. (2003). Therapist self-disclosure: Research-based suggestions for practitioners. *Journal of Clinical Psychology, 59*(5), 529–539. doi:10.1002/jclp.10157

Lindsay, P., Breckon, J. D., Thomas, O., & Maynard, I. W. (2007). In pursuit of congruence: A personal reflection on methods and philosophy in applied practice. *The Sport Psychologist, 21*(3), 335–352. doi:10.1123/tsp.21.3.335

MacIntyre, T., Campbell, M., & Turner, M. (2014). From baptism to immersion: How wet should we get in consulting. *Sport & Exercise Psychology Review, 10*, 65–74.

McEwan, H. E., & Tod, D. (2015). Learning experiences contributing to service-delivery competence in applied psychologists: Lessons for sport psychologists. *Journal of Applied Sport Psychology, 27*(1), 79–93. doi:10.1080/10413200.2014.952460

Petitpas, A. J., Giges, B., & Danish, S. J. (1999). The sport psychologist-athlete relationship: Implications for training. *The Sport Psychologist, 13*, 344–357. doi:10.1123/tsp.13.3.344

Poczwardowski, A., Sherman, C. P., & Ravizza, K. (2004). Professional philosophy in the sport psychology service delivery: Building on theory and practice. *The Sport Psychologist, 18*(4), 445–463. doi:10.1123/tsp.18.4.445

Ruddle, A., & Dilks, S. (2015). Opening up to disclosure. *The Psychologist, 28*(6), 458–461.

Shiv, B., & Fedorikhin, A. (1999). Heart and mind in conflict: The interplay of affect and cognition in consumer decision making. *Journal of consumer Research, 26*(3), 278–292.

Simons, J. P., & Andersen, M. B. (1995). The development of consulting practice in applied sport psychology: Some personal perspectives. *The Sport Psychologist, 9*, 449–468. doi:10.1123/tsp.9.4.449

Tod, D. (2007). The long and winding road: Professional development in sport psychology. *The Sport Psychologist, 21*(1), 94–108. doi:10.1123/tsp.21.1.94

Vernon, A. (2019). *Mind Games.* London: Bloomsbury Sport.

Way, W., & Vosloo, J. (2016). Practical considerations for self-disclosure in applied sport psychology. *Journal of Sport Psychology in Action, 7*(1), 23–32. doi:10.1080/21520704.2015.1123207

Woolway, T., & Harwood, C. G. (2020). Consultant characteristics in sport psychology service provision: A critical review and future research directions. *International Journal of Sport and Exercise Psychology, 18*(1), 46–63. doi:10.1080/1612197X.2018.1462230

11

PERSONALISING A SPORT PSYCHOLOGY STYLE FOR INDIVIDUAL AND TEAM CONSULTING

Megan Gossfeld

Introduction

Individual sport psychology consulting styles are not just developed after years of work, but as soon as one's career begins. In many cases, personal life experiences long before our introduction to the field contribute to professional approaches. Beginning sport psychology practitioners can work towards creating an authentic consulting style by making the most of graduate training experiences, experimenting with public speaking, identifying a theoretical orientation, coming to terms with mistakes, and exemplifying mental wellbeing in our personal lives. Dare to ask the hard questions: What do I believe about athletic potential? How do I impact people? What am I doing wrong? What can I do with my precious time on this planet? I encourage readers to view development of a consulting style not just as choosing interventions, but as a journey of self-exploration. My former professor used to say, 'You are your best tool'. Avoid searching for the perfect approach to consulting, and instead look inward to grow into a stronger consulting 'tool'. This chapter will explore how beginning sport psychology practitioners can enrich their consulting style through a culmination of personal aspiration, mistakes, team workshop experience, stories, and values.

Gleaning Inspiration from Graduate Training

From the very onset of graduate training programs, beginning sport psychology practitioners can develop unique consulting styles. Although accumulated experience and education are undoubtedly key to seasoned sport psychology careers, there is also much to gain from early exposure to everything the field offers. I chose to attend my specific master's program because it provided the opportunity

DOI: 10.4324/9781003263890-15

to start working with sport teams right away. My first-year colleagues and I began shadowing second-year students during the very first week of the program. Immediately I fell in love with the applied nature of sport psychology. Before even fully understanding what sport psychology career options lay before me or how to navigate them, I was suddenly collaborating with classmates to serve local teams. Early on, I observed elder colleagues form connections with coaches, establish rapport with new teams, and brainstorm mental skills workshops catered to a team's specific needs. How thrilling to bring empirical research into a living, breathing, competitive field! As a hands-on learner, I much preferred working with real athletes and teams over learning only from textbooks and lectures. Soon enough we also learned about empirical sport psychology theories and mental training skills, but I believe our program's strength was early exposure to consulting work.

While graduate school offers many chances to learn about sport psychology, only a small fraction takes place within the classroom. Supplementing one's graduate training with extra projects and events can offer real-world inspiration. I seized every opportunity within my program to learn what sport psychology has to offer, helping colleagues by conducting research, assisting with presentations, and attending conferences. By observing more service delivery in action, learning new research techniques, and meeting some of the best sport psychology practitioners in the world, I gained a sense of what direction to take my own career. It is not always easy to accept every opportunity presented, as the basic human needs of eating, sleeping, exercising, and relaxing are all too often neglected in graduate school. While I deeply believe in embracing every learning opportunity, I caution graduate students not to glamorise the idea of overworking oneself through 'the grind'. By establishing a routine of regular self-care, graduate students can best muster the energy to seek out enriching opportunities.

Aside from exposure to a myriad of different sport psychology settings and workshops, graduate school also prompts early career practitioners to develop interpersonal styles of delivering content to athletes and teams. Early on I learned this field is just as much about sport and psychology as it is about public speaking. While many early career practitioners find this aspect of consulting intimidating, the associated stress and anxiety can be combatted with our own use of psychological skills like deep breathing and self-talk (Tod et al., 2011). Beginning sport psychology practitioners can reference self-practice resources like *The Mindful Athlete*,[1] *Beyond Grit*,[2] or *Mind Gym*[3] to improve our own delivery skills using the same psychological training skills we share with athletes.

---

[1] Mumford, G. (2015). *The Mindful Athlete: Secrets to Pure Performance*. Berkeley, CA: Parallax Press.
[2] Kamphoff, C. (2017). *Beyond Grit*. Minneapolis, MN: Itasca Press.
[3] Mack, G. (2002). *Mind Gym: An Athlete's Guide to Inner Excellence*. New York, NY: McGraw-Hill.

In overcoming these initial jitters, sport psychology practitioners can more comfortably settle into their authentic tone of presenting. Some of my mentors were loud and energetic, while others were soft-spoken and thought-provoking. After trying and failing to copy other's boisterous or scholarly styles, I eventually settled into a presentation mode of my own. I use visual demonstrations, humorous anecdotes, and concrete acronyms to make my workshops instructive and engaging. When preparing to deliver sport psychology content, also bear in mind one's reasons for selecting mental training interventions. A professor of mine always asked us if we knew which theories or models grounded our workshops. I realise now when sports psychology work loses scientific rationale, it dissolves into motivational speaking or pep talks. To balance delivery of educational content with entertaining interactions, our supervisors often used the term 'edutainment'. This reminder helped me and my colleagues in delivering informative yet fun and memorable services. Depending on the audience's age, maturity, or mood, a practitioner can adjust their delivery to prioritise engagement, promote retention, or infuse enjoyment. To this day I still ask myself if my services speak to an appropriate edutainment ratio, reflect my authentic interpersonal style, and are grounded in theory. All practitioners continue to develop personal consulting styles throughout their careers, so it is important to initiate a sense of comfort with public speaking early on. While personal consulting styles are evident in both individual and team settings, our work impacts exponentially more athletes through public speaking, thus necessitating a comfort with team delivery style.

Developing a Theoretical Orientation

It is valuable for sport psychology practitioners to develop authentic styles of working with athletes. Although competence in many mental training interventions and approaches is useful, all practitioners inevitably gravitate towards specific styles (Keegan, 2010). For early career practitioners to identify their theoretical orientation, three questions can be particularly helpful: 'What is my role as a practitioner?', 'What do I believe?', and 'How do I make that happen?' The first question regarding our role offers a clue to our natural working style. Personally, I see my role as a guide alongside athletes' mental training journeys, positioning athletes as autonomous experts in their craft. That said, one can understand why I typically use a humanistic or person-centred counselling style (Walker, 2010). The second question about beliefs informs the psychological theories we draw upon in our sport psychology practice. For example, I truly believe in an athlete's ability to overcome, heal, evolve, and improve no matter how challenging the circumstances are. Whether I meet an athlete performing at the peak of their career or struggling to manage a seemingly impossible obstacle, I always desire to instil hope and motivation in whatever form someone needs. After a practitioner identifies their role and beliefs, they can consider the third question, 'How do I make that happen?' This prompt clarifies the actual approaches we use to act out our roles and beliefs. My mental training workshops typically involve movement-based activities so athletes can remember the content with muscle memory. Tangible interventions are integral to my consulting style because they align with my role as a demonstrator and my belief that athletes can master mental training skills in their own way. Once a sport psychology practitioner pinpoints their ideal role, beliefs, and approaches, they can develop a consulting style aligned with their theoretical orientation.

When developing a personal consulting style, beginning sport psychology practitioners should keep in mind how our personal life experiences impact the development of our professional style. Best practices encourage the separation of personal and professional aspects of life to maintain ethical and healthy boundaries (Anderson et al., 2000). Yet we would be remiss to ignore the human emotions encountered while guiding athletes through their journeys of growth. The earliest impact of sports on my life was the comfort from rituals and routine. I remember looking forward to Fun Run 5K races, rooting for beloved teams on TV, and showing up to daily practices with a team which felt like family. Throughout the highs and lows of life there always remained weekly football broadcasts, afternoon practices, and a never-ending cycle of training seasons. What I enjoyed most about life as a young athlete was not a pursuit of victory but simply showing up every day, putting effort into something I loved, and getting a bit better along the way. Early on, sport inadvertently taught me to value progress over perfection.

This process-oriented mindset helped me through my lowest of lows after losing my father suddenly when I was 16 years old. When faced with something as incomprehensible and unfixable as death, there is no way to find the right way to move on, because there is none. Yet despite my utter disbelief, there was still a certainty of 3:30 PM practices. Even when my head felt confused, my body still knew how to put one foot in front of the other. Even when no words of sympathy were helpful to hear, I loved listening to the inconsequential chatting and gossip of my teammates. Even when my body felt numb, there was amazing relief in sprinting, sweating, and racing. Eventually the workouts turned into weeks, the weeks turned into seasons, and the seasons turned into years, until I did not feel so numb anymore. At this point, my athletic career was not about winning or losing, but trying. Of course, it felt nice to win, but I knew better than most athletes of my age there are more important things in life to cherish and much harder things in life to lose than a competition. To this day, I am grateful for every opportunity to train hard and have fun in sport, just as I see every day as a gift. Since I personally believe in the power of the process, I can bring this perspective of hope within my applied practice too.

The reason I fully embrace mental training skills like mindfulness, gratitude, and resilience is because I witnessed their effectiveness through personal experiences, not just from textbooks and lectures. In fact, many sport psychology practitioners report personal use of mental training skills apart from working with athletes (Pack et al., 2014; Filion, Munroe-Chandler & Loughead, 2021). Personally, my existential outlook on life as a teenager contributed to the very theoretical orientation which grounds my sport psychology practice today. My approach is also heavily influenced by Jungian therapy of striving towards a whole, balanced self (Jung, 1914). Beginning sport psychology practitioners would benefit from reflecting on experiences or values which led them to their sport psychology role. Try as we might to support athletes' mentality from a neutral stance, we are not impartial beings. Rather, every practitioner is a concoction of past experiences, values, and goals. Not only is it practically impossible to fully remove personal attributes from our professional role, but a missed opportunity in authentically enriching our professional consulting style.[4]

'I Am Sure We Will Look Back and Laugh One Day!'

Creating a personal consulting style is just as much about fine-tuning our strengths as it is about coming to terms with our weaknesses. One of my biggest improvements in delivering team workshops was learning from mistakes. It can be a tough realisation for highly motivated and perfectionistic graduate students when workshops do not go as planned. We learn about theories to improve athletes' confidence, motivation, and focus, but when our first workshop is about to begin, suddenly our own confidence, motivation, and focus go out the window. Ironically, as much as we pursue expertise in the science of high performance, every early career practitioner still has fears, doubts, and, of course, imposter syndrome.[5] Anyone who finds themselves in a workshop with sweaty hands, trembling words, or wondering 'What on earth am I doing here?' should remember that the biggest mistake is not from imperfection but failing to learn from errors.

The first team workshop I ever led was frankly a disaster. I remember my colleagues and I were told to expect 20 athletes, but we arrived to a room full of well over 80 attendees. My heart dropped through my stomach when I saw athletes leaning on walls and sitting on the floor. Not only was there inadequate seating, but we also lacked enough handouts and pens. I felt my face flush and limbs tremble. Never before had I spoken in front of such as large team. My memory of the workshop content was a blur, but I recall trying and failing to project my quivering voice to everyone in the room. Afterwards my colleagues gently informed me I stood so far back from the team that my back literally touched the front wall. It was the worst team workshop I ever led and probably the most embarrassing experience of my life. However, I'll be damned if I ever make those same mistakes again! Now I bring extra supplies, arrive early, and overly communicate logistics with coaches. I chuckle to think of my younger self squished against the wall as I now walk around a room full of athletes, weaving

---

4   Early career practitioners looking to explore various theoretical models can reference *The Routledge Handbook of Applied Sport Psychology* by Hanrahan et al. (2010) detailing the distinctions among theoretical models including person-centred, cognitive-behavioural, positive psychology, existential, psychodynamic, family systems, acceptance-based, and various Eastern philosophical approaches.

5   Early career practitioners facing these barriers may appreciate self-practice resources such as '*You are a Badass; How to Stop Doubting Your Greatness and Lead an Awesome Life*' by Jen Sincero or '*The Subtle Art of Not Giving a F*ck*' by Mark Manson.

around tables, asking for volunteers, and projecting my voice. Some lessons are hard to learn, but they also lead to our biggest improvements.

One of my fondest mistakes from a team workshop I led took place on a grassy playing field. The topic was control, so my colleagues and I invited the athletes to consider how they can focus on athletic abilities within their control compared to external factors outside their control. The team wrote examples on post-it notes which we stuck onto a poster board. I remember it was a beautifully warm day, but very windy. Of course, when my colleagues and I held up the poster board, saying 'There are always elements of performance outside your control', a strong gust of wind ripped the papers off, scattering them across the entire field. The athletes' surprise turned into amusement as we added, 'Indeed, there are always things we cannot control!' Yet another valuable lesson cemented into my memory while picking up papers afterwards: No detail is too small to overlook, especially with outdoor workshops!

I now anticipate worst-case scenarios when preparing individual sessions and team workshops: What if the room is locked? What if the team does not show up? What if the facility does not have the correct laptop adapter? What if my car battery does not start in the cold weather? What if I become ill the night before the workshop? What if the coach makes a last-minute request for a 15-minute workshop instead of 50 minutes? What if there is a global pandemic? Although these real-life situations were frustrating at the time, they presented opportunities to sharpen my skills. It is extremely humbling to study the science of high performance, only to find yourself trembling against a classroom wall or chasing papers across a field. Looking back, these memories have become reminders that despite mistakes, improvement is possible. In fact, moments of painful growth are the very experiences we strive to help athletes overcome. By trusting in our own abilities and believing in ourselves despite challenges, athletes may appreciate we too are imperfect yet choose to keep trying. By allowing athletes to witness our imperfections, we invite them to join alongside us in a pursuit of growth.

The Bigger Picture

There are many powerful ways sport psychology practitioners can embody the very mental performance messages we deliver to athletes. Our very ambitions, values, and habits are all evident to athletes. There is a large responsibility and opportunity to use our authentic selves as helping professionals. One way sport psychology practitioners can form personal consulting styles is by considering how we approach our own aspirations. I personally benefitted from processing my career aspirations throughout a period of self-doubt. After earning my master's degree, I felt drawn to expand my sport psychology opportunities by starting a private practice, but worried about lacking business, finance, and entrepreneurship training. Sure enough, there were several obstacles. It felt daunting to watch veteran entrepreneurs expand their successful practices to reach larger, more elite populations. I stressed about gaining enough clients and profit. Although my perfectionism and comparisons were well-intentioned, I eventually realised I needed to transition to an intrinsic source of motivation (Vallerand, 1997). I was so determined to create a perfect private practice that I lost sight of the bigger picture: my original goal to expand my sport psychology skills. In refocusing my entrepreneurial efforts inward, I chose to practice gratitude for areas of growth like marketing skills, social media use, web development, networking, and continuing education. With this mindset adjustment, I felt much more enjoyment and motivation towards my private practice. If I want athletes to practice the mindset of 'progress over perfection', I should do the same in my professional life too. It takes a lot of courage and risk to try something completely new, but I believe that is exactly where we have the most potential for growth.

Another aspect of sport psychology practitioners' consulting styles that become evident to athletes are our values. In the helping professions, we interact with hundreds of individuals throughout our career which means the messages we convey through our work reach a lot of people. Therefore, we must consider how we intentionally or unintentionally convey values through our work. The reality is there are always values at play when working with athletes. Not only do athletes have unique backgrounds of different sports and regions, but also intersecting identities of gender, age, race, ethnicity, sexual orientation, nationalities, socio-economic status, religions, and abilities. That said, practitioners should picture athletes as more than just the person in front of them, but also their experiences outside of sessions. In looking at the bigger picture of our work, we can determine what we value about working with athletes, and how our professional goals can support those values. For instance, in wanting to convey my willingness to serve LGBTQIA+ (lesbian, gay, bisexual, transgender, queer, intersex, plus) and BIPOC (Black, Indigenous, and people of colour) athletes, I added a statement of allyship to my private practice's mission and vision web pages. While this was an incredibly minor action, I continuously evaluate how to advocate more for athletes of underserved communities. Just like any other goal-setting experience in mental training, transferring personal values to professional goals requires intentional action steps and accountability. Many of us will be in this profession for decades, so we have a lot of opportunities to support our values through our work, as long as we keep the bigger picture of professional goals in mind.

Finally, sport psychology practitioners can appreciate the bigger picture of consulting work through personal habits. To succeed through a long process of training, responsibilities, and years of hard work, practitioners must develop habits of setting healthy boundaries and engaging in regular self-care. Boundaries look different for every professional, depending on how someone needs to prioritise their mental energy (Quartiroli et al., 2021). For instance, boundary-setting may involve clearly communicating one's priorities or turning down requests (i.e., 'I do not offer weekend sessions, but I can be flexible with evenings'). For me, boundaries involve sticking to a schedule, so work does not infringe upon time to relax. In graduate school I aimed to complete coursework during the week, so I had the weekend free. Even if that meant staying up later during the week, those two days of rest were incredibly rejuvenating. Self-care is also important for helping professionals, who offer so much support to athletes but often neglect personal needs. I know I provide the best services when I feel focused and excited, which can only happen if I engage in enough self-care. My self-care often exists in the form of kind self-talk, like being gentle with myself after making a mistake or missing a deadline. Other times, self-care prioritises my physical and mental health. Regularly exercising outdoors and going to therapy are two ways I keep myself healthy to continue serving athletes well. Oftentimes the boundaries and self-care we initiate early in our sport psychology training transfer to our post-graduate careers. By viewing self-care and boundaries as necessary, proactive job requirements rather than last resorts when we feel burned out, early sport psychology practitioners can extend that same message to athletes.

Conclusion

Beginning sport psychology practitioners can learn about personal consulting styles from far more than lectures and readings alone. By leaning into the most vulnerable moments of failure, asking oneself deep questions, and diving headfirst into public-speaking responsibilities, practitioners will undoubtedly find professional and personal growth. Although everyone's journey in developing a sport psychology consulting style is unique, one commonality is the journey rarely goes easily or predictably. Yet in these very moments of challenge or uncertainty, beginning practitioners can find the greatest opportunities for improvement. In graduate school, embracing mistakes and new consulting responsibilities can provide unforgettable learning experiences. When contemplating which theoretical approaches resonate most with one's consulting work, personal beliefs and experiences can reveal many insights. For further evidence of theoretical style, one can look to the very values, ambitions, and habits made evident to the athletes we serve. Through brave ambitions and self-reflection, one can find inspiration to continuously grow an applied sport psychology career.

REFLECTIVE QUESTIONS

- How will I embrace training opportunities outside my comfort zone?
- How do I most naturally engage in public speaking?
- What psychological skills have I gleaned from life experiences?
- What do my consulting mistakes tell me I can improve upon?
- How do I embody my professional beliefs through ambitions, values, or habits?

References

Anderson, M., Van Raalte, J. L., & Brewer, B. W. (2000). When sport psychology graduate students and consultants are impaired: Ethical and legal issues in training and supervision. *Journal of Applied Sport Psychology, 12*(2), 134–150. 10.1080/10413200008404219

Filion, S., Munroe-Chandler, K., & Loughead, T. (2021). Psychological skills used by sport psychology consultants to improve their consulting. *Journal of Applied Sport Psychology*, *33*(2), 173–191. 10.1080/10413200.2019.1647475

Hanrahan, S. J., Anderson, M. B., Todd, D., & Hodge, K. (Eds.). (2010). *Routledge Handbook of Applied Sport Psychology*. New York, NY: Routledge.

Jung, C. G. (1914). On the importance of the unconscious in psychopathology. *The British Medical Journal*, *2*(2814), 964–968.

Kamphoff, C. (2017). *Beyond Grit*. Minneapolis, MN: Itasca Press.

Keegan, R. J. (2010). Teaching consulting philosophies to neophyte sport psychologists: Does it help, and how can we do it? *Journal of Sport Psychology in Action*, *1*(1), 42–52. 10.1080/21520704.2010.518663

Mack, G. (2002). *Mind Gym: An Athlete's Guide to Inner Excellence*. New York, NY: McGraw-Hill.

Manson, M. (2016). *The Subtle Art of not Giving a F*ck: A Counterintuitive Approach to Living a Good Life*. New York, NY: Harper.

Mumford, G. (2015). *The Mindful Athlete: Secrets to Pure Performance*. Berkeley, CA: Parallax Press.

Pack, S., Hemmings, B., & Arvinen-Barrow, M. (2014). The self-practice of sport psychologists: Do they practice what they preach? *The Sport Psychologist*, *28*, 198–210. 10.1123/ijsnem.2012-0085

Quartiroli, A., Wagstaff, C. R. D., & Thelwell, R. (2021). The what and how of self-care for sport psychology practitioners: A Delphi study. *Journal of Applied Sport Psychology*. *34*(6), 1352–1371. 10.1080/10413200.2021.1964107

Sincero, J. (2013). *You Are a Badass. How to Stop Doubting Your Greatness and Lead an Awesome Life*. Philadelphia, PA: Running Press Adult.

Tod, D., Andersen, M. B., & Marchant, D. B. (2011). Six years up: Applied sport psychologists surviving (and thriving) after graduation. *Journal of Applied Sport Psychology*, *23*(1), 93–109. 10.1080/10413200.2010.534543

Vallerand, R. J. (1997). Toward a hierarchical model of intrinsic and extrinsic motivation. *Advances in Experimental Social Psychology*, *29*, 271–360. 10.1016/S0065-2601(08)60019-2

Walker, B. (2010). The humanistic/person-centered theoretical model. In S. J. Hanrahan, & M. B. Anderson (Eds.), *Routledge Handbook of Applied Sport Psychology* (pp. 123–130). New York, NY: Routledge.

12

THE WORLD IS YOUR OYSTER: IDENTIFYING AND SELECTING OPPORTUNITIES FOR PRACTICE

Alban Dickson

Sport Psychology Practice

In recent years, the role of the applied Sport & Exercise Psychologist has emerged prolifically. Despite this, the associated responsibilities and outcomes remain unclear to the general public, coaches, and athletes, with perceptions spanning everything from mind-reader to miracle-worker. As a result, stakeholders within sport can hold expectations of practitioners without understanding the training required to be a Sport and Exercise Psychologist. With a growing interest in the appealing prospect of sport and exercise psychology as a profession, early-career (trainee or 'in training') practitioners increasingly find themselves facing diverse opportunities in the pursuit of experience. Although often welcomed, the selection and management of applied work prospects remains a vital yet challenging process. This chapter will use examples from the world of applied practice to guide emerging Sport & Exercise Psychologists in key considerations for the selection of opportunities; namely knowing your context, knowing what matters, and knowing your options.

My Journey So Far

In 2018, having recently completed my post-graduate degree – and vowing never to write anything again – I eventually relented and punched my ticket to ride upon the Qualification in Sport & Exercise Psychology (QSEP). Applied practice was my desired destination and, at such a time, there was no alternative route to practising legitimately as a Heath and Care Professions Council (HCPC) registered Sport and Exercise Psychologist in the UK. As I suspect many encounter, my enthusiasm was equally matched by uncertainty as to how I would achieve the minimum – let alone indicative – hours I was required to fulfil. With my supervisor in place, even before formally embarking I expected the value of my work to fluctuate massively in the

DOI: 10.4324/9781003263890-16

years ahead. To date, my portfolio has captured private consultancy, working across Governing Bodies of Sport (NGBs), and Higher Education.

Training Pathways and Expectations

In the United Kingdom, the designation of a practitioner 'Sport and Exercise Psychologist' is a protected title, reflective of extensive years dedicated to study and supervised practice (Hings et al., 2018). Whilst variations upon this title can be ambiguous, there remain several formal routes for legally referring to oneself as a Sport & Exercise Psychologist. The most established of these is provided by the British Psychological Society (BPS). First made available in 2009, it has encountered an extensive growth in popularity over the past decade (Eubank, 2016). The Qualification in Sport & Exercise Psychology (QSEP) is not the most accessible path to certification, requiring an undergraduate honours degree in Psychology (typically obtained after three years study in England, or four in Scotland) and a BPS-accredited Master of Science degree in Sport & Exercise Psychology. Together, these steps constitute 'Stage 1', with 'Stage 2' spanning the next stretch of the journey. A recent development for this pathway to registration was a comparative route offered by British Association of Sport and Exercise Sciences (BASES). The Sport & Exercise Psychology Accreditation Route (SEPAR) also requires relevant academic grounding and would similarly allow – upon completion – registration with the HCPC. Finally, a further option of completing a Professional Doctorate is available, operating within the structures of a university and further recognising achievements with the associated academic credentials for doctoral-level study.

Although QSEP further offers use of the Chartered Psychologist title (CPsychol), and SEPAR removes the requirement for a research component, these two paths have much in common. Both expect the candidate to source and complete set hours across consultancy, dissemination and professional practice development while using 'in training' titles. These are obtained while operating under the supervision by a qualified practitioner, of which there are many, each offering their own unique style of support.

No One Path

Whilst some may be fortunate to commence QSEP having secured a placement providing many of their required consultancy hours, few will earn respectable financial compensation for a service worth extensive years of university education. Whilst Stage 2 permits a great deal of flexibility and choice in gaining the necessary applied experience, it is important to acknowledge that everyone will pursue their own plan. It can be distracting and futile to expect that others' paths will be comparable with our own; each candidate will plot a unique course over the months and years that lie before them.

What constitutes the great strengths of QSEP – flexibility, choice, freedom – also presents the greatest obstacle for candidates. It is easy to look ahead (or parallel) to understand how others have gained access to great institutions or opportunities. Yet it can be equally *unhelpful* if overlooking the nuances of each practitioner's networking and selection processes. Embracing that we each shape our own progress should be a powerful action, helping tether expectations and attention firmly on the here and now. By contrast, when making comparisons to others it would be easy for a practitioner to overthink and grow concerned about progress. If we lose sight on our long-term aspirations or professional philosophy or our attention drifts from our own development, then our actions can become limited and compensatory. For example, if one trainee sport psychologist considered that another was investing considerable hours in football academy setting, they might feel obliged to emulate this, concerned that not doing so may disadvantage them in the future. If we strive solely to keep up with the pack, we may find ourselves straying from our personal values.

At an early stage in developing one's portfolio, all opportunities to gain hours can feel irresistible. Despite the utility of embracing all that comes our way, the experience can ultimately be exhausting. Working with disengaged coaches, awkwardly integrating into programmes, and investing additional hours due to early misunderstandings is neither rewarding nor sustainable. Challenging encounters can prove useful – to permit a flexing of ethical practice and reflection – but too much can quickly drain one's resource of resilience. It is therefore important to carefully evaluate each opportunity before progressing. Such encounters are moments of judgement, best supported through considering three aspects of awareness: *knowing our context, knowing our values, and knowing our options.* When we find ourselves in a difficult situation, our self-awareness can be our greatest asset. At onset, we should plot where our own applied practice may emerge from.[1] Gradually, our own unique map may emerge, but be prepared for wrong turns and changes in direction. As we learn through mistaken turns and shortcuts, there is clearly no one path.

Knowing Your Context

Whilst literature emphasises the context surrounding our practice, we must consider our individual context too. The situation in which sport psychology – particularly with respect to performance – is provided, challenges many of the traditional assumptions of psychological intervention (Keegan, 2016). This can cover limitations of time, informal settings, and brief contact (Aoyagi & Portenga, 2010). Even if we are confident in our understanding of the environment we are working in, we should consider our personal context too; resources available, compatibility of ourselves with the client, even our own career trajectories. Should we find ourselves in what appears to be a psychologically informed setting,

---

[1] For further insight into a range of topics related to being a psychology practitioner including how to run a private practice, promoting your work on social media, and how to set your fees, check out 'The Business of Psychology' podcast with Dr Rosie Gilderthorp.

working as part of a multi-disciplinary team in an organisation that values our expertise (somewhat a gold standard setting to conduct work in!), we should still evaluate our awareness and suitability within a setting for applied work. Our assumptions can be quick to form based either on first impressions, or previous involvement in a sport or organisation, so an objective and critical lens as we assess the viability of a role can be very helpful in the long term.

To illustrate, imagine the prospect of working in an exemplary youth tennis academy. This could be desirable either as an open door to working in a sport of particular interest or a chance to diversify upon past experiences – a valuable aspect in pursuit of Stage 2. On the contrary, perhaps it is a deviation for a practitioner interested in community, grassroots, or even exercise domains for their applied practice? As we pause to consider our own context, a decision presents itself. What if we disagree with the principle of early specialisation? Even if this academy has robust ethical foundations, we may consider that this context does not align with our own values or beliefs (explored in more detail later). Perhaps most critically, what resources do we have at our disposal? This wonderful placement may require more time than we can afford to do the job – and ourselves – justice. Have we factored in the time for preparation, travel, observation, and stakeholder meetings?

The above passage attempts to indicate that we should not only pay attention to the context we would operate within, but also how compatible we are with that context, at that time. It could well be that a reputable and well-organised club approaches you for sport psychology support only for you to realise that their expectations are not aligned to your own approach; certaintism of measurable questionnaires versus a person-centred, construalist tradition, for example (Keegan, 2016). Awareness of our own context is vital in ensuring we work in line with our preferences, and that an opportunity does not become a burden upon our already busy schedules. Reflective practice can help build our awareness, particularly paying attention to our thoughts and feelings as they emerge (Gibbs, 1988).

Knowing What Matters

In the pursuit of appealing opportunities – or reaching a quota of applied hours – the in-training practitioner may feel inclined to overlook or bypass some of their integral beliefs or values, which could be to their detriment. Just as we would not disregard the codes and standards of ethics and conduct set out by the representative body or professional regulator, we should equally preserve our own lens on the world. Awareness of our fundamental beliefs and values is critical in navigating the twists and turns that inevitably emerge, especially with selecting and committing to work opportunities. For example, I strive to embody honesty, integrity, and professionalism in all that I do. I hold the belief that context shapes how we behave, and that unwanted thoughts and feelings are generally treated with suppression, which may not be one's most helpful reaction. Values and beliefs are presented as the foundation for our professional philosophy for a reason; they should be stable and never freely compromised (Poczwardowski et al., 2004). When new opportunities present, I cycle through these values and my belief system. If I sense that an opportunity is simply sourcing psychological input (a standalone workshop, for example) as lip service, or that at point of intake the client confesses to not believing that psychology is important – in accordance with my personal value of integrity – I would look to decline or refer on, where appropriate. Conversely, when working with volunteer coaches whose dedication and structure match my own aspiration for professionalism, a positive and enduring working relationship develops. Our beliefs and values are shaped by our own experiences and can adapt during our life. With this in mind, consider your own core values, their origins, and their influence upon how you conduct yourself professionally (in psychology, as a student or in another domain entirely). Would you be willing to compromise on your beliefs and values in the pursuit of applied work?

Knowing Your Options

Just as a Sport & Exercise Psychologist must reflect on any ethical considerations before engaging with a client, one should adopt a process of identifying and evaluating the possible implications before accepting an invitation to provide services. Whilst generating sufficient income as a practitioner is particularly challenging or concerning (Hemmings, 2015) it is often a priority. Accepting work is – and should be – dependent upon various factors, far beyond a simple distinction of 'paid' versus 'unpaid'.

Unpaid work encapsulates multiple levels; it is not simply the act of providing a service without payment as there may be multiple other factors to consider. An intervention programme agreed on a voluntary basis, perhaps to help a population close to one's heart (such as athletes with disabilities or disadvantaged populations), differs markedly from a project undertaken to help build professional relationships (which may yield benefits further in one's career). As such, our choices surrounding when to offer our services without financial compensation may make sense in a particular context. Working unpaid in a professional setting (such as a football academy) is in stark contrast to a practitioner intentionally gaining experience in a new environment (Eubank, 2013b). There may be times we find ourselves compromised to not receive payment, but there may be other scenarios that serve a clear purpose in developing a portfolio or supporting a community.

Sport and Exercise Psychology trainees identify working 'gratis' and the lack of remunerated consultancy opportunities as the most challenging aspect in pursuit of qualification (Eubank, 2013a). The depiction of hours in-training equating to little financial return poses other issues in turn; expenditure of time, and requirements to source additional employment (effectively a double jeopardy scenario), with working for free and maintaining other employment acknowledged as somewhat the norm (Davies, 2019).

When alternative phrases are used to denote work where the practitioner is not financially compensated it can feel disingenuous. In contracting, *gratis* has Latin roots shared with the concept of favour, defined as 'without charge or recompense' (Merriam-Webster, n.d). Work considered to be *pro bono* may be interpreted differently, perhaps empowering for the service provider. Also derived from Latin – typically found in legal contexts – the full phrase *pro bono publico* is defined as 'for public good' (Merriam-Webster, n.d.) or 'without asking for payment' (Cambridge, n.d.). This conveys a sense of generosity or altruism on the part of the provider. Our choice of language can reflect subtle differences to the recipient of such services.

The acceptance of paid work should also only occur after some consideration. For example, it raises ethical questions should a Sport & Exercise Psychologist be enticed financially to work in a psychologically unsafe environment (e.g., one emulating a 'win at all costs' ethos or with a toxic power imbalance across coaches and athletes). With those examples being one extreme, further down the sliding scale of risk, should an invitation to take employment in a completely unfamiliar context be accepted without due diligence? For example, what if you chose work in a new context only to discover that the coaches and performance director view impact solely in terms of performance, at the possible expense of athlete well-being? Consideration of each opportunity in its own right is vital to progress and maintain the reputation of oneself and the profession. Any trainee Sport & Exercise Psychologist will likely have come across situations similar to those outlined above, and many more. Regardless of the form of payment, psychologists are reminded to strictly adhere to applicable ethical codes of conduct; even if simply obtaining placement experience, a psychologist must put the needs of the client ahead of any personal gain (Keegan, 2016). How we come to define personal gain may prompt further reflection; does this include growth, payment, respect, glory?

Deciding on Opportunities

To offer some assistance with the decision-making process of selecting appropriate opportunities, a framework is offered (Figure 12.1). This may serve a trainee Sport & Exercise Psychologist to identify, consider, and act accordingly as new opportunities present on their path to qualification and future career.

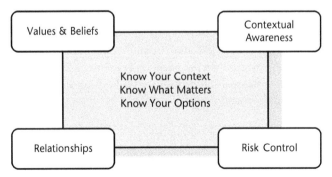

FIGURE 12.1 Overview of key considerations in deciding upon applied practice opportunities

Each trainee and early career Sport & Exercise Psychologist will have their own destination in sight. That may vary across individuals; HCPC registration, Chartered Psychologist status, full-time employment, and so forth. Even the notion of 'a successful career' is dependent on personal aspirations: working domestically, working internationally, specialisation, or adaptability. Others may choose to emphasise not the destination but rather the direction, based on their personal values; being caring, seeking challenge, or achieving self-sufficiency. Whether adopting a goal- or value-directed approach, broadly speaking we share the intention to move forward.

Throughout training and early stages of one's career, the starting points and markers of progress vary. As we reflect upon our peers, we would unlikely identify two practitioners embarking from the same place pursuing identical destinations. I would propose that in our trainee journey we should consider four essential elements in pursuit of work: Values & Beliefs, Contextual Awareness, Relationships, Risk Control (Figure 12.1).

Values and Beliefs

Values and Beliefs are integral as the foundations of a professional philosophy for practice or consultancy. Poczwardowski and colleagues explain that knowing these may help us direct our actions and shape our understanding of the world (2004). My professional values influence the way that I work and include authenticity and humility. Expressing one's values and beliefs when first engaging with a client can be helpful early in discussions, setting expectations, and exploring viability.

Contextual Awareness

Contextual Awareness reflects our understanding of the environment we are going to enter. This is underpinned by what we would seek to establish from the intake and needs assessment (Keegan, 2016). Without developing an understanding of the environment and expectations upon entering a new context, we could find ourselves limited in delivering the scope and quality of work we aspire to. For example, if a coach has commissioned a team-building intervention but it quickly becomes apparent the leadership have 'lost the dressing room' then we will struggle to deliver the service or standard we intended to. We must ensure that we derive sufficient and relevant contextual information early; both of the situation we will work in and our own reflections.

Relationships

Relationships require consideration of the benefactors. From my experience, this is critical when delivering work *gratis*, even accepting any work at all. With an existing relationship, evaluate if and how you are being appreciated, valued, or respected; do the stakeholder's core beliefs and values align with your own? For new relationships, explore your instincts; if your relationship with the key point of contact doesn't feel right, then take notice and make adaptive changes that may protect your reputation. When encountering gatekeepers – those people essential for access and eventual delivery – who seem disinterested, you should consider whether a fruitful relationship can be formed. When I have felt a good connection with a stakeholder (such as a coach, committee member, or captain) the provision of sport psychology has tended to be a successful one.

A critical element of developing relationships is the fostering of rapport. Rapport has been cited extensively as an important attribute of a sport psychologist (Sharp & Hodge, 2014). Researchers and practitioners have identified important behaviours for building rapport including making a good first impression, applying humour, displaying appropriate body language, and careful use of personal disclosure (Pack et al., 2019; Pearson & Bulsara, 2016; Way & Vosloo, 2016). Broadly speaking, displays of openness, interest, and warmth are noted as important throughout the literature, yet examples appear sparse. To illustrate rapport in practice, I have reflected on some of my own interactions. When engaging with athletes – in line with embodying my own authenticity – I often have to outline my own limited knowledge of their sport and do so with a degree of humour. You could define my style as slightly self-deprecating, although I make sure this only applies to a lack of sporting accomplishment, separate from my own area of expertise. When connecting with coaches, I'm careful not to emphasise my own coaching experience or credentials. Often, this will be insignificant in comparison, but could also imply to the coach that I could overstep my boundaries. Instead, I look to show interest in their background or approach. Displaying body language is challenging when operating online, as so many practitioners have transitioned to in recent years. Here, non-verbal cues such as nodding and smiling are essential; when sharing my screen, the occasional disparaging comment on my own drawing abilities can help too!

Risk Control

Risk Control presents as an extension of core ethical conduct and considerations. Once necessities of ethical practice are ensured, a Sport & Exercise psychologist should consider the consequences of either accepting or declining an available opportunity. Does undertaking a prospective project create a reputational risk for ourselves or the profession (e.g., devaluation if undertaken without payment)? As the role of identity has been flourishing in applied practice (Rees et al., 2015), we must consider the implications of our own professional identity. I have previously declined to continue providing services where I felt as though the sport psychology component, and my involvement, was simply a 'tick-box'. I wouldn't want recipients to receive a tokenistic experience of my subject, nor work in such a way that my own value could be diminished.

Example

What follows is an anonymised example exploring how issues across each of our four cornerstones of decision-making (see Figure 12.1) can jeopardise the prospect of delivering an effective and efficient service. Only when each aspect has been thoroughly considered should a decision to proceed then follow.

The following illustration of evaluating an opportunity comes in the form of a junior football academy who approached me during my first year of QSEP training. An interest was expressed to provide sport psychology workshops to an Under-16 group of male footballers.

- **Values & Beliefs.** There was an initial alignment across my own values system and that of the academy as it promoted 'lifelong' learning, health, and well-being. With no issue presenting here, there was a solid foundation for the delivery of workshops. However, incongruence emerged as I realised my core values of integrity, professionalism, and family were compromised. With no opportunity for payment, nor travel expenses available, the result was a three-hour round trip to provide the workshops. This immediately compromised my own sense of value as a professional and would restrict me in spending time with my child. I concluded that this situation would restrict me being able to live by my core values, which should encourage us to question our willingness to proceed.
- **Contextual Awareness.** Through my coaching background, previous experience of delivering sport psychology and understanding of the national context of the sport, I felt satisfied in my understanding of the context. I reflected on being unaware of specifics, such as the coaching style and dynamics of the team but saw opportunity to clarify this through observation of training and engagement with the stakeholders. I was familiar with the sport, the wider environment of football in that geographical area, and saw opportunities to quickly learn more about the applied setting itself.
- **Relationships.** My relationship with the contact – head coach – was circumstantial and in its infancy. This meant there was a prospective relationship and room to enhance my reputation. Yet, with no prior relationship the prospects were also obscured. It was unclear whether sport psychology would be well-received, integrated into the environment, or if further opportunities would emerge beyond this project. Initial contact had been face-to-face, and via telephone, and e-mail; though beyond the first meeting the communication had been somewhat brief, which made it difficult to gauge rapport.
- **Risk Control.** The prospect of providing work without payment or expenses carries a risk to reputation. The BPS Code of Ethics & Conduct embodies Responsibility (BPS, 2018) as one of four cornerstone principles for all psychologists. This includes a responsibility to the profession which can lead to a reputational compromise or de-valuation of the services provided. When informed that no compensation or payment would be available there posited a risk to my reputation and that of sport psychology in football settings.

Whilst it may seem pedantic to have declined this opportunity on grounds of non-payment for services or incurred travel expenses, it should be considered from a perspective of the emerging thoughts and feelings (Gibbs, 1988). When informed there would be no financial compensation, I attended to how I felt before making my final decision. In discussing the arrangements with the coach, I felt hesitant and uncertain, so followed my intuition that this opportunity was not likely to be an effective use of my time. These thoughts emerged when travel expenses were swiftly ruled out; was it therefore reasonable and professional for me to provide my own investment of time and costs to provide these services? I decided it was not in my own interests (I could use this time beneficially in other ways) nor that of the profession (to suggest that a sport psychologist can be expected to make such a commitment). I was uncertain of the benefit to myself; what would I gain from investing in this experience? It may have established new relationships but would not add any diversity to my portfolio of work at that time. In fulfilling the consultancy hours for QSEP, I did not feel this placement would contribute to demonstrating my own competencies more broadly. My intuition concluded this was not a viable option for me and so I declined the opportunity, expressing my reasoning, in an effort to embody my integrity and professionalism once more.

Whilst some may not identify with the considerations I made, I believe that if feeling uncomfortable regarding boundaries and professionalism then we should stand our ground. Although it can be disappointing when our work concludes prematurely, by acting upon our values we can negate any negative consequences of guilt, regret, and frustration.

Conclusion

The training journey of becoming a Sport & Exercise Psychologist is challenging. Beyond those initial years of study are the twists and turns of gaining applied practice and valuing oneself, while simultaneously avoiding the temptation to make comparison to others moving in a similar direction. The most successful travels are those that apply judgement and selection to the available opportunities. In other words, mapping out the route by knowing our context, knowing our options, and knowing what matters to us. By identifying and considering values, context, relationships, and risk, we can embark on our journey towards qualification, confident in our approach.

REFLECTIVE QUESTIONS

- What are your minimum requirements for undertaking applied work? Do you have non-negotiables and how do you articulate these?
- From your experiences to date, what circumstances or events have made you question your decision to accept or agree to applied opportunities? What have you learnt from these occasions?

> • Upon concluding your training pathway, what aspects of applied work would you like to demonstrate in your portfolio? What challenges or compromises might you anticipate in achieving this?

References

Aoyagi, M. W., & Portenga, S. T. (2010). The role of positive ethics and virtues in the context of sport & performance psychology service delivery. *Professional Psychology: Research and Practice*, *41*, 253–259. 10.1037/a0019483

British Psychological Society. (2018). *Code of Ethics & Conduct*.

Cambridge Dictionary. (n.d.). Pro bono. In *dictionary.cambridge.com* dictionary. https://dictionary.cambridge.org/dictionary/english/pro-bono

Davies, J. (2019). QSEP Stage 2 candidate reflection: The reality of being a trainee. *Sport & Exercise Psychology Review*, *15*(2), 3–13.

Eubank, M. (2013a). Professional training experiences on the Qualification in Sport and Exercise Psychology: A supervisor and candidate experience. *Sport & Exercise Psychology Review*, *9*(1), 45–60.

Eubank, M. (2016). Guest editorial. *Sport & Exercise Psychology Review*, *12*(2), 5–8.

Eubank, M., Ronkainen, N. & Tod, D. (2020). New approaches to identity in sport. *Journal of Sport Psychology in Action*, *11*(4), 215–218. 10.1080/21520704.2020.1835134

Eubank, M. R. (2013b). Evidencing and assessing trainee competence on the Qualification in Sport and Exercise Psychology: The consultancy case study. *Sport and Exercise Psychology Review*, *9*, 11–14.

Gibbs G. (1988). *Learning by doing: A guide to teaching and learning methods*. Further Education Unit, Oxford Polytechnic: Oxford.

Hemmings, B. (2015). A week in the life of an Applied Sport Psychologist. *Sport & Exercise Psychology Review*, *11*(1), 82-88.

Hings, R. F., Wagstaff, C. R. D., Anderson, V., Gilmore, S., & Thelwell, R. C. (2018). Professional challenges in elite sports medicine and science: Composite vignettes of practitioner emotional labor. *Psychology of Sport and Exercise*, *35*, 66–73. 10.1016/j.psychsport.2017.11.007

Keegan, R. (2016). *Being a Sport Psychologist*. London: Palgrave Macmillan

Merriam-Webster. (n.d.). Gratis. In Merriam-Webster.com dictionary. https://www.merriam-webster.com/dictionary/gratis

Merriam-Webster. (n.d.). Pro bono publico. In Merriam-Webster.com dictionary. https://www.merriam-webster.com/dictionary/pro%20bono%20publico

Pack, S., Hemmings, B., Winter, S., & Arvinen-Barrow, M. (2019) A preliminary investigation into the use of humor in sport psychology practice. *Journal of Applied Sport Psychology*, *31*(4), 494–502, 10.1080/10413200.2018.1514428

Pearson, M., & Bulsara, C. (2016). Therapists' experiences of alliance formation in short-term counselling. *European Journal of Psychotherapy and Counselling*, *18*(1), 75–92. doi:10.1080/13642537.2015.1131729

Poczwardowski, A., Sherman, C. P., & Ravizza, K. (2004). Professional philosophy in the sport psychology service delivery: Building on theory and practice. *The Sport Psychologist*, *18*(4), 445–463. 10.1123/tsp.18.4.445

Rees, T., Haslam, S. A., Coffee, P., & Lavallee, D. (2015). A social identity approach to sport psychology: Principles, practice, and prospects. *Sports Medicine*, *45*(8), 1083–1096. 10.1007/s40279-015-0345-4

Sharp, L. A., & Hodge, K. (2014). Sport psychology consulting effectiveness: The athlete's perspective. *International Journal of Sport and Exercise Psychology*, *12*(2), 91–105. 10.1080/1612197X.2013.804285

Way, W. C., & Vosloo, J. (2016). Practical considerations for self-disclosure in applied sport psychology. *Journal of Sport Psychology in Action*, 7, 23–32. 10.1080/21520704.2015.1123207

13

EMBEDDING EXERCISE PSYCHOLOGY IN THE FITNESS WORLD

Clara Swedlund

A Clear Beginning with a Foggy Horizon

Introduction

If I was to ask my younger self what I might be doing with my life at my present age, a 'self-employed online fitness coach and trainee exercise psychologist' would have been one of the most unlikely responses. Even when I realised, as a psychology undergraduate student, that exercise psychology was my passion, I did not picture myself working in the fitness world, both as a trainee psychologist and fitness coach. However, as life and pandemics have it, I am now fully dedicated to both; therefore, this chapter is a reflection on my experience of forging a career path as an exercise psychologist in the fitness industry (based on Anderson, 1999a's model in Anderson et al., 2004). In the next pages, I will share with you how the lack of awareness regarding exercise psychology has shaped my career and my role as a trainee so far; how having a dual role as both a fitness professional and psychologist has helped me gain entry and work in the fitness industry as an exercise psychologist; and how my experience has highlighted the importance of collaborating with, and working through, fitness coaches. My hope is that this chapter inspires you to consider similar avenues of work.

What Is Exercise Psychology, and What Does an Exercise Psychologist Do?

'Exercise psychology is primarily concerned with the application of psychology to increase exercise participation and motivational levels in the general public' (British Psychological Society [BPS], n.d.). Applied exercise psychologists can work with individuals on a one-to-one basis, in group settings, or at an

DOI: 10.4324/9781003263890-17

organisational level (e.g., multidisciplinary team), in the same way that applied sport psychologists do. Whilst they are not primarily concerned with competitive athletes, anyone in any age category who takes part, or would like to take part, in physical activity can work with an applied exercise psychologist (Perry, 2020).[1]

Getting Started in Exercise Psychology

Although I have never been a sporty person, my interest in exercise psychology was sparked when I joined a gym as an undergraduate student. Understanding what separated the people who exercised regularly and stuck to their intentions from those who did not, fascinated me and I immediately saw myself as someone who could support individuals in their uptake, maintenance, and long-term relationship with physical activity. This passion led me to qualify as a fitness coach and later work in this role while completing my masters in sport and exercise psychology. By the time I graduated in 2019, it was clear to me that I wanted to work in the fitness industry as an exercise psychologist, but at the time, there was little precedent for this type of work. Acutely aware of the specificity of my interests, I decided that I'd enrol in the British Psychological Society's Qualification in Sport and Exercise Psychology (BPS, QSEP), which is an independent training pathway, part-time. I felt that this approach would be most suitable for my own personal and professional development for multiple reasons. Firstly, I felt it was important to have the formal evidence-base, supervision, credibility, accountability, and endorsement that comes with acquiring the appropriate qualification to engage in this avenue of work. Secondly, I wanted to have sufficient time to build relationships that would facilitate work opportunities, without feeling pressured to do work that I was not passionate about. Finally, I sensed that this training pathway would help me develop my own ways of working and philosophy of practice.

Thus, while working at a private gym, I simultaneously commenced a job in my local council's sport and leisure department, supporting their exercise referral pathway as a fitness instructor, holding both positions until the Coronavirus pandemic shut the world down. My intention had been to use these workspaces as placements to kick-start my trainee role: my fitness qualifications had allowed me to get one foot through the door, but both settings offered opportunities for me to develop as an applied exercise psychologist. Unfortunately, the pandemic delayed my formal enrolment with the BPS.

This setback came with a silver lining: coinciding with gym closures, I started working as an online fitness coach, and spent the rest of 2020 nurturing relationships within the fitness community, with clients and coaches alike. Notably, this coaching role allowed me to see that there was a palpable interest and demand within the fitness industry for the expertise of applied (sport and) exercise psychologists: for

---

[1] 'The Psychology of Exercise' by Perry (2020) uses real-life case studies to discuss the psychology of exercise across the lifespan.

example, many of my coaching colleagues would regularly ask me questions concerning behaviour change, and about how I applied my exercise psychology knowledge into the fitness context to help my clients when they were stuck. This confirmed my previous impressions and experiences about how exercise psychology could benefit the fitness world. Therefore, I set out to pursue the goal of bridging the gap between the fitness industry and applied exercise psychology in the only way that seemed feasible to me: with one foot in each world.

Defining My Role with a Blank Canvas

Lack of Awareness of Exercise Psychology

Although working as a fitness coach and applied trainee psychologist, with ongoing supervision, has been beneficial for my professional development, I have had to grapple with the many discomforts and lessons that come with positioning myself both in the psychology and fitness space at the same time (Jones et al., 2007), not least because at the start of my career, there was a lack of awareness around the existence of exercise psychology as a profession. This was true even within the psychology community itself[2] as well as amongst the populations and environments which could most benefit from the support of an applied exercise psychologist.

As you can imagine, this presented some unique challenges. Prior to 2021, I did not know of anyone who was working as an applied exercise psychologist, which meant that I did not have any role models to look up to or be guided by. Moreover, I could not find any research or published case studies that suggested there might be a precedent for the type of work I was trying to do (i.e., working in the fitness world as a coach and applied psychologist). Consequently, I had to be very proactive: I purposefully spent time networking with anyone who I thought might be of help to my professional development (e.g., sport psychologists, health psychologists, clinical psychologists, personal trainers, gym owners), to get an idea of what needs I might be able to meet as an exercise psychologist. In addition, I was able to find an incredibly supportive supervisor, who I trusted to help me identify and reflect on how I wanted to do 'this exercise psychology thing'.

Although my supervisor primarily works in sport psychology, she has been instrumental in the process of defining my role, namely by supporting my interests and curiosity, and nudging me towards practitioner philosophy literature (e.g., Poczwardowski et al., 2004; Castillo, 2020). Developing my own philosophy of practice early on in my training helped me determine that my core values and beliefs were centred around the importance of collaboration (Poczwardowski et al., 2004; Collins et al., 2013). I viewed myself as the expert in applying psychological principles to exercise but saw the client as the expert on themselves;

---

[2]   In 2021 the Applied Psychologists in Physical Activity Network was founded. You can find out more about the network by following @APPANetwork on social media platforms.

thus, my role was to facilitate conversations that would allow us to generate solutions together, to support them in whichever way was relevant and important to their relationship with physical activity (Friesen & Orlick, 2011). Although I initially only considered my philosophy to be relevant to my applied psychologist role, I soon realised that the work I do as a trainee exercise psychologist is inextricably linked to the work I do in my role as a fitness coach, a lesson which was fast-tracked through my involvement in, and reflections stemming from, delivering a weight-loss intervention.

The Necessity of a Dual Role: Two Hats, One Head

I know it sounds like an oversight, but I was neither expecting, nor prepared for, the challenge of defining my role and responsibilities as an exercise psychologist when I put myself forward to lead a weight-loss program at my gym. This was because the gym owners and I had decided that, given my qualifications – and for the sake of consistency, coherence, and ease (Keegan, 2010) – I would deliver and monitor both the psychoeducational and the exercise component of this intervention. In other words, my first piece of applied work required me to have a dual role, and I was very pleased to be able to take this on: it felt like a superpower! What I had not considered, however, was that any gym members who signed up for the weight-loss program already knew me as Clara the fitness coach. This required me to ask myself who Clara the fitness coach was relative to who Clara the exercise psychologist was. Were they different? Did I view myself as a different person when I switched between my roles or personas as an applied psychologist and fitness coach? Why was I even switching between different personas in the first place? (Hings et al., 2020). Beyond this self-inquiry, when an intervention participant asked me a question, who was answering it: was it Clara the coach or Clara the psychologist? Would they provide different answers? And why did they have to be different or separate from one another? Did I want them to be different?

Having to reflect on my professional identity at this early stage, when I still felt like I barely had a grasp on the things I had learnt as a master's student, was incredibly helpful in defining my role and its aims (Tod et al., 2020). I observed that when I applied knowledge from my two roles, I could provide better quality support to clients who were choosing to work with me – for example, by creating periodised physical activity routines, designed to simultaneously help my clients develop their sense of autonomy, competence, and relatedness (Silva et al., 2008), to support their long-term exercise motivation and health-behaviour change. Having this realisation in the first few months of my training has been instrumental in shaping my career: that is, drawing on expertise from both professions makes me a better professional. It allows me to remain authentic, work with integrity, and always be one and the same person for everyone (Friesen & Orlick, 2010). As a result, I now proactively integrate my roles of applied psychologist and fitness coach to help me embed exercise psychology in the fitness world: I might wear two hats, but they both go on the same head.

Gaining Entry

Having a Dual Role: An Ethically Challenging Entry Pass

Placing myself at the intersection between fitness and psychology has meant that I have used my two roles to better assist my clients with their physical and/or mental objectives. Although most clients will only contract to work with me as either a fitness coach or an exercise psychologist, sometimes clients will contract to work with me in both spaces: I support them with their fitness goals (e.g., through a supervised exercise program), while incorporating a psychological intervention (e.g., developing a more autonomous motivation) that will facilitate the behaviour change process necessary to achieve their fitness goals. Therefore, whilst I do not *always* have a 'dual role', in my experience this crossover has enriched my practice, because I have been able to adapt my skillset and role to the requirements of the client or environment within which I am working.

Despite my dual role benefitting my clients, it is also true that in maintaining both roles, I am presented with specific challenges around boundaries (i.e., where does one role end and the other one begin?) as well as in the dual-role contracting process, particularly when a client's fitness goals and psychological needs are mutually exclusive to begin with: for example, when a client wants to lose weight (fitness) but is not at present engaging in the behaviours that would facilitate this change (psychology of motivation). Noticing the mismatch between what might be deemed a successful psychological intervention versus the accomplishment of a specific fitness goal gives rise to ethical dilemmas that I need to be very explicit about in my contracting processes: I always consult with my supervisor first, and then ensure I share my thoughts with my clients, usually agreeing to prioritise working on their psychological processes first before we set explicit fitness goals.

In addition, by virtue of being trained in two professions, I am also aware of the fact I might make assumptions about an individual's behaviour or language as it relates to physical activity. Consequent to reflecting on these professional issues, I am now very deliberate in how I practice (Cropley et al., 2007). For instance, when a client uses specific terminology to describe exercise, I always seek clarification as to what they mean, to avoid erroneous assumptions in our shared language (e.g., if a client refers to high-intensity interval training workouts, I ask them to describe what that means to them). Similarly, following an intake and needs analysis, I ensure that the definition of 'a successful intervention outcome' is generated by the client and not influenced by my own bias and experience. This is particularly important when I am working with a client as both a fitness coach and psychologist, because of the added difficulty of maintaining consistency and coherence between the psychological intervention and the fitness goals we have established together. Additionally, I need to be very aware of how my passion for exercise might negatively influence the process of building a therapeutic alliance with someone who is sedentary, and/or someone who does not enjoy exercise. These are just some examples of the types of professional challenges I encounter because of my dual role.

Do You Need to Dual Role?

Considering the implications of not having a dual role and the significance it would bear on my current position has been an important reflection for me to undertake. I have often wondered whether having a different experience at the start of my career, one in which I was not working both as a fitness coach and as an applied psychologist, would have led me to arrive at the same conclusion of 'needing' to dual role. In saying that, given that my knowledge and expertise in the fields of both exercise psychology and fitness coaching have developed simultaneously, I struggle to think of how I could have 'gained entry' and found suitable employment as an exercise psychologist in the fitness industry, had I not already been working in a gym as a fitness coach (see Woolway & Harwood, 2018). How else was I going to embed applied exercise psychology into the fitness world, when this was an unexplored and unmapped territory?

Given the novelty of positioning applied exercise psychology in fitness communities, being a part of the fitness industry, as a coach and exerciser, has helped me develop trust and connect with my clients (individuals, coaches, and organisations) in a more meaningful way, which has in turn paved the way for paid employment as a psychologist. In many cases, the opportunity to work with my consulting clients began with them first getting to know me as a coach, and then enquiring about my role as a psychologist. That is, leveraging society's trust in fitness coaches has allowed me to gain entry by positioning exercise psychology on the fitness world's map and subsequently generating applied work opportunities, by promoting myself as a 'jack of two trades'. Notably, by using social media to talk, post, and write about how specific exercise psychology concepts apply to fitness (e.g., goal setting, motivation theories, self-efficacy), I have tried to cultivate a sense of curiosity amongst exercisers, that has led to exchanges about how exercise psychology can positively impact the realisation of their health and wellbeing goals (HCPC, 2020). Not only has this generated interest from clients who have later benefitted from 1:1 support, but it has also sparked conversations with fellow fitness coaches who have subsequently worked with me to learn how to better support their clients.

In short, openly talking about my dual role and its transferability to fitness contexts has enabled me to create work opportunities, by letting people know that exercise psychology exists, and by discussing how it might be of benefit to them. This has enabled me to work in the fitness industry as a trainee applied practitioner despite the relative infancy of the field (BPS, 2022). However, having one foot in each world is just one way of approaching this line of work, and there are many equally successful alternative strategies.[3]

---

[3] The Fitness Psych podcast is a useful resource if you are looking to find out more about exercise psychology.

Similarities Between Working in Sporting and Fitness Environments

As I reflect on how other applied (sport and) exercise psychologists might choose to integrate their work into the fitness industry, I keep coming back to the advantage of doing so through established fitness organisations. Gaining entry into the fitness industry is a process not dissimilar to that which is seen in applied sport psychology settings: adopting a top-down approach by networking with 'gatekeepers' (i.e., gym owners, managers, personal trainers) seems to be the most sensible starting point, as the fitness industry has a well-established level of credibility amongst members of the public. Consequently, working in recognised settings – such as gyms, personal training qualification providers, or fitness coaching companies – helps us raise awareness of the field, but also facilitates visibility, increases trust, and creates easier access for those people who could most benefit from our support.

As in applied sport psychology, knowing the language of the environment facilitates the process of gaining entry (Woolway & Harwood, 2018). Positioning yourself as an 'insider' with the shared identity of being an exerciser also helps clients build trust in a profession they probably know very little about (Hogg & Reid, 2006). This will undoubtedly assist you in the initial stages of collaboration, as you observe and notice opportunities for intervention and support. Thus, you do not have to be a psychologist and fitness coach to do this work effectively, in the same way that you don't need to be a professional athlete to be an effective sport psychologist: attentiveness (e.g., observing a client interact with their trainer), open questioning, and reflective skills are sufficient to perform a needs analysis and show how your input can make a difference to the specific fitness environment you are working in.

Advancing the Field Through Collaboration

Our Unique Selling Point (USP)

I still struggle to understand why so few practitioners work as applied (sport and) exercise psychologists in the fitness industry, as from my standpoint, the opportunities seem endless. As we think about gaining entry, it is important to remember that (sport and) exercise psychologists bring an evidence-based practice to an industry which is ripe to benefit from our knowledge. Critically, our skillset is applicable across many diverse contexts. For example, knowledge of mental skills could support a gym-goer who freezes every time they attempt a heavy lift (see Behncke, 2004); an understanding of irrational beliefs could help people engage with physical activity in a more sustainable way (see Turner & Barker, 2014);[4] and

---

[4] For a discussion about how Rational Emotive Behaviour Therapy (REBT) can be used with exercise addiction, check out the MyoMinds Podcast entitled 'Rational Emotive Behaviour Therapy and Exercise Addiction'.

helping someone identify their values can be of assistance in the process of developing a healthier motivation to be active (see Ciarrochi et al., 2015).[5] In short, although *the way in which* principles of sport and exercise psychology are applied might be contextually dependent, the *principles* themselves are not. Therefore, any applied psychologist can expand their work opportunities by stepping into the fitness industry: the key lies in being able to effectively communicate and showcase the applicability of your skillset, whilst being relatable, realistic, and open-minded (Woolway & Harwood, 2018).

Next Steps: Working Through Coaches

Despite our options being plentiful, the low recognition of our field within the fitness industry means that people who could benefit from our input may never consider themselves to be potential clients. For example, someone who historically keeps 'falling off the exercise bandwagon' might not know that support from an applied psychologist could help them break their unhelpful behavioural cycles. In addition, we face the possible stigma of our title carrying the word 'psychologist', which may suggest why people seeking support with their physical activity – from an initiation, safe execution, motivation, and maintenance perspective – may be more likely to contact a fitness coach in the first instance.

Nonetheless, I believe that this 'drawback' presents a great opportunity in itself. With fitness coaches already being established as sources of credible information in the fitness field, we psychologists are much more likely to have a greater reach and impact on the general population if we can work through them. Critically, many people's relationship with exercise could improve without the need for a 1:1 intervention if the fitness environments they were entering were already psychologically informed. As such, one of our best opportunities for thriving as a profession within the fitness industry exists in working alongside fitness coaches, gym managers, and other stakeholders; assisting them in learning how to work in psychologically informed ways, and simultaneously creating appropriate referral pathways for them to use when the direct support of an applied (sport and) exercise psychologist is required.

Collaboration in Action

One way in which I see applied exercise psychologists situating themselves in the fitness community is by replicating the multi-disciplinary team approach that is seen in sport, within gym settings. Being 'the exercise psychologist on site' would provide the opportunity to observe gym managers and fitness coaches at work, communicating with their clients and one another. This insight would create an array of opportunities for intervention, from training coaches in communication

---

[5] *The Weight Escape: Stop Fad Dieting, Start Losing Weight and Reshape Your Life Using Cutting-edge Psychology* is a fascinating book if you're looking to find out more about weight loss and psychology.

methods that could improve coach–client relationships (e.g., COMPASS model; Rhind & Jowett, 2012) to undertaking organisational work (e.g., creating thriving gym environments; Fletcher & Sarkar, 2016). These are just some of the ways in which an exercise psychologist can support the creation of psychologically in-formed fitness environments.

Another example of collaboration is an exercise psychologist who is working directly with a fitness coach and providing psychoeducation regarding basic psy-chological needs, self-determined motivation, and helping them apply autonomy-supportive coaching behaviours and language when working with their clients[6] (see Mageau & Vallerand, 2003). This could influence how the coach responds to a client who is struggling with exercise non-adherence, as rather than telling the client that they need to 'want it more', the fitness coach may be open to exploring a variety of different physical activity modalities in which the client can participate. If this client was still struggling with behaviour change, they could get referred on to a (sport and) exercise psychologist. Meanwhile, for others who work with this given coach, exploring ways in which their need for autonomy, competence, and relatedness can be satisfied in an exercise context may be sufficient to improve long-term exercise adherence (Gorin et al., 2014). Alternatively, applied exercise psychologists could collaborate more closely with fitness coaches by providing consulting services in which fitness professionals can learn about behaviour change that is specific to their client niche, problem-solve specific client issues, and reflect on how their coaching style and virtual set-up can influence client outcomes (e.g., how their coaching check-in forms might reinforce a client's sense of competence).

In these instances, fitness coaches and organisations would have access to the support of applied (sport and) exercise psychologists, as well as appropriate referral pathways should they need it for themselves or for their clients. Not only could this ensure better outcomes for clients, but it could also enhance these fitness professionals' working experiences, knowing that they are working more effec-tively, as well as within their scope of practice (see Jowett, 2017). To that end, I think that collaboration with coaches is at the centre of how we – as applied psychologists – might begin working within the fitness industry. Importantly, as the number of exercise psychologists grows in conjunction with society's recognition of our field (Wood et al., 2021), sharing our experience of successful collaborative strategies with one another will be the essential next step in con-tinuing the integration of exercise psychology into the fitness world.

Concluding Remarks

To summarise, forging my career path as an exercise psychologist in the fitness industry has been a challenging but rewarding journey so far. Having a dual role by

---

[6]   For further insight into working as an exercise psychologist alongside fitness coaches, check out 'The Performance Psychcast' episode 22 'Exercise Psychology and Working with Fitness Coaches'.

virtue of my position in both worlds has helped me shape and define how I practice as a professional. Knowing who I am and what I am trying to do has facilitated many of the work opportunities that I have been granted, despite the lack of awareness regarding the field of applied exercise psychology. Admittedly, despite being at the start of my career, I feel I have found myself in a position of relative expertise, as there are perhaps only a handful of applied exercise psychologists currently working within the fitness industry. Thus, I hope that sharing my experience as a trainee can provide an example of 'how to do this exercise psychology thing', as well as facilitate reflection on what this might look like for anyone with an interest in working within fitness spaces.

Moving forward, I am optimistic about the many different avenues applied sport and exercise psychologists can explore when it comes to working with fitness communities. As a final note, it is worth mentioning that the frequently cited link between mental health and physical activity during the COVID pandemic (Wood et al., 2021) means that there is perhaps no better time than the present to start embedding ourselves within the fitness world, to do our part in integrating both domains in a mutually beneficial way. As they say, the best time to start was yesterday, and the next best time is today.

REFLECTIVE QUESTIONS

- How might being a personal trainer as well as an exercise psychologist enhance or hinder one's applied work?
- What other similarities exist between the process of gaining entry into high-performance vs. fitness environments?
- What are the main challenges our profession might encounter when it comes to working in the fitness industry?

References

Anderson, A. G., Knowles, Z., & Gilbourne, D. (2004). Reflective practice for sport psychologists: Concepts, models, practical implications, and thoughts on dissemination. *The Sport Psychologist*, *18*(2), 188–203.

Behncke, L. (2004). Mental skills training for sports: A brief review. *Online Journal of Sport Psychology*, *6*(1), 1–19.

British Psychological Society. (n.d.). *Careers: Sport & Exercise Psychology*. Retrieved from https://careers.bps.org.uk/area/sport-exercise

British Psychological Society. (2022). *Member Conduct Rules*. Retrieved from https://www.bps.org.uk/news-and-policy/member-conduct-rules

Castillo, E. A. (2020). Developing a professional philosophy for applied exercise psychology: Integrating theory and practice. *Journal of Sport Psychology in Action*, *11*(3), 183–195.

Ciarrochi, J., Harris, R., & Bailey, A. (2015). *The Weight Escape: Stop Fad Dieting, Start Losing Weight and Reshape Your Life Using Cutting-Edge Psychology*. UK: Hachette.

Collins, R., Evans-Jones, K., & O'Connor, H. L. (2013). Reflections on three neophyte sport and exercise psychologists' developing philosophies for practice. *The Sport Psychologist, 27*(4), 399–409.

Cropley, B., Miles, A., Hanton, S., & Niven, A. (2007). Improving the delivery of applied sport psychology support through reflective practice. *The Sport Psychologist, 21*(1), 475–494.

Fletcher, D., & Sarkar, M. (2016). Mental fortitude training: An evidence-based approach to developing psychological resilience for sustained success. *Journal of Sport Psychology in Action, 7*(3), 135–157.

Friesen, A., & Orlick, T. (2010). A qualitative analysis of holistic sport psychology consultants' professional philosophies. *The Sport Psychologist, 24*(1), 227–244.

Friesen, A., & Orlick, T. (2011). Holistic sport psychology: Investigating the roles, operating standards and intervention goals and strategies of holistic consultants. *Journal of Excellence, 14*(1), 18–42.

Gorin, A. A., Powers, T. A., Koestner, R., Wing, R. R., & Raynor, H. A. (2014). Autonomy support, self-regulation, and weight loss. *Health Psychology, 33*(4), 332.

Health and Care Professions Council. (2020). *Guide on Social Media.* Retrieved from https://www.hcpc-uk.org/globalassets/resources/guidance/guidance-on-social-media.pdf

Hings, R. F., Wagstaff, C. R., Anderson, V., Gilmore, S., & Thelwell, R. C. (2020). Better preparing sports psychologists for the demands of applied practice: The emotional labor training gap. *Journal of Applied Sport Psychology, 32*(4), 335–356.

Hogg, M. A., & Reid, S. A. (2006). Social identity, self-categorization, and the communication of group norms. *Communication Theory, 16*(1), 7–30.

Jones, L., Evans, L., & Mullen, R. (2007). Multiple roles in an applied setting: Trainee sport psychologist, coach, and researcher. *The Sport Psychologist, 21*(2), 210–226.

Jowett, S. (2017). Coaching effectiveness: The coach-athlete relationship at its heart. *Current Opinion in Psychology, 16*(1), 154–158.

Keegan, R. J. (2010). Teaching consulting philosophies to neophyte sport psychologists: Does it help, and how can we do it?. *Journal of Sport Psychology in Action, 1*(1), 42–52.

Mageau, G. A., & Vallerand, R. J. (2003). The coach–athlete relationship: A motivational model. *Journal of Sports Science, 21*(11), 883–904.

Perry, J. (2020). *Psychology of Exercise.* London: Routledge.

Poczwardowski, A., Sherman, C. P., & Ravizza, K. (2004). Professional philosophy in the sport psychology service delivery: Building on theory and practice. *The Sport Psychologist, 18*(1), 445–463.

Rhind, D. J., & Jowett, S. (2012). Development of the coach-athlete relationship maintenance questionnaire (CARM-Q). *International Journal of Sports Science & Coaching, 7*(1), 121–137.

Silva, M. N., Markland, D., Minderico, C. S., Vieira, P. N., Castro, M. M., Coutinho, S. R., … & Teixeira, P. J. (2008). A randomized controlled trial to evaluate self-determination theory for exercise adherence and weight control: Rationale and intervention description. *BMC Public Health, 8*(1), 234.

Tod, D., McEwan, H., Chandler, C., Eubank, M., & Lafferty, M. (2020). The gravitational pull of identity: Professional growth in sport, exercise, and performance psychologists. *Journal of Sport Psychology in Action, 11*(4), 233–242.

Turner, M. J., & Barker, J. B. (2014). Using rational emotive behavior therapy with athletes. *The Sport Psychologist, 28*(1), 75–90.

Wood, C. J., Barton, J., & Smyth, N. (2021). A cross-sectional study of physical activity behaviour and associations with wellbeing during the UK coronavirus lockdown. *Journal of Health Psychology, 27*(6),1432–1444.

Woolway, T., & Harwood, C. G. (2018). Gatekeepers' experiences of hiring a sport psychologist: A phenomenological study. *Journal of Applied Sport Psychology, 31*(4),474–493.

14

WHAT DREAMS ARE MADE OF? A SPORT PSYCHOLOGIST'S REFLECTION OF THEIR FIRST INTERNATIONAL TOURNAMENT

Erin Prior

Introduction

Working with elite athletes and experiencing elite sporting events is often considered to be the pinnacle of the sport psychology profession, with travelling to an international tournament (whereby athletes represent their country at European, World, Olympic or Paralympic level) being a major milestone within a sport psychologist's career. While this experience may be seen as 'perks of the job' from an outsider's perspective, upon closer inspection, international travel with an elite team may be one of the most challenging aspects of a sport psychologist's role.[1] This chapter will explore my experience of working as a (trainee) sport psychologist at an international tournament for the first time. I am writing this as a chartered Sport and Exercise Psychologist, however, at the time of the tournament, I had recently completed a 1-year Master's degree and been in training to become chartered for merely one year (a process which in the UK typically takes 2–4 years). Therefore, my career was (and still is) in its infancy.

Background and Context

My work with the team in question began within my first year of supervised training, with this role being my first position within a team. The role involved ad hoc – and at times sporadic – contact time with the team, limited to 6 two-day training camps prior to the tournament (this is how the governing body structures training around a tournament). With limited contact time, I focused on

---

[1] See '*Preparing our Greatest Team: The Design and Delivery of a Preparation Camp for the London 2012 Olympic Games*' by Arnold, Hewton, & Fletcher (2015) for an insight into sport psychology provision for international tournaments such as the Olympic Games.

DOI: 10.4324/9781003263890-18

introducing the team to sport psychology, exploring psychological skills training (e.g., developing pre-performance routines), and beginning longer-term work on team culture.[2] Delivery consisted of team workshops and one-to-one sessions with the athletes. Despite my efforts to include both athletes and staff in the psychology sessions, certain challenges within the environment (e.g., coaching staff prioritising analysis meetings over attending psychology sessions) resulted in most sessions involving athletes only. This chapter will explore four key areas of challenge within this role: understanding my role at a tournament, considering how I will work throughout the tournament, working impactfully in the tournament environment, and engaging in self-care.

Understanding My Role at a Tournament

Research across both sport and business promotes the importance of role clarity in determining a practitioner's ability to maximise their impact and provide the best service to their clients by establishing roles, responsibilities, and expectations (Cotterill, 2018). When a lack of clarity is achieved – resulting in role ambiguity – this may become a key stressor for a practitioner (Olusoga et al., 2009), resulting in a range of challenges including issues meeting performance expectations, and a subsequent negative impact on a practitioner's mental health and well-being (Cotterill, 2018).

Reflecting on my work with the team has led me to consider the importance of role clarity, both for my benefit as a practitioner, and the benefit of those I work with. Firstly, I have found that role clarity can increase your confidence in your ability as a practitioner. Feeling competent and confident in my role has not only been important for me on a personal level, but also in effectively communicating my role and intentions to others within the sporting environment (i.e., athletes and fellow staff). Crucially, demonstrating confidence can be important to achieve buy-in from others, whether that be those in managerial positions who may be involved in hiring practitioners, or athletes you work with day-to-day (see Woolway & Harwood, 2019).

Clearly articulating your role and approach can be particularly important when your client(s) has not worked with a Sport Psychologist previously, as there can sometimes be a sense of uncertainty around your role, or perhaps misconceptions that may be misaligned with the reality of your role and way of working.[3] In my experience, uncertainty, and misconceptions can lead to challenging conversations

---

2   Check out the 'Eighty Percent Mental' podcast entitled 'To Yell or Not to Yell: How Do We Get Our Team Culture Right?' with Dr Pippa Grange and Rebecca Levett (née Symes) for a discussion on how we define success, creating an environment where people can freely express themselves, and the potential dangers of romanticising 'winning' cultures.

3   See Pain & Harwood (2004) for an interesting discussion of the barriers sport psychologists face due to perceptions of the profession. Although published almost 20 years ago at time of writing, practitioners still face these challenges today.

surrounding your approach and the impact of your work. This can be particularly difficult to navigate if there is a disconnect between your clients' perceptions and expectations, and your own. For example, does your client expect to see 'results' or an evident change after one session? If so, what do they specifically mean by 'results'? For example, are they simply looking for more match wins, or might they also consider an improved team dynamic a 'result' and a sign of progress? What specific changes are they looking for and how are they assessing this (e.g., via statistics or exploring athlete and staff experiences of your service)? Equally, from your viewpoint as a practitioner, are these realistic expectations for your client to have of your services? If not, how, and when do you have this conversation with your client?

Across training camps prior to the tournament, I had attempted on several occasions to establish my role and work more closely with the coaching staff. These efforts involved initiating meetings with coaches to discuss player progress, standing with the coaches on the side-line during training, and requesting that staff attend the team psychology sessions. Despite these efforts, the coaching staff appeared inattentive during meetings, and rarely attended team psychology sessions – instead using this time for performance analysis. This lack of engagement with sport psychology led me to reflect on whether I had given the coaches a clear understanding of my role, and the role of sport psychology more broadly. Perhaps the coaching staff perceived that sport psychology is only beneficial for athletes and that they had a minimal role to play in this area? Perhaps they prioritised other aspects of performance? Despite an increase in coach education surrounding sport psychology in recent years, lack of coach engagement can still present challenges for practitioners due to lack of knowledge and awareness of psychology from those in senior roles (Fletcher & Wagstaff, 2009).

It can be tempting to reflect on these challenging scenarios and tell ourselves that the client simply does not understand how we work – that they have misconceptions about our profession, our role, and are therefore judging our work based on inaccurate expectations. Whilst this may help us feel better by trying to absolve ourselves of our responsibility in these challenging moments, it is important to ask ourselves: where have these misconceptions come from? Have I articulated my role and approach with clarity? Have I done enough to resolve any disconnect between myself and my client? It could be argued that sport psychology as a profession lacks a consistent identity (Portenga et al., 2011), resulting in a lack of clear understanding of what the field encapsulates.[4] Therefore, as practitioners, what are we doing to encourage a sound understanding of what sport psychology is, and what it can offer? These can be uncomfortable questions at times, as they demand that we consider our own part in the more challenging moments with clients. However, engaging in these testing, uncomfortable, and awkward reflections is crucial to improve our work as practitioners, and the perception of our profession.

---

[4] See '*Applied Sport Psychology: A Profession?*' by Winter & Collins (2016) for a compelling discussion on this.

Whether working as part of a national team, or working with private clients, I have experienced a (perhaps unexpected) level of freedom within my roles which demand me to establish boundaries and expectations. I would encourage you to consider your role as a practitioner; how you would like to work and whether this is feasible; which key stakeholders need an understanding of how you work; and how and when you communicate your approach effectively – all the while considering the various contexts you operate within. Once you have developed a sense of role clarity and have expressed this appropriately to key stakeholders, you are then in a position to consider *how* you are going to work within the context you find yourself in.

How Do I Work Throughout the Tournament?

A Balance of Proactivity and Reactivity

When considering how I would work with the team throughout the international tournament, I was unsure whether to take a proactive approach (e.g., delivering psychoeducation), or be more reactive (e.g., supporting the players with challenges as they arise).[5] On one hand, I was unsure how much new content I wanted to introduce throughout the tournament – with many other demands being placed on the team. On the other hand, I felt reluctant to take a largely reactive approach for fear of being seen as not doing enough work throughout the tournament. I began to discover that both a proactive and reactive approach would be necessary to support the team which involved finding a balance between managing anticipated challenges (e.g., nerves in the early moments of a match), and addressing unexpected challenges (e.g., supporting a player being repeatedly fouled by other teams). The reactive work took more of a precedence and appeared to be particularly effective within the ever-changing competitive environment.

Ad hoc, but meaningful conversations became key moments throughout the competition. This may have been during mealtimes, while travelling to the venue, or during downtime in the evenings (see Bull, 1995; Simons & Andersen, 1995). Essential to this approach was to be present and approachable within the environment. As the tournament progressed, I would be sure to work while sitting in the communal area within the hotel where the players often relaxed after the competition day. By making myself more visible and accessible to the players and my fellow staff, I presented the team with the opportunity to engage in ad hoc – but nonetheless important – conversations. I was particularly pleased when a player approached me in this setting for the first time and engaged in an open and honest conversation regarding his playing time during recent matches. Whilst I simply provided him with an opportunity to discuss his feelings and consider how he

---

[5] Check out the 'Eat Sleep Repeat' podcast entitled 'Talking Teams: An Interview with Dr Pippa Grange – Head of Team & Culture at the England Football Team' for a fascinating insight into Pippa's work building a winning culture, working with athletes before a big game, and her experience of being a woman working in sport.

would like to approach this with the coaching staff, I felt that this conversation improved our rapport in addition to supporting him with his next steps.[6] This first instance demonstrated to me the importance of these meaningful conversations and how I must put myself in the position to engage with these conversations as much as possible throughout the tournament.

As the competition progressed, I felt more confident initiating these ad hoc conversations, feeling they were beneficial to the team (e.g., helping to continue building relationships with the team, providing social support, and enabling me to influence how the coach engaged with players, particularly after difficult matches). I began observing the team dynamic and would seek out conversations with players and staff where I felt some difference could be made. This involved carefully considering who to initiate discussions with. Here, I would be thinking about what impact I was looking to facilitate, and who would be best placed to achieve that impact. For example, after a challenging match, I felt the team needed a regroup, and a morale boost. Reflecting on who could motivate the team effectively, I approached the team captain and head coach, shared my thoughts around what may help the team, and encouraged them to call a team meeting to debrief the previous match and prepare the team for the next match later that afternoon. It was also important to consider when and where to have these conversations, as many situations in a tournament are time-pressured, therefore, I had to make swift decisions, and take opportunities for these discussions when they were presented. This means a lot of thinking of your feet!

It became clear that an important part of how I worked throughout the tournament was orchestrating these conversations to get people thinking about their approach to their performance, or perhaps even mediating challenging discussions within the team. During the tournament, one of the players' parents approached me about his dissatisfaction with his son's lack of playing time, stating the player would be embarrassed and disheartened. He requested I raise this with the coaching staff. Sensing this could become contentious, I sought the advice of the team doctor with whom I had developed a good working relationship. Through discussing various courses of action, we decided to speak to the player about their thoughts on their playing time. While travelling back from the venue, I seized the opportunity to speak to the player. To my surprise, the players' feelings about his playing time were completely different to his father's, as he suggested he was relatively satisfied given it was his first international tournament. By carefully considering who best to approach in this situation, I not only gained insight into the players' thoughts and experiences of the tournament, but I was also able to avoid what may have been a heavy-handed approach if I had brought this complaint to the head coach. This was a valuable lesson in considering how best to approach situations before jumping in headfirst, and crucially, listening to others' views and experiences – gathering all the facts – before acting.

---

6   'The High-Performance Podcast' episode 51 entitled 'Empathy over Engineering' with Toto Wolff gives a fascinating insight into creating an environment for performers to achieve their potential and doing this with respect and empathy for others.

Although orchestrating ad hoc conversations with clients can be initially daunting, I have found this to be an important skill as a sport psychologist, and something that improves with thought, practice, and the willingness to listen – rather than focusing too much on what you want to get across in a conversation. This approach also requires flexibility and adaptability, particularly when engaging in conversations at unconventional times (e.g., during meals). Whilst some practitioners may prefer to conduct such conversations at a set time, in a set location, with plenty of planning involved, sometimes this just isn't feasible within applied settings – particularly during tournaments with hectic schedules. Of course, there are times when a set meeting time and private location is more appropriate and necessary, however, practitioners must be willing to be somewhat flexible with this. In my experience, those who are new to working with a sport psychologist sometimes prefer a more relaxed, ad hoc style of working (e.g., engaging in casual conversations, with practitioners asking some open questions but mainly focusing on listening and providing a sounding board).

The challenge in this way of working surrounds the ability to think on your feet and make decisions swiftly, often under time pressure. As much as there is a need for evidence-based practice, in fast-paced, dynamic, applied environments, practitioners often simply don't have the time to consult literature for guidance. Imagine, the head coach approaches you 15 minutes before a match and asks you to manage the challenging on-court dynamic between two senior players. Would the best use of your time to be to run to your laptop and seek out the latest research on team dynamics? Yes, these moments require background knowledge, but more importantly, they require initiative in abundance. This is a skill that practitioners develop by proactively familiarising themselves with literature and seeking out development opportunities throughout their careers, which allow them to be effective when working reactively in the moment. Ultimately, practitioners need to find their own balance of working proactively and reactively to provide effective support.

Working as Part of a Multi-disciplinary Team

When considering how I planned to work throughout the tournament, I felt a distinct pressure for both athletes and staff to feel that I knew what I was doing. This may partly be due to my awareness that clients can sometimes be uncertain of the approach and impact of sport psychologists, but also my own doubts surrounding my competence at such an early stage in my career (see Tonn & Harmison, 2004). Therefore, I felt the need to have a clear sense of my role throughout the competition and how this would be enacted, and that I could not 'rely' on anyone else to do my job for me. My initial feelings of needing to work independently (to demonstrate my competence) led me to feel reluctant to share my professional challenges with the multi-disciplinary team (MDT). The ability to work as part of an MDT is often cited as a key aspect of the sport psychologist role (see McCalla & Fitzpatrick, 2016) and has been raised in many job interviews I have attended. Despite being familiar with the literature surrounding the benefits of working cohesively within an MDT,[7] I now realise that prior to gaining personal experience of working in this way, I never fully appreciated the value of this approach.

During the tournament, members of the MDT were: the head coach, the supporting coach, the team manager, the team doctor, the physiotherapist, the operations manager, and myself as the sport psychologist. Although the MDT staff members were relatively consistent throughout the training camps, we often worked in silos, with the coaches and team manager often working separately from the rest of the staff. This meant that working collaboratively as an MDT did not occur until we were away at the tournament. My first experience of working more collaboratively with the coaching staff during the tournament came after the first practice session when the coaches felt that the players appeared nervous, lacked focus, and weren't implementing the psychological skills we had developed during training camps. The coaches expressed their concern over lunch at the hotel. Although this seems like an incidental detail, had I not sat with the coaches, I may not have been made aware of their concerns, due to their tendency to work largely separately from the rest of the team. This further highlights the importance of positioning yourself to be present for such conversations where possible. During this conversation, I felt that the coaches really listened to my views – particularly the head coach – which had not always been the case during training camps. We planned for me and one of the coaches to engage in one-to-one check-ins with the players to discuss how they were feeling, and their mental approach to the tournament. Through these one-to-ones, we were able to re-engage the players with their psychological preparation for the upcoming matches. At this early stage in the tournament, I began to experience the benefit of working closely with the coaching staff in encouraging buy-in from the players and working as part of the team rather than independently.

While grappling with the desire to be considered professionally competent, I found that when I expressed my challenges to my colleagues within the MDT, they became a valuable source of support. Supporting others with their issues can place a potential strain on practitioners (Winstone and Gervis, 2006), therefore, developing a support network is of paramount importance, particularly when working away for a prolonged period. By recognising the benefit of social support in enhancing my work (e.g., using others as sounding boards) and maintaining my well-being throughout the week (e.g., by taking the opportunity for an emotional outlet), I was able to move away from the view that I needed to work independently to be seen as professionally competent within my role. Although being more open with my colleagues was challenging and somewhat uncomfortable at first, working closely and receiving their support reduced the pressure I felt to be

---

[7] See 'Multidisciplinary Sport Science Teams in Elite Sport: Comprehensive Servicing or Conflict and Confusion?' by Reid et al. (2004) for an interesting discussion surrounding the challenges of working within an MDT.

wholly responsible for the psychological support of the team. I also felt this moved us towards developing a more psychologically informed environment[8] as the MDT were now actively reflecting on the psychology of the team.

As the tournament progressed, I began to seek out more opportunities to liaise with my fellow staff members (mainly the team doctor, operations manager, and physiotherapist) as it became clear that they had formed positive working relationships with the players which could be helpful in further supporting the team. By recognising and tapping into the rapport that the team doctor had with the players, we were able to effectively communicate key techniques and ideas that were well-received by the team. This approach was particularly impactful when the team doctor overheard another team discussing their tactics which involved deliberately fouling one of our players to provoke a reaction, and potentially cause conflict between our player and the referee. The team doctor and I approached the player with this information, encouraging him to consider his previous behaviour towards the referee, and how he may adopt a more helpful approach if a contentious situation was to arise in the next match. Feedback from this player after the tournament was that this conversation had made a substantial difference to his approach and performance in the following matches. Experiences like this cemented the value of collaborating within an MDT, learning from your colleagues' skills and experience, and most importantly, letting go of the feeling that you and you alone must be responsible for supporting athletes with their mental approach.[9]

Working Impactfully in a Tournament Environment

Underlying all my reflections above is a desire for my work to be impactful – whatever that means. Reflecting on my goals for the tournament, there was an overwhelming sense that I needed to make a difference to the team's performance, and in so doing, prove my worth as a practitioner, and as part of the team. This was perhaps due to both my own feelings surrounding my role, and that I was the first sport psychologist to work with the team. Sport psychology as a profession can often find itself in a tenuous position in terms of receiving acceptance in its target markets (Aoyagi et al., 2012). Consequently, many practitioners place themselves under increasing pressure to 'perform' effectively to satisfy expectations and promote the profession (Sharp and Hodge, 2013; Barker and Winter, 2014).

Firstly, in unpicking my perceived pressure to 'perform', I must explore what 'performance' means to me as a practitioner. At the time of the tournament, making a difference to the team's performance was a key marker of 'success'. Of course, some element of this is necessary as a practitioner working within elite sport. However, much as I encourage my clients to do, since the tournament I

---

[8] Check out 'The Sport Psych Show' podcast episode 167 with Dr Mustafa Sarkar entitled 'How to Create a Psychologically Safe Environment'.

[9] See Tod & Bond (2010) for a discussion on developing working relationships and an appreciation for how others can influence service delivery.

have reflected on not only my performance-based goals, but also my process. Consequently, I have broadened my perception of what success means for me as a practitioner. This is in no way an attempt to negate the value of, or demand for performance results within elite sport, but more an effort to consider more critically my role as a sport psychologist and how it may be pertinent to appraise my effectiveness based on a variety of indicators. Secondly, given that we often aim to satisfy our clients' expectations, we must first clarify what those expectations are, and whether they are aligned with our own expectations and ways of working. Neglecting to establish expectations early in the process can result in a disconnect between practitioners and their clients. Therefore, when considering what we mean by working impactfully we must take into account the impact both we and the client are looking for and any (in)congruence.

Both players and staff gave positive feedback regarding my impact on the team's performance, describing the team's mindset as a key aspect of their victory. Of course, I would not be so bold as to suggest that our psychology work was (wholly) responsible for the team's success, however it interests me that when the players and staff were asked to reflect on the impact of the psychology work, they focused largely on the outcome of the tournament. I, on the other hand, reflected on the improved closeness of our working relationships, the openness with which players shared their thoughts and feelings with me for the first time, and those understated but effective conversations throughout the week. This experience demonstrates that considering your 'performance' as a sport psychologist is far more nuanced and complex than simply looking to performance results and that an appreciation for the more subtle pieces of work is necessary, while understanding that your clients may appraise you based on performance results.[10,11]

Engaging in Practitioner Self-care

When reflecting on the importance I placed on working impactfully and essentially proving my worth throughout the tournament, it was impossible to ignore the feeling that I had to be seen to be working all day, each day. However, I soon realised that I needed to strike a balance between working hard for the team and being present – often at unconventional times such as late evening team meetings – and finding opportunities for downtime. In my view, part of the role of a psychologist is to prioritise supporting your clients and being largely selfless in your work with them. This may feel fairly straight-forward in some contexts we work in as sport

---

[10] 'The Long Win' by Cath Bishop provides a compelling argument for adapting our view of 'success' in sport to not only enhance performance but more importantly positively influence our mental health long-term. Cath has also been interviewed in a range of fascinating podcasts on the topic.

[11] 'Becoming a True Athlete: A Practical Philosophy for Flourishing Through Sport' by Laurence Cassøe Halsted draws on ancient wisdom and modern psychology to show how athletes and those supporting them can harness their lived experience of sport to contribute to a healthy, meaningful, and fulfilled life and lead to improved performance.

psychologists (e.g., one-to-one sessions), but when working at a tournament where you may be away for days if not weeks at a time, often working longer hours, away from your support networks, and sometimes unable to find sufficient opportunities for downtime, it can be challenging to find the balance between supporting your clients, and maintaining your own well-being.[12]

As practitioners, discussions of our roles and responsibilities are – rightly – turning more and more towards our duty of care to the athletes we work with. However, such a focus on the athletes' needs can sometimes leave us as practitioners neglecting to engage in the self-care that we need not only to ensure we can perform in our careers, but more importantly, thrive as people. Of course, there may be practical and logistical barriers to practitioner self-care at times, but in my experience, it is important to establish boundaries to maintain your mental health and well-being and to communicate these boundaries to those around you. In sport psychology we often hear the phrase 'person first, athlete second', but do we consider this when we are attempting to balance work demands with our own mental health as practitioners? Person first, practitioner second.

By setting these self-care boundaries and giving yourself time to be you, rather than 'the sport psychologist', you are more likely to maintain your own mental health and well-being, perform more effectively within your role, and model behaviours you may be encouraging from your athletes and coaches. If practitioners can establish what they need as downtime during work trips (for me it's having time to sit down with a good book and to phone home occasionally!), set those boundaries and communicate them clearly, they will be in a good position personally and professionally to bring their best selves to their careers.

Concluding Thoughts

Travelling internationally as part of a team can often be considered a highlight in a sport psychologist's career, but the experience is not without its challenges. This chapter has given an insight into my experience as a trainee practitioner when approaching some of the more challenging moments. It is my hope that by candidly sharing my thoughts and experience, practitioners may reflect on how they can relate to the themes explored and develop their own practice by considering how they would approach these – often complex – situations. Whilst this chapter has focused on the challenges of this experience, I want to express the immense privilege and excitement I felt at being part of the team, travelling internationally, and experiencing the tournament as a sport psychologist. The rush of happiness, pride, and adrenaline I experienced when the team achieved their goal and won the tournament – becoming European Champions – brought home to me why I love my job and it is a feeling I will never forget. Longer-term, the

---

[12] See Quartiroli et al. (2019); Quartiroli, Wagstaff & Thelwell (2021); and Quartiroli et al. (2021) for literature on practitioner self-care.

working relationships I developed throughout the tournament are not only meaningful to me in terms of facilitating future work with the team, but they also made the tournament experience much richer, and more satisfying on a human level. Whilst it is important to consider the moments that will challenge you as a person and a practitioner, it is also important to embrace the life experience and enjoy it (this is what you've been working so hard for!). By reflecting on this chapter – and indeed all chapters within this book – I hope that you will be best placed to thrive in an enjoyable and rewarding career.

REFLECTIVE QUESTIONS

- Consider how you establish your role, expectations, and approach when working at a tournament. How will you develop your own understanding of your role? How and when will you communicate this? Who will you have these discussions with?
- What would working impactfully at a tournament look like for you?
- What do you need to maintain your own mental health and well-being and how will you establish opportunities for self-care when working at training camps or tournaments?

References

Aoyagi, M. W., Portenga, S. T., Poczwardowski, A., Cohen, A. B., & Statler, T. (2012). Reflections and directions: The profession of sport psychology past, present, and future. *Professional Psychology: Research and Practice, 43*(1), 32.

Arnold, R., Hewton, E., & Fletcher, D (2015). Preparing our greatest team. *Sport, Business and Management: An International Journal, 5*, 386–407. 10.1108/sbm-01-2014-0003.

Barker, S., & Winter, S. (2014). The practice of sport psychology: A youth coaches' perspective. *International Journal of Sports Science & Coaching, 9*(2), 379–392.

Bishop, C. (2020). *The Long Win: The Search for a Better Way to Succeed*. Practical Inspiration Publishing.

Bull, S. J. (1995). Reflections on a 5-year consultancy program with the England women's cricket team. *The Sport Psychologist, 9*(2), 148–163.

Cotterill, S. (2018). Working as a sport psychology practitioner in professional cricket: Challenges, experiences, and opportunities. *The Sport Psychologist, 32*(2), 146–155.

Fletcher, D. (2012). An introduction to the special edition: Sport psychology in action at the Olympic and Paralympic Games. *Journal of Sport Psychology in Action, 3*(2), 61–64.

Fletcher, D., & Wagstaff, C. R. (2009). Organizational psychology in elite sport: Its emergence, application, and future. *Psychology of Sport and Exercise, 10*(4), 427–434.

Halsted, L. C. (2021) *Becoming a True Athlete: A Practical Philosophy for Flourishing Through Sport*. Sequoia Books.

McCalla, T., & Fitzpatrick, S. (2016). Integrating sport psychology within a high- performance team: Potential stakeholders, micropolitics, and culture. *Journal of Sport Psychology in Action, 7*(1), 33–42.

Olusoga, P., Butt, J., Hays, K., & Maynard, I. (2009). Stress in elite sports coaching: Identifying stressors. *Journal of Applied Sport Psychology, 21*(4), 442–459.

Pain, M. A., & Harwood, C. G. (2004). Knowledge and perceptions of sport psychology within English soccer. *Journal of Sports Sciences, 22*(9), 813–826.

Portenga, S. T., Aoyagi, M. W., Balague, G., Cohen, A., & Harmison, B. (2011). Defining the practice of sport and performance psychology. *Manuscript Submitted for Publication.*

Quartiroli, A., Etzel, E. F., Knight, S. M., & Zakrajsek, R. A. (2019). Self-care as key to others' care: The perspectives of globally situated experienced senior-level sport psychology practitioners. *Journal of Applied Sport Psychology, 31*(2), 147–167.

Quartiroli, A., Wagstaff, C. R., & Thelwell, R. (2021). The what and the how of self-care for sport psychology practitioners: A delphi study. *Journal of Applied Sport Psychology*, 1–20.

Quartiroli, A., Wagstaff, C. R., Zakrajsek, R. A., Knight, S. M., & Etzel, E. F. (2021). The role of self-care and professional quality of life in sustaining a long-lasting career in sport psychology: A qualitative exploration. *Journal of Applied Sport Psychology*, 1–18.

Reid, C., Stewart, E., & Thorne, G. (2004). Multidisciplinary sport science teams in elite sport: Comprehensive servicing or conflict and confusion? *The Sport Psychologist, 18*(2), 204–217.

Sharp, L. A., & Hodge, K. (2013). Effective sport psychology consulting relationships: Two coach case studies. *The Sport Psychologist, 27*(4), 313–324.

Simons, J. P., & Andersen, M. B. (1995). The development of consulting practice in applied sport psychology: Some personal perspectives. *The Sport Psychologist, 9*(4), 449–468.

Tod, D. A., & Bond, K. (2010). A longitudinal examination of a British neophyte sport psychologist's development. *Sport Psychologist, 24*(1), 35–51.

Tonn, E., & Harmison, R. J. (2004). Thrown to the wolves: A student's account of her practicum experience. *Sport Psychologist, 18*(3).

Winstone, W, & Gervis, M (2006). Countertransference and the self-aware sport psychologist: Attitudes and patterns of professional practice. *The Sport Psychologist, 20*, 495–511. 10.1123/tsp.20.4.495.

Winter, S., & Collins, D. J. (2016). Applied sport psychology: A profession? *The Sport Psychologist, 30*(1), 89–96.

Woolway, T., & Harwood, C. G. (2019). Gatekeepers' experiences of hiring a sport psychologist: A phenomenological study. *Journal of Applied Sport Psychology, 31*(4), 474–493.

15

THE THINGS YOUR TRAINING DIDN'T TEACH YOU: CHALLENGING CONVERSATIONS AND SPEAKING TO POWER

Joseph G. Dixon and Jennifer A. Hobson

Introduction

Having a challenging conversation is part of everyday life (Levine et al., 2020). Despite the potential benefits of these interactions, communicators approach them with trepidation, 'in part, because they perceive them as involving intractable moral conflict between being honest and being kind' (p.38). In addition to being feared, challenging conversations can be executed poorly or even avoided completely (Bradley & Campbell, 2014). The impact of such situations on sport psychology practitioners can be significant; Champ and colleagues (2021, p. 855) described how one such occurrence caused the lead researcher to experience 'a range of deep-rooted emotions that resulted in me questioning every aspect of my identity'. Furthermore, in their work examining sport psychologists' experiences in applied sport McDougall et al. (2015, p. 272) found that providing 'an alternative or challenging opinion was considered to be a demanding task, often associated with high risk'.

In the following discussion, two sport psychologists share candid experiences of having difficult conversations within their applied work. They reflect on each situation, highlight what made the situation "difficult" and how they navigated it, and identify recommendations for early-stage practitioners facing similar situations.

We encourage the reader to consider the following whilst reading this chapter:

- How would you define a *difficult* or *challenging* conversation?
- How does this definition relate to your own needs as a practitioner?
- How could (knowing) your core values and strengths help you to approach and navigate these difficult conversations?

DOI: 10.4324/9781003263890-19

Practitioner Conversation

JD: As practitioners, there have been times when we've had to have 'difficult conversations'. What would you define as a difficult conversation, something that perhaps traditional training doesn't prepare you for?

JH: I think it is a situation I feel worried about, something I want to put off or avoid. Because I feel that sense of uncertainty and not feeling comfortable with how it might go. It probably relates to having a negative conversation with someone, because those are more uncomfortable than positive conversations. Everyone's quite happy with giving positive feedback. So difficult conversations from my perspective involve giving critical feedback, or an observation of someone's negative behaviour.

JD: I can relate to that. Reflecting on what you're saying there, the situations I find easier are ones where I know the individual a bit more, rather than if I am critiquing someone who I don't have a strong relationship with. I tend to find I can prepare and tailor my approach for those that I know and I'm more able to anticipate what is the best way to frame a particular message, so it lands with optimal impact.

JH: Yeah. If you compare it to people interacting online, it's much easier to criticise or offer a point of view which differs from someone else's, because you don't have that relationship or there's distance between you. However, when you interact face to face with someone who you're going to continue working with, you might need to keep them on board, maintain their buy-in with your role and work. They might be doing you a favour later down the line … supporting you in your role or even helping you keep your job or renew your contract if they are in a position of power! Therefore, there is more pressure for the conversation to go well. Even if it is critical, or negative in tone.

JD: Yes, and I guess by definition, we are in a supportive, helping profession. I know I find the natural desire to help, to please and support can be a barrier to that direct challenge. What are your thoughts on that? You might be different, but certainly I feel that at times, discomfort is required to have those challenging and difficult conversations.

JH: Yes, we need to feel like we are helping and supportive. And when people first think of a psychologist or the psychologist's role, it is often expected to be a more positive kind of a conversation you are likely to have with someone. Obviously, it can be about negative things, but overall, the expectation is probably that this person's going to be encouraging or going to be supportive. A lot of it is positive, but it also involves the flip side; challenging people on their behaviour or language, disagreeing with someone, or providing critical feedback, which training doesn't necessarily prepare you for, certainly MSc level, going into Stage 2 or SEPAR training.

JD: I think it is important to note everyone will have their natural approach to these kinds of situations, and there is not a specific 'right way' to do things. However, for the reader we will share some of our own experiences of challenging situations and discuss how we've navigated them based on our own approach. Okay, can you describe a specific situation in this territory?

JH: So, there was an academy coach who was the head of a developmental phase, consisting of four age groups. As part of this role, they supervised coaches working across the age groups, so this individual was in a position of power. They also had their own age group of children to coach. I was asked by their superior, the Head of Coaching, to provide specific feedback on the coach's behaviour, which, in short, was that their behaviour was too negative.

JD: So, you were actually feeding back information from another staff member. How did you feel about that?

JH: It was difficult. I didn't feel comfortable passing on his feedback as if it were my own. I didn't want to feel like a puppet. But knowing and reflecting on my core values helped me to resolve this internal conflict. I knew it was important for me to be authentic and honest in my work with others. So, thinking about how that would look in this situation really helped me. I took on board the Head of Coaching's feedback whilst making sure I collected my own observations and referred to those in any conversation with that coach. So, I could use my own judgement as a rationale rather than referring to somebody else and relying on their testimony, so to speak.

JD: So, there are two dynamics going on there in terms of having a senior individual, a Head of Coaching that wants you to give feedback and then actually going to give your version, your own feedback to the coach themself.

JH: Yes, building the case of my own feedback involved being pitch side and making sure I had the opportunity to observe. When I did that however, I felt like I saw the coach on their best behaviour because they knew I was observing. I had to use opportunities to covertly observe … turn up unexpectedly or stand out of view so that I could see the behaviour and record observations in that way. I also used a video camera because once set up, it can be easy for people to forget it is there. I set that up during training sessions, so I had visual data to show the coach and present back, which was helpful.

JD: Talk me through the conversation that followed.

JH: After collecting the footage, I made clips of the most salient behaviours for the conversation. I was sure to clip good practice as well as poor practice, because I didn't want the conversation to just be a fault-finding exercise.

JD: Yeah, I guess it is not like you are an investigator going in trying to prove that the coach is guilty, right?

JH: Exactly. I wanted to role model the behaviour I wanted the coach to show. So, I needed to balance good examples with poor examples. And by having the two side by side, or sequential in this order of clips, it also helped to highlight the point, because the poor practice contrasted so much with the good practice. So, I had the clips ready. But due to feeling a bit concerned or worried about having the conversation, I didn't go out of my way to arrange the meeting. I was putting it off.

JD: Why?

JH: Because I felt uncomfortable with the prospect of having the conversation and calling the coach out on these behaviours, which I fully agreed needed addressing and weren't the best for the players. I always had it in my head it was going to happen, but I just didn't make sure the conversation happened quickly. Listening to my own language there, viewing it as 'calling the coach out' probably isn't the best way to frame it. I was making it out to be something more confrontational than it needed to be or ended up being.

Anyway, we did meet. But it was at the end of a very long day as I was leaving the building. The coach said, 'can we go through that footage now?'. I was struggling to keep my eyes open but felt I couldn't turn down the opportunity because the coach went out of their way to initiate the conversation. That's a brilliant opportunity; whilst there was willing, I felt I had to go with it. Had I said 'no, can we catch up another time?' it is possible the next free opportunity would be weeks away and I wanted the event to still be quite fresh in our minds. I was also concerned the coach may devalue me and my feedback, if I failed to provide it when asked … perhaps I was overthinking it but that's how I felt.

So, I agreed, and we watched each clip together, in real time. I first asked for the coach's thoughts on the clip or the behaviour on show. The coach highlighted positive things and I agreed, explained why it was good and the impact it could have on the players. Then, we watched the less positive examples. Again, I asked for the coach's thoughts and explained why certain behaviours might be unhelpful. So, I was engaging the coach in that process of feedback and education. Not just me lecturing. I felt this was an important approach to take because I didn't want the coach to feel threatened or criticised by me, that I was 'calling them out'. I was under the impression the coach did feel this way when they received feedback directly from the Head of Coaching, so I wanted to contrast with that style. I also wanted the coach to understand not just the 'what' but also the 'why' of what needed to change, since this can help with behaviour change.

One thing I haven't mentioned was that I was up front with the coach, highlighting the Head of Coaching, their superior, had asked me to feedback on these things; I didn't shield that from the coach. I wanted to be clear 'the Head of Coaching recommended I feedback on your behaviour, but these are my observations, not the Head of Coaching's observations' ... . being transparent with the intervention. This was important to me again given that my core values are to be authentic and honest, so it really felt right for me to be upfront about that, and I think they respected that.

JD: A couple of things I'm hearing when thinking about advice for early-stage practitioners is the idea of planning; if you can anticipate a difficult conversation, 'being able to prepare' is helpful in these situations. For instance, preparing data and thinking about how you might approach the conversation. Also, knowing your core values but even simple things like the timing of the conversation ... when you'll be at your best with the right energy to push yourself out of your comfort zone. What happened next?

JH: We summarised the key things the coach wanted and needed to work on. First, I asked if the coach had any ideas that might help them be quieter when a player makes a mistake, rather than highlighting it or showing frustration. The coach suggested one idea from a training course. So, we agreed to try that, which was to write down one's thoughts instead of being verbal. Therefore, the intervention was to try to practice that strategy. We also discussed beliefs about mistake making, which was part of the conversation that I led and ended with. By this point in the conversation, I think I had grown in confidence. I was also reassured by how I felt our relationship had strengthened. So, I felt comfortable presenting these comments more directly. I explained that changing their beliefs about the meaning of mistakes could be very helpful; a mistake shows a player has tried and is at the edge of their comfort zone, pushing the boundary. Mistakes do not mean they are not trying hard enough. Players aren't there to please the coach by performing mistake-free; they need to explore and stretch themselves. Things like that, to help the coach challenge their beliefs about player mistake making and produce more helpful behaviours. I wanted to challenge the belief that 'a session is only good if it is mistake-free'.

JD: Tell me about how you were feeling during the interaction.

JH: It didn't feel anywhere near as bad as I thought it was going to since I tapped into my listening, conversation, and therapeutic skills.[1] Being able to communicate properly with another human being and knowing what constitutes good communication with another human being. Knowing I felt comfortable with my skills in that area I think helped because that's all I needed to do on that occasion.

JD: So, leaning back into what you know and your training. Good advice. Would you do anything differently if that situation arose again?

JH: I would definitely take more control over when we catch up. I was planned and prepared, I had created the clips and thought about the key points but

---

[1] In this podcast, Sheila Heen makes tough talks easier by breaking down the three layers that make up every difficult conversation: https://fs.blog/knowledge-project-podcast/sheila-heen/

ideally it wouldn't have happened at the end of the day unexpectedly. One thing I think helped me to approach the conversation and feel comfortable doing so was considering 'why do I need to give this feedback?'

I felt really passionately about the dynamic between the coach and those players. I felt like the players were being silenced. The players were being told off for making mistakes. And, because they're young children, they are unlikely to challenge that person above them. Doing so could cost them in their reviews, and it could potentially make the coach view them less favourably, and negatively impact their journey through the academy system. In that situation I thought it was so important to be a voice for the players, I just had to put aside how I felt because I felt so passionately about making sure the coach was aware of the impact of their behaviours. So, reminding myself of why it was important for me to have the conversation was helpful, as was connecting with my core values and understanding how I was enacting them even in this difficult and uncomfortable situation.

JD: It is a really good reflection. So going back to your own 'why' and purpose to give you the motivation to do something that might not be high on your list of wanting to undertake.

That leads into my example, like yours it is focused on coach engagement and speaking to power, working directly with a head coach on their impact on the team. It centres around engaging with a coach and providing feedback on how they are communicating to players on a match day, during half-time and post-game, and the impact this is having on the group and specific individuals.

Typically, this is not something I've naturally felt comfortable doing, providing direct constructive feedback. We both work in environments where an individual's specific role can play a big part in the nature of the relationships you have and how you approach these types of conversations. So, just speaking from experience, I think there are times when I might have refrained from being directly critical and challenging because I've had the longer-term view in mind and was wary of such an approach damaging a relationship.

I also think you might need to establish if that's part of the expectations around your role (coach feedback). This is something that happened over time with this particular coach, where a relationship was built through spending time together, engaging in both informal and formal feedback on a regular basis.

It became evident there was a pattern of communication on match days that was having a negative impact on players. This was a result of the coach being highly critical at times. Through the way messages were being delivered in the volume, tone and language used you could immediately see the detrimental effect it was having on the players, through their body language and, the knock-on impact on their performance.

At the time I was concerned about whether this feedback could land badly, and if so, my opportunity to be as effective or even be part of the team could be impacted. However, my inner voice was ultimately saying 'I'm here to have an impact' and, part of that impact, as we had scoped out previously is that the coach wanted and stated they would value feedback.[2] Having said that, I've also seen times where people say they want feedback and then when it's given, the truth is that they don't always respond consistently with that message.

JH: Yeah, because that's another dimension of providing feedback, isn't it? Do they want it, and even when they say that they do, do they really?

JD: Similar to your first example, it was important to undertake a little bit of planning to ensure this feedback landed well. So, I reflected on how to best highlight how they were delivering excessive amounts of detail in quite a critical manner. Not necessarily wrong information, but the way it was delivered was highly negative. Just like you, I felt gaining evidence was important. I did this through observation; looking at the impact on players' body language, on their energy levels or confidence levels, which you could see visually but also through players reporting back to me the negative impact it was having on them. Next, finding a set time to sit down away from the hassles and distractions of the day job where I would have their full attention was also important.

I can see similarities between your approach to the conversation and mine; starting by asking their perception on how the messaging was landing with the team, and where they thought they could be better. Actually, they did allude to, when their emotions had settled down, they recognised they could be more positive and less critical. So, one of the big learnings for me is giving the individual space to reflect and articulate things to you first before you go in and lead with the feedback.

However, this was a situation where the individual disagreed with a couple of things and provided a plausible and logical rationale for their approach; 'no, the reason for this was … .' for instance, if a piece of tactical information was not being listened to after being delivered several times. So, I also think there needs to be a willingness from us as practitioners to accept that we're not always right and, accepting that sometimes, a message can be delivered directly, if there's a rational thought process behind it.[3]

JH: Similarly, thinking back to my example, when we discussed the clips, there was also to-ing and fro-ing; 'well I thought I was doing it like this', and I

---

2 In this blog post, Brené Brown discusses how having clear conversations with others is kind: https://brenebrown.com/articles/2018/10/15/clear-is-kind-unclear-is-unkind/

3 In this podcast, Simon Sinek talks further about how to navigate difficult conversations: https://simonsinek.com/podcast-episodes/how-to-have-difficult-conversations-with-david-harris/

had to highlight how the players likely interpreted this in a different way. It is a situation where you might disagree. We have to accept that but try to find a way to explain where we're coming from … why you are saying what you are saying and why you've given the feedback that you've put together.

JD: In this scenario I think it was important to listen to the coach articulate his reasoning to ensure that he felt involved in the discussion and it not appearing like a lecture. In doing so, he actually talked himself round to recognising how he could be perceived as overly detailed and underutilising positive feedback. I had some more examples ready to further evidence the point if greater challenge was required, however that was not necessary. I think that is also an important reflection; that you don't have to reference and discuss every piece of available evidence. Sometimes it only requires one or two impactful examples for the feedback to strike the right chord.

JH: In our examples, perhaps we have used a 'softer' approach to delivering feedback compared to being overly critical; by asking for their thoughts then providing our own. I think that approach meets the need for us to be or feel like we are being supportive.

But have you ever found times where, when the message is delivered in this way, it hasn't 'gone in'? And thought 'I need to actually be direct and blunt with this person'? I have had to address behaviours of colleagues in the past where I have had to stand up and go, 'No, that's wrong'. Really *call people out*. But I guess that is very few and far between. We know the 'preferred' or 'better' ways of approaching this type of situation, but what if that isn't working?

JD: We are not necessarily trained for that, those blunt conversations and being direct. Where I have tried to pitch it, and by no means got it right, is to almost allude to the fact that I'm stepping into the coaches' world and do it how they might do it, almost get permission through asking 'how do you want this to go?' and get them to lead on this. Some coaches say, 'just tell me the bad stuff' or 'what do I need to fix?', and are used to a more direct, fast-moving approach. When that happens, that doesn't always go down well either, but you can highlight how this was what was agreed. And naming disagreements; 'perhaps we disagree on this', rather than leave it unsaid or go back and forth. It is okay and healthy to disagree on certain things and then move on. It is part of being in an environment with different disciplines and personalities.

If I was to reflect on this example I think if you define success as behaviour change, there was acknowledgement from the individual that there could be some more balance in what they were delivering in terms of detail and critique versus positive praise. Not just a 'fix it' mindset that could be perceived as quite negative. There was also a continued response in asking for more feedback in relation to these areas, so that suggested they had taken it on board and wanted to hear more about it, perhaps because it was a bit of a blind spot for them. Because initially, the challenging part of the conversation was, they didn't quite see things that way. Other reflections: I think what was challenging was probably the fear of wrecking a relationship. In hindsight you end up being ineffective in these situations because you are not able to get to the point quickly enough and the individual can spot the cautiousness. The irony being, this is more likely to negatively impact the relationship; would you want a sport psychologist who isn't giving you the truth through fear of upsetting you? Probably not.

JD: Any other situations that you would draw on as powerful for your own learning in this territory?

JH: An example of speaking to power was a situation involving someone at senior management level in a sporting organisation.[4] Essentially, I went to them with a proposal about the psychology programme that would shift the approach for the next season. Basically, idea pitching. It was challenging because there was pressure for me to make a good impression.

JD: A 'dragon's den-type' situation?

JH: Yeah, but with the back story of not having a close or strong relationship with this individual, which added to the challenge. Through reflecting on my prior interactions with this individual, I sensed my natural approach might not be the best way to go. Specifically, my use of humour and a more laid-back style. Knowing this approach didn't really fit with this person, and being a bit demoralised by that as well, I went into this pitch being calmer, more reserved, and straight talking, without being overly enthusiastic or excited. You probably think that is the opposite to how you should present an idea. You should show enthusiasm, you should show passion! However, I felt this wouldn't land since this person had previously rapidly batted away my ideas or shut me down. So, I wanted to go in more level to avoid a similar response.

JD: There is something in that, if you talk practitioner skills, showing flexibility and being adaptable.

JH: Something that you are not necessarily taught about too much in your training. You craft an approach, and you use your strengths, but if your strengths don't fit with someone else you have to do something else.

JD: Yes, in our types of roles, you can be talking to a child one minute and in your example, a member of senior management the next. So, tell me about what happened.

JH: The pitch was well planned for. I created a presentation to talk through, illustrating my ideas. I guess I didn't come across as being attached to the ideas. I didn't go into the conversation thinking 'this is what it must be', and I verbalised that flexibility. I said things like 'these are my initial thoughts, what do you think?', and 'I'm not precious on it being exactly like this, but this is what I think will work because x, y, and z'. I just calmly described everything. At times I was

---

4 Reitz and Higgins (2020) provide a commentary on speaking truth to power and why leaders cannot hear what they need to hear: https://bmjleader.bmj.com/content/5/4/270

stopped, and devil's advocate-type questions were put to me. I think because I had tempered my enthusiasm, positivity, and excitement and, came across quite calm, when those more challenging questions were put to me, I was able to remain balanced rather than show a change of tone which could have been perceived as a defensive reaction. Because in my own mind I was flexible about how it could go, that helped me to keep calm, not react defensively and, answer each question genuinely without frustration. As the pitch progressed, I was able to provide applied examples of how these ideas would work. I applied the ideas to key athletes we both knew. Using these as case studies to bring my ideas to life and add impact was a helpful approach, since we had that shared knowledge of stories of success and failure that fed into the ideas associated with this proposal.

JD: So, it sounds like the hardest part was how you perceived the conversation was going to go based on some previous baggage associated with the relationship with this individual. Were there any difficulties during the conversation?

JH: Yes, I wasn't looking forward to the conversation at all. I personally had to put issues from the past aside when presenting. I was dubious about how well things would go. Still, the outcome was really positive. All the ideas were complimented and given approval to prepare for implementation in the next season. I don't think I would do it differently next time around, but I do wonder if I had been really passionate and excited, what impact that might have had on the conversation. I think being calm helped me to appear more confident and that is often the most important thing!

JD: So, what's the advice for early-stage practitioners going to a senior-level colleague and pitching an idea or selling their services?

JH: I think being willing to be flexible, open minded to changes and being prepared and planned so that you're capable of answering challenges you might receive. We know there are drawbacks and benefits to different ideas including some logistical challenges. So, I think going over those sorts of things, pre-empt the critique you might receive.

Avoid going in with the mentality of 'this person must agree with everything I suggest' and 'it has to look like this'. Be comfortable with the process being collaborative and be happy for it to look a little different in the end. Expect it to be different from what you originally suggested because, then we are not so attached to this 'idea'. I think that was helpful for me on this occasion. Being less attached meant I was calmer and better prepared to respond to challenge and critique.

Conclusion

Sport psychologists are required to have *challenging conversations,* often with in-dividuals in positions of power. This can feel very daunting, not least because, aside from confiding in a supervisor, there is little in the way of training and guidance available to early-career practitioners faced with such a task. In this chapter, two practitioners immersed within a sport organisation candidly shared their own early-career experiences with having challenging conversations and speaking to individuals with power. It is hoped through providing such honest insight and reflection on these experiences, other early-career practitioners can benefit through thinking more positively about such situations and feeling better prepared for them. The key recommendations for early-career practitioners are summarised below.

TIPS FOR EARLY-CAREER PRACTITIONERS

- Prepare for challenging conversations; what will you discuss? How will you discuss this? Where may there be challenge? How could you respond?
- Be willing to be flexible regarding your ideas.
- Put yourself in their shoes; what do you know about them and their personality? Where might you disagree? How could you respond to that?
- Have evidence to back up your points.
- Where possible, agree some ground rules with the individual
- Draw on support of mentors/supervisors.
- Remember conflict and difficult conversations can often lead to strengthened rather than weakened relationships, if approached and delivered with openness and respect.
- Consider your core values; what makes you *'you'* and underpins your approach? How could your values *look* within the challenging conversation?
- Use your strengths; what are they? How could you use these (if appropriate) within the conversation?
- Engage in reflective practice following challenging conversations to refine your approach to these types of situations.

References

Bradley, G., & Campbell, A. C. (2014). Managing difficult workplace conversations: Goals, strategies, and outcomes. *International Journal of Business Communication*, *53*(4), 443–464. doi: 10.1177/2329488414525468

Champ, F., Ronkainen, N., Tod, D., Eubank, M., & Littlewood, M. (2021). A tale of three seasons: A cultural sport psychology and gender performativity approach to practitioner identity and development in professional football. *Qualitative Research in Sport, Exercise and Health*, *13*(5), 847–863. doi: 10.1080/2159676X.2020.1833967

Levine, E. E., Roberts, A. R., & Cohen, T. R. (2020). Difficult conversations: Navigating the tension between honesty and benevolence. *Current Opinion in Psychology*, *31*, 38–43. doi: 10.1016/j.copsyc.2019.07.034

McDougall, M., Nesti, M. S., & Richardson, D. J. (2015). The challenges of sport psychology delivery in elite and professional sport: Reflections from experienced sport psychologists. *Sport Psychologist, 29*(3), 265–277. doi: 10.1123/tsp.2014-0081

Reitz, M, & Higgins, J (2020). Speaking truth to power: Why leaders cannot hear what they need to hear. *BMJ Leader, 5*, 270–273. doi: 10.1136/leader-2020-000394.

REFLECTIONS: IN CONCLUSION

Erin: *So, in bringing the reflections section to a close, I'm aware that the authors of each chapter have been very generous in sharing their experiences and they've been quite open and vulnerable when talking about the more challenging moments in their careers which I think can be quite difficult to do. One of the chapters that has a particular focus on some of the more challenging moments as a practitioner is Joseph and Jennifer's chapter (Chapter 15). They've really given us a look at the nitty gritty of the more difficult and testing conversations practitioners may need to have. In sharing with us her experience of needing to adapt her approach due to her ideas previously being dismissed, Jennifer demonstrates the importance of being flexible and adaptable as a practitioner, with both authors sharing how they have navigated the more challenging moments of their careers.*

Tim: And what readers may have also picked up on is some of the connections between the reflections. One example that caught my attention when I was reading the chapters was your own chapter Erin (Chapter 14) and Megan's chapter (Chapter 11), as you both talk about how regularly you might find yourself in uncomfortable situations. You both talk very openly about how you have been able to overcome uncomfortableness in that practitioner role. Another example of chapters with connecting themes would be Charlotte's (Chapter 8) and Steven's (Chapter 9). Both Steven and Charlotte talked about the way in which their different experiences have transferred across into different contexts. So, for Charlotte, the notion of doing a PhD alongside professional training and how those two pathways can be complementary to each other. Then Steven shared how he's been able to positively transfer learnings from his previous career to aid his development in a new career. So, both practitioners share how skills can be transferable

DOI: 10.4324/9781003263890-20

and can help you be efficient in your working practices as you develop as a practitioner.

Erin: *And I think the reflections really give the readers a sense of what it's like to be a practitioner. Whether you're new to the field and just starting out, or whether you're a few years down the line, having an awareness of some of the highlights, but perhaps more importantly, the challenges that other practitioners who have come before you have experienced can be reassuring and can prompt further reflection on our own personal experiences.*

Tim: And the personal nature of these reflections in this section of the book gives a great opportunity to develop the next generation of practitioners – giving them a sense of what they need to be aware of and how they can perhaps shortcut some of the challenges that others have navigated in the past.

CONCLUSION

Erin: *Okay, in bringing the book to a conclusion, what next? Now people have read the book, what are we hoping will come from it?*

Tim: Firstly, I'd like to think that the book will provide practitioners with a resource that is valuable in future years and something that practitioners can return to and benefit from throughout their years of practice.

Erin: *And I think as you gain more experience, dipping in and out of the book will be a useful approach – I know I certainly will be from time to time! As we're faced with new challenges – perhaps ones that remind us of a chapter from the book – coming back to the book, having another read through a fellow practitioner's approach and experience I think will offer some inspiration and maybe some reassurance too.*

Tim: And each of the chapters has reflective questions at the end for practitioners to use as a sounding board, to encourage thinking further beyond the chapter and prompt engagement with the book over time.

Erin: *Throughout the book, the authors have also signposted a range of resources from podcasts to blog posts – consciously moving away from a reliance on academic literature and thinking outside of the box when it comes to expanding our applied knowledge. Exploring these resources will be great to tap into different voices and different perspectives on some of the topics explored in this book to further our understanding and introduce us to new ideas.*

Tim: And I think this is the book we wish that we'd have had when we were going through our training. When I was starting out as a practitioner, the resources were very limited and there weren't many people sharing their experiences. So, I hope that this book provides an honest and open insight into what it is like to be an early career practitioner, sharing some of the lessons that others maybe haven't had access to in the past.

DOI: 10.4324/9781003263890-21

Erin: *And I think over the past few years, still being an early career practitioner, I've been really struck by how useful it's been to be able to share my own experiences and hear about other early career practitioners' experiences of navigating their way through the profession. But for some practitioners, there isn't always a lot of opportunity to learn from their peers who are at a similar stage in their career, particularly if they're working on a self-employed basis. So, I hope this book can develop a feeling of community, openly and honestly exploring our shared experiences to help us grow as practitioners as we navigate the profession of sport and exercise psychology.*

INDEX

Milton Keynes UK
Ingram Content Group UK Ltd.
UKHW021856271223
434958UK00001B/3